GW00601432

Elisabeth Farnell .

DIMENSIONS OF CHANGE IN A GROWTH AREA

Dimensions of Change in a Growth Area

Southampton since 1960

Edited by
C M MASON
and
M E WITHERICK
Department of Geography,
University of Southampton

Gower

© Geography Department, University of Southampton 1981

All rights reserved. No part of this publication may be reproduced, stored in a retrieval system, or transmitted in any form or by any means, electronic, mechanical, photocopying, recording, or otherwise without the prior permission of Gower Publishing Company Limited.

Published by
GOWER PUBLISHING COMPANY LIMITED,
Gower House, Croft Road, Aldershot, Hants., England

 British Library Cataloguing in Publication Data

Dimensions of change in a growth area: Southampton
   since 1960.
   1. Southampton (Hampshire)—Population—Addresses,
   essays, lectures
   I. Mason, C.M.   II. Witherick, M.E.
   304.6'2'0942276   HB3586.S/

   ISBN 0-566-00426-7

Printed and bound in Great Britain by
Biddles Ltd, Guildford and King's Lynn

Contents

Figures

Tables

ix

Preface

The publication of this book has been timed to coincide with the
holding of the Annual Conference of the Institute of British
Geographers at the University of Southampton in January 1982. It has
been general practice in the past for the geography department of the
host university to produce for the benefit of Institute members either
a general introduction to the geography of the area or a collection of
local excursion guides. Not wishing to depart too far from this
convention, we have sought to compile a collection of essays which
indicates some of the current research being undertaken by members of
the Geography Department, but which might also serve as an introduction
to the Southampton area. This part of southern England offers much of
geographical interest, not least of which is its remarkable record of
growth sustained throughout the post-war period. The last
comprehensive review and analysis of the state of the area was
completed some seventeen years ago to mark the meeting of the British
Association for the Advancement of Science at this University. It
would seem that sufficient time has now elapsed to warrant another
stock-taking of developments in the Southampton city region. Pitfalls
frequently associated with collaborative exercises such as this are
that the final outcome can so easily become both disparate and
parochial. It is hoped, however, that these particular essays gain
cohesion from reference to the same area and from pursuit of a common
theme of growth and change, and that by striving to raise broader
issues each will prove to be of relevance in a wider context.

Many individuals and organisations have contributed in various ways
to the preparation of this book and their help and cooperation are very
gratefully acknowledged. In particular, we wish to record our thanks
to the following: the Hampshire County Planning Department and the City
of Southampton Planning Office for providing much data; to our
contributing colleagues for meeting the deadlines and for useful
comment; to Mr A S Burn and other members of the Cartographic Unit
(University of Southampton) for preparing the maps and diagrams,
and lastly, but by no means least, to Angela Ali for typing the
camera-ready copy.

Geography Department,
University of Southampton

September 1981

Colin Mason
Michael Witherick

1 Growth and Change in the Southampton Area: An Overview

C M MASON AND M E WITHERICK

No matter what the indicator, there is repeated confirmation that Britain is currently in the midst of its worst economic recession since the 1930s. Industrial output and investment have declined; both private and public sector house building are at their lowest levels since the Second World War; 1.1 million manufacturing jobs have been lost between mid-1979 and mid-1981; even service sector employment has now begun to contract, and over 2.9 million people are at present out of work, that is nearly one in eight of the national workforce. Unemployment seems set to reach 3 million by the end of 1981, and there are commentators who expect that figure to touch the 4 million mark by the mid-1980s. The prevailing economic circumstances may be seen as merely an acceleration in the long-term decline of the British economy, a downturn which, according to some observers, had its roots in the late 19th century, but less contentiously can be seen to have started in the early 1960s (Bacon and Eltis, 1978). Moreover, it is unlikely that the current recession is a transient phenomenon; indeed, one school of thought believes that there will be no economic recovery in the foreseeable future, simply a 'flattening out' at present low levels of activity.

Given the persistence of this cyclical economic downturn and the evidence of a longer-term secular decline in the British economy, it might seem unduly perverse to be producing here a study of growth. However, the widespread tendency to discuss the malaise of the British economy in macro-scale terms frequently masks the fact that, despite the general economic decline, there are certain areas in the country which remain dynamic and continue to experience growth. These persistently

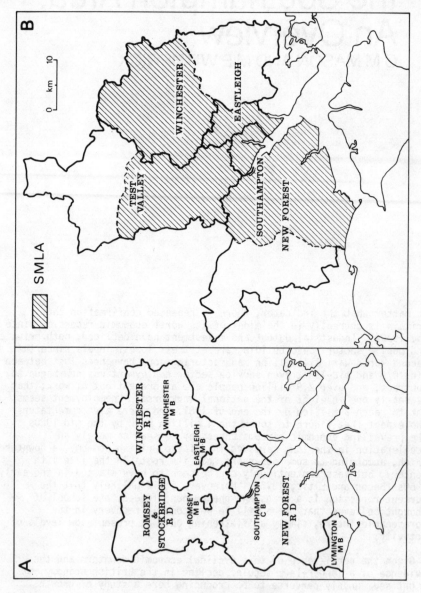

Figure 1.1 The Southampton SMLA :
A Pre - 1974 local authorities
B Present authorities.

prosperous parts of contemporary Britain are, in the main, towns and
cities not too distant from London, most of them being located along a
broad axis extending from Norfolk to Avon and Dorset. Such urban
centres are still characterised by high rates of industrial investment
(especially in high technology industries and in the quaternary sector),
by job creation and by rapid population growth, particularly of white-
collar workers. Paradoxically, when northern Britain is willing to have
new jobs at almost any price, these southern counties are "the places
where planners have been desperately trying to restrict growth these
past thrity years" (Hall, 1980, 54) in order at a local level to
conserve historic environments and the "agreeable semi-rural lifestyle
of their existing inhabitants" (Hall, 1981, 1), and at a regional scale
to redirect growth to the declining, peripheral areas of Britain.

Arguably, there is as much, possibly more, to be gained from the
investigation of growth as there is from the apparent national
preoccupation with stagnation and decline. Thus it is that this
collection of essays is unashamedly about a growth area, being
specifically concerned with Southampton, one of the dynamic cities of
southern Britain. The purpose is to address three interrelated themes.
First, using the conventional indicators of population, employment and
built-up area, there is an attempt to establish the scale of growth
which has taken place over the last two decades and to identify its
major components. Secondly, some of the diverse consequences of growth
are examined. These range from socio-economic considerations such as
the effects of development on demographic, occupational and industrial
structures to its consequences for the spatial form of the built-up area
and its relationship to the physical environment. Finally, an
assessment is made of the planning issues posed by growth, together with
a review of the planners' attempts to accommodate and direct development
in this part of the country.

An important point to consider at this stage is the definition of the
study area. Are we concerned simply with the City of Southampton or
with the wider city region? Administrative boundaries often reflect
historical factors and in some cases even jerrymandering, and as a
result fail to coincide with 'natural' economic areas. This is
particularly the case with Southampton. In 1971 the City of Southampton
received a daily inflow of some 32,000 workers from neighbouring local
authority areas, while some 14,000 city residents found employment
outside its boundaries (Southampton City Council, 1981). Consequently,
the most appropriate spatial framework in which to discuss population
and employment trends is provided by the 'travel-to-work area' or 'daily
urban system', that is, a region defined on the basis of commuting flows
and largely self-contained in terms of journey-to-work patterns.
Although a number of different attempts have been made to define
functional urban areas, the approach favoured here is that of the
Standard Metropolitan Labour Area (SMLA), a spatial unit which consists
of an employment core and a related commuting hinterland (Chapter 6).
Using 1971 commuting data and pre-1974 local authority areas as the
basic 'building blocks', Drewett et al. (1976) have defined SMLAs for
the entire country. The Southampton SMLA comprises Southampton CB (the
employment core) and a commuting hinterland for ring which includes
Eastleigh, Romsey and Winchester (Fig.1.1A); Lymington has been added to
the original SMLA definition because of its close economic links with
the City of Southampton (Hampshire County Council, 1978a). This area is

3

less easily identifiable when post-1974 local authority areas are used, since the SMLA boundary does not coincide with those of the New Forest, Test Valley and Winchester districts (Fig.1.1B).

The Southampton SMLA is by definition largely self-contained in commuting terms. In 1971 only 14.4 per cent of jobs in its five main employment nodes were filled by non-SMLA residents, a slight increase from 12.8 per cent in 1961 and suggestive of a small outward extension of its commuter catchment. The City of Southampton was the principal focus of journey-to-work flows, attracting a significant number of commuters from the New Forest RD, Winchester RD and Eastleigh MB, as well as from outside the SMLA (mainly from South East Hampshire). The only other significant journey-to-work flows were from Southampton CB to Eastleigh MB and to the New Forest RD (specifically to the Waterside Parishes) and to Winchester MB from Winchester RD and from outside the SMLA (Fig.1.2).

Southampton and its near neighbour and 'rival', Portsmouth, are united under a common planning regime, that of the South Hampshire Structure Plan. Nevertheless, this study excludes any direct consideration of Portsmouth, for the simple reason that it is so very different from Southampton, notably in terms of its economic base, socio-economic composition, post-war prosperity and appearance. Southampton has the more significant and fully developed regional role. The South Hampshire Study (Buchanan, 1966), for example, noted Southampton's clear dominance as a commercial and financial centre, and this is indeed reflected in its large office sector. Portsmouth, on the other hand, remains very dependent upon the large Ministry of Defence presence in the city and its hinterland. The Royal Naval Dockyard is still the largest single employer in the area (Riley and Smith, 1981), although the government has recently announced its intention to run this down during the first half of the 1980s. In addition, manufacturing is more important in the Portsmouth area than in Southampton, and perhaps for this reason has suffered higher rates of unemployment than Southampton. With its cramped island site and grid plan, Portsmouth looks (and, for the south of England, is) a poor city, in contrast to the spacious, airy and prosperous appearance of Southampton (Gladstone, 1976).

Not only are Southampton and Portsmouth two substantially different cities, there is also relatively little economic interaction between them, and this despite the short distance separating them. For example, although Southampton does recruit some of its labour from the general direction of Portsmouth, the principal source is quite clearly Fareham rather than Portsmouth itself. In addition the flows of heavy commercial vehicles are much greater in a north-south direction from Southampton than east-west (Hampshire County Council, 1977a). However, it can be speculated that the improvement in east-west traffic which will result from the completion of the 'missing part' of the M27 motorway during the early 1980s might promote greater interaction between the two cities in the future.

Although much of the material and discussion embodied in this collection of essays relates to the Southampton area, the intention is that it should assume wider relevance and raise broader issues. For example, to date much research on urban growth and change has been directed towards the 'million cities'. The concern here is instead with

4

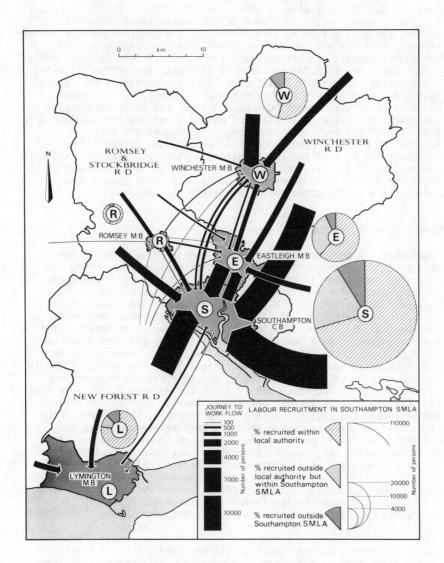

Figure 1.2   Journey-to-work flows in the Southampton SMLA, 1971.

5

a medium-sized, free-standing city, an altogether more commonly
encountered order in the urban hierarchy. Perhaps even more important,
by embracing the demographic, economic, social and environmental
dimensions of growth, collectively the essays offer a much broader
perspective than is customarily adopted. However, although the overall
cover is deliberately wide-ranging, the treatment of topics is
inevitably selective, conditioned by the expertise of individual
authors and by the availability of spatially disaggregated data. Some
aspects of change are, therefore, given detailed consideration in
subsequent essays; others are briefly reviewed in this chapter, whilst
still others are excluded by force of circumstance. Above all else,
the principal concern of this book is with the events of the last 20
years, a period of very rapid growth for Southampton. Such an
examination of developments during the 1960s and 1970s also serves to
complement an earlier collection of essays about the area published in
1964 to mark the hosting of the annual meeting of the British
Association for the Advancement of Science by the University of
Southampton. Most of the contributions in this publication dealt with
the systematic analysis and monitoring of change up to the very
beginning of the 1960s (Monkhouse, 1964). For this reason they
constitute a useful datum for this present discussion.

SOME DIMENSIONS OF GROWTH

Proof that the Southampton city region qualifies as a growth area is
most readily evidenced by the expansion of employment. During the 1961-
71 period employment increased by some 15,000 jobs (+8.7 per cent)
compared with a national growth rate of 1.5 per cent (Fig.1.3A).
Between 1971 and 1977 (the latest date for which information is
available) a further 26,500 jobs (+13.5 per cent) were created in the
Southampton SMLA. Over the same period, employment in Great Britain as
a whole increased by a modest 2 per cent and by less than 5 per cent in
the ROSE area (South East England outside Greater London), the sub-
region of which Southampton is part (Fig.1.3B). Employment growth in
the Southampton SMLA has, therefore, not only clearly outstripped
national rates of increase, but it has occurred at a faster rate than in
the ROSE area, recognised as one of the fastest growing sub-regions in
the UK during the past two decades. Furthermore, this expansion of
employment in the Southampton area has been achieved despite the
existence in 1961 of an industrial structure in which nationally
declining activities, notably water transport, and shipbuilding and
marine engineering, were prominent. Indeed, if national rates of growth
in each industry had been replicated in Southampton during the 1960s and
1970s, then SMLA employment would actually have declined. In fact,
Southampton's industries 'performed' substantially better in terms of
employment creation than their national counterparts (Hampshire County
Council, 1977b).

The main source of employment growth has been the service sector,
particularly finance industries and certain public sector activities
such as education and health. Almost nine out of every ten net new jobs
created between 1961 and 1977 were in this sector. Employment in
manufacturing also expanded in absolute terms, although at a much slower
rate than for services. Consequently, manufacturing's share of total
SMLA employment fell from 34 per cent in 1961 to 28 per cent in 1977.

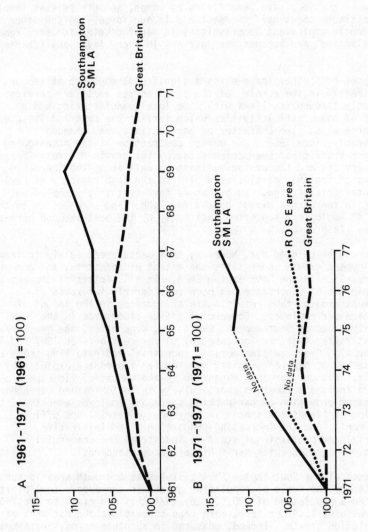

Figure 1.3 Employment growth, 1961–77.

Events since 1977 suggest that this sector has further declined in significance as a source of employment. Redundancies have been declared by a number of local manufacturing firms and there has been an absence of compensating job-creating investment, whereas in contrast, the service sector appears to be weathering the recession with relatively little adverse effect. A large proportion of the additional service sector jobs have been filled by women, so much so that females now constitude about half the sector's labour force. On the other hand, female employment opportunities in manufacturing industry remain fairly limited and account for just one in every five jobs (Chapters 3 and 4).

The port of Southampton remains a significant employer of labour, both directly in the running of the port and its ancillary services and indirectly through its links with some local manufacturing and a variety of commercial activities which service the port and its users in diverse ways. The character of port activity has changed considerably since 1960. The marked contraction of the ocean-going passenger traffic has been compensated by the growth of cross-Channel ferry services and the cruise business as well as by the increased handling of freight, particularly oil (to the Esso refinery at Fawley) and containerised cargo. Such changes have certainly prompted both a decline in the port's direct demand for labour and a reduction in the amount of employment supported indirectly by the port through port-city linkages (Chapter 2).

It should be pointed out, however, that measurement solely in terms of employment growth understates the extent of industrial and commercial expansion in the Southampton SMLA. In all sectors of the economy, the expansion of floorspace has been considerably in excess of employment growth, thus resulting in an increase in the amount of floorspace per employee. Commercial office floorspace in the local authority areas of Southampton, Eastleigh, Winchester, the New Forest and Test Valley together increased by 93 per cent between 1967 and 1979 (Chapter 4). Over the same period, industrial and retailing space each increased by 30 per cent, whilst warehousing floorspace expanded by 150 per cent. Reasons for this expansion in the amount of floorspace per employee include automation (particularly in factories and warehouses), the greater provision of car-parking space and employee amenities, the inclusion of 'landscape space' in many new industrial and office developments, and the increasing proportion of administrative, managerial and professional staff in industrial and commercial occupations (grades which merit higher space standards).

Evidence of the Southampton SMLA's status as a growth area is further indicated by the scale of population growth in the area. In 1961 it contained a population of 430,500; by 1971 this had risen to 496,750, an increase of 15.4 per cent, more than three times the national rate of population growth. Indeed, measured in absolute terms, Southampton was the fifth fastest-growing urban centre in Great Britain (Chapter 6). At the time of writing detailed results from the 1981 Census are not available. However, estimated 1981 population data have been provided by the County Planning Department 'Small Area Population Forecasting Model' which based its predictions on information derived from population surveys undertaken in 1977 and 1978 (Hampshire County Council, 1979a). These estimates indicate that population growth between 1971 and 1981 took place at an appreciably reduced rate of 3.7 per cent, but nonetheless at a rate three times the national average. However, provisional results from the 1981 Census, so far released only for local authority areas and hence not conforming precisely to the SMLA definition of Southampton, suggest that the County Planning Department's estimates may have been somewhat conservative. The five local authority areas covering the Southampton SMLA (but collectively embracing a much larger area) recorded a total population increase of 33,000. Although the 5.6 per cent growth rate was much lower than that for the previous inter-censal period, it was nevertheless well in excess of the 0.5 per cent growth rate for the whole of England and Wales (Hampshire County Council, 1981).

The number of dwellings in the SMLA has increased at an even faster rate than the growth of population would suggest, increasing by 25 per cent between 1961 and 1971 and by 19 per cent between 1971 and 1978 (Hampshire County Council, 1973 and 1978b). In part at least, this rate of addition to the housing stock has been a function of a high rate of household formation. The average size of household in the SMLA has fallen from 3.06 persons in 1961 to 2.67 in 1981, mainly as a result of the increase in one- and two-person households. Elements which have contributed to this trend include the contracting of younger marriages and the tendency for more young people to seek a house of their own earlier in the life cycle. In addition, the number of one-parent families has increased, although their significance is still fairly limited and they account for under 2 per cent of all households in Hampshire (Hampshire County Council, 1980b). However, by far the most significant factor in the expansion in the number of households has been the growth in the number of independent pensionable households. Well over half of all the one- and two-person households in the SMLA contain at least one pensioner. This is not simply a reflection of the fact that pensioners are now proportionately more significant in the local population; rather it is also that elderly residents appear more willing than ever before to form separate households (Hampshire County Council, 1980b). Retirement migration into the area has also contributed considerably to the increase in the number of elderly households living in the Southampton city region, especially in the Lymington area which is one of the main areas of retirement migration in Great Britain (Law and Warnes, 1976).

As it has increased in size, so the structure of Southampton's population has changed. Three main trends may be observed (Chapter 6). First, there has been an upward shift in occupational status, reflecting the changing nature of the local economy, notably the rapid growth of the service sector and of the science-based industries which employ large numbers of white-collar staff. Secondly, there has been a growing ethnic diversity in Southampton, as its New Commonwealth population has increased in relative significance. Even so, the size of the coloured population, both in absolute and relative terms, remains small by national standards, so that Southampton fails to figure amongst the first 25 British cities ranked according to the size of their 1971 coloured population (Jones, 1978). Thirdly, Southampton's age structure has changed. As mentioned above, the proportion of people of pensionable age increased (thereby necessitating the much greater provision of welfare services for the elderly). But in addition, the population under 30 years of age has also increased,

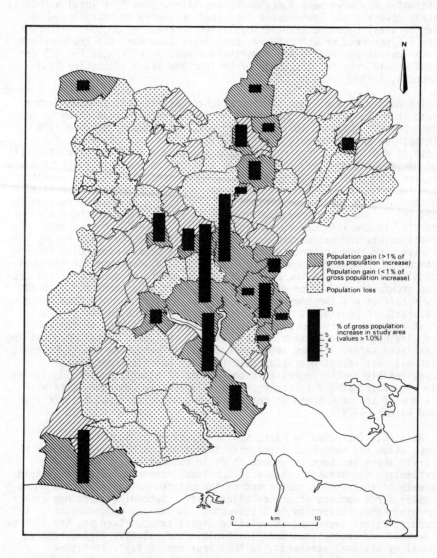

Figure 1.4 Population change in the Southampton SMLA, 1961–71.

Population gain (>1% of gross population increase)

Population gain (<1% of gross population increase)

Population loss

% of gross population increase in study area (values >1.0%)

N

prompted by a relatively high birth rate and by the substantial migration of young families into the area. The 'baby boom' of the 1960s has now reached the late teenage and early 20s cohorts, thus increasing the proportion of the population of working age and unhappily also resulting in rising levels of youth unemployment (Chapter 12). In addition, the decline in the birth rate during the 1970s now means that many primary schools are faced with falling rolls.

SOME CONSEQUENCES OF GROWTH

Undoubtedly the principal spatial trend associated with this economic and demographic growth in the Southampton SMLA has been its progressive decentralisation over much of the study area. This 'spillover' of development has, in its turn, led to the emergence of new patterns and to a whole range of consequences not only for the general settlement system (Chapter 8), but also for the physical environment (Chapters 9 and 10).

The increase in employment and population has, for the most part, been accommodated outside the SMLA core (as represented by the City of Southampton). Admittedly, Southampton itself was the main focus of absolute population growth during the 1960s, accounting for 15.2 per cent of the net increase in SMLA population (Fig.1.4). However, its rate of population growth was only 5 per cent compared with 25 per cent in the rest of the SMLA. Outside the city, but within its immediate orbit, three separate and essentially suburban areas have contributed significantly to population growth, namely along the west side of Southampton Water (a corridor known as the Waterside Parishes), to the north and north-west of Southampton in Eastleigh MB, North Baddesley and Romsey MB, and on the eastern side of the river Itchen from Fair Oak southwards to Bursledon. Further afield, population growth was also evident in Lymington MB and along a small axis running northwards from Winchester. But despite the overall substantial increase in population, there were parts of the SMLA which actually lost population during the 1960s, particularly the outlying rural areas such as the New Forest, the Test Valley and the downland tracts of Winchester RD. In these parts, the proportional importance of the elderly in the population has been increased as younger people have left in search of employment elsewhere (Hampshire County Council, 1980b).

Between 1971 and 1981, however, there was a substantial reversal of trends in that according to the provisional results of the 1981 Census, the City of Southampton sustained an 11,000 decline in its population, equivalent to 5 per cent of its 1971 population (Hampshire County Council, 1981). In fact, population loss was experienced in nearly all parts of the city during the 1970s. In the 1960s 10 of the city's 18 wards, all in the inner city, had declined in population, but this had been more than compensated by growth in the remaining wards. Between 1971 and 1981 there was an acceleration in the rate of population loss in those 10 wards, whilst another five suffered a reversal of population trends. As a result, from a situation of accounting for 47.6 per cent of SMLA population in 1961, the City of Southampton's share had fallen to 39.3 per cent by 1981, and its population in 1981 was smaller than 20 years earlier. However, population continued to increase in the rest of the SMLA; the four peripheral local authority areas embraced by the SMLA

11

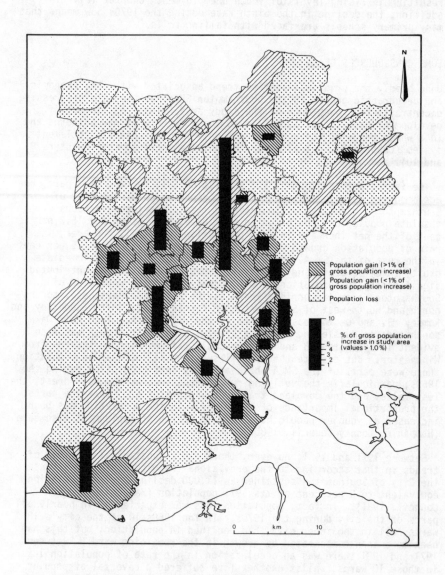

Figure 1.5 Population change in the Southampton SMLA, 1971–81.

Legend within figure:

Population gain (>1% of gross population increase)

Population gain (<1% of gross population increase)

Population loss

% of gross population increase in study area (values > 1.0 %)

10
5
4
3
2
1

0   km   10

N

showed an inter-censal increase of 42,000 residents (+11 per cent) (Hampshire County Council, 1981). To an even greater extent than in the 1960s, the city was surrounded by an almost continuous belt of population growth, largely of a suburban character and related for the most part to the continuing buoyancy of the local economy and to the exhaustion of building-land supply within the city boundaries (Fig.1.5). Further afield, only Lymington made a substantial contribution to aggregate population growth, increases in the Winchester area being much reduced compared with those experienced during the 1960s. Population loss was again conspicuous in the rural fringes of the SMLA, although to a lesser degree in the case of the New Forest than had been so during the previous decade.

In summary, therefore, the Southampton SMLA has during the past two decades experienced two distinct phases of population decentralisation. During the 1960s the decentralisation was relative, with the core (the City of Southampton) growing at a slower rate than the periphery or ring (the rest of the SMLA). During the 1970s, however, the decentralisation became absolute, with population loss occurring in the core and so contrasting with continued growth in the periphery (Chapter 6). This observed transformation suggests that Southampton has been faithfully following the 'city life-cycle' path as proposed by Drewett et al. (1976).

The main process contributing to the growth of population outside the City of Southampton has been in-migration both from the SMLA core and from other parts of the country. Migration to the periphery has been selective in terms of both age and social group. Because household mobility is generally related to changes in the family 'life cycle', particularly the setting up of an independent household (usually on marriage) and because of increasing space requirements at the child-bearing, child-rearing and child-launching stages, it is not surprising to find that it is the young and child-rearing age groups which have increased most rapidly in the periphery. However, as indicated earlier, there are certain parts of the periphery, notably the Lymington area, which have been a focus for retirement migration (Barnard, 1978). In addition, increased representation of the higher-status social groups in the periphery has occurred at a faster rate than for other social groups. This is borne out by the housing tenure characteristics of the periphery; for example, in both Eastleigh and the New Forest around two-thirds of housing is owner-occupied compared with only one half in Southampton. Semi- and unskilled social groups, on the other hand, have displayed the least ability to move to the growth areas of the SMLA ring. Their apparent exclusion is related to a range of factors, notably low incomes that inhibit their ability to enter the owner-occupied sector of the housing market, but also because of the time and cost involved in a longer journey-to-work, and the general difficulty of inter-authority moves within the public-housing sector (Chapter 6). There is, therefore, some suggestion of social polarisation within the Southampton SMLA and that this has been an integral part of the broad process of decentralisation.

As population has decentralised, so population-serving activities (most notably retailing) have also expanded outside the core area, albeit sometimes only after a substantial time-lag. There has been relatively little retail development in central Southampton in recent

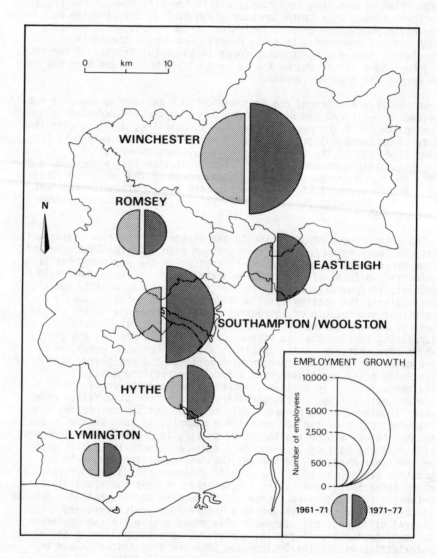

Figure 1.6 Employment growth by employment office area, 1961–77.

years, in marked contrast to the experience of most other British cities (Chapter 5). However, the city centre was extensively rebuilt immediately after the Second World War on account of severe bomb-damage, and as a result there have been few sites suitable for redevelopment during the past two decades. Most new retail schemes have occurred in suburban locations, for example with the development of a number of district centres and hypermarkets. In part, this reflects the aim of retail organisations to seek out convenient locations for the attraction of the affluent and generally car-owning suburbanites. It also reflects their policies of product diversification and the concentration of retail floorspace in fewer, larger and supposedly more efficient units, often necessitating sizeable greenfield site developments (Chapter 5). Paralleling this suburbanisation of retailing and other population-serving activities has been a tendency for those services within the periphery to become more spatially concentrated. This rationalisation has meant that many of the more rural parts of the SMLA periphery have been progressively deprived of certain amenities, such as the village shop, the local doctor, the branch post office and the bus service, and thereby posing particular problems for the elderly and for those who lack access to a car (Hampshire County Council, 1980b).

Although to a lesser degree, the pattern of employment in the SMLA has also shown signs of decentralisation since 1961. A considerable number of new jobs have been created in the SMLA core (Southampton-Woolston), but the rate of job creation has been much slower than within the periphery, where Winchester and, to a less extent, Eastleigh have emerged as employment growth centres (Fig.1.6). So, the share of total SMLA employment contained in the Southampton-Woolston area has fallen from 64 per cent in 1961 to 58 per cent by 1977. A number of factors can be offered in an attempt to explain this decentralisation of employment. First, local government reorganisation in 1974 was associated with a considerable expansion in the number of local government employees working in Winchester. In some cases staff were physically relocated to Winchester from offices elsewhere in the county. In many other cases, there was no change in the place of work, merely that they were now paid from Winchester; however, for statistical purposes employees are allocated to the location from which they are paid, hence this change in the source of remuneration has served to greatly enlarge the number of workers ascribed to Winchester (Chapter 4). Secondly, the City of Southampton has suffered from an acute shortage of land for industrial development, and this has prevented any large-scale industrial estate construction within its boundaries during the last 20 years. Instead, the development of industrial estates has been undertaken in the peripheral districts, particularly in Totton, Romsey, New Milton and at a number of locations in Eastleigh. Superior accessibility has further encouraged industrial development in certain parts of the ring. Because of its site characteristics, Southampton has for long suffered severe traffic congestion, especially during the rush hours. Technological developments, road improvements and changes in the character of the port have contributed to a weakening of the ties which necessitated the location of port-related activities within, or close to, the dock gates, permitting their dispersal over a much wider area. Suburban population growth has also played its part in encouraging industrial and commercial growth outside Southampton, in order to tap local labour supplies and also because of the creation of a local market of sufficient size to sustain a greater number and range of population-related activities. Indeed, the decentralisation of retailing, and especially the development of superstores and hypermarkets, has been a major, although rarely acknowledged source of employment opportunity in the suburbs, particularly for married women wishing to work on a part-time basis and constrained by the need to seek employment close to the home (Alexander and Dawson, 1979). For example, the Carrefour hypermarket at Eastleigh employs approximately 500 staff, of whom three-quarters are female and mainly work part-time.

The changing location of homes and workplaces, allied to the general increase in car ownership, have had implications for journey-to-work patterns. Particularly in Southampton, although also in other parts of the SMLA, there was a reduction between 1961 and 1971 in the proportion of employees both living and working within the same local authority area. Although the 1981 Census results are needed for an adequate appraisal, there is evidence to suggest that the degree of 'self-containment' has further declined during the 1970s, resulting in a significant increase in commuting both into and out of the City of Southampton (Hampshire County Council, 1980a). Furthermore, the size of journey-to-work flows within the periphery also seems likely to have increased, possibly at a faster rate than flows to the city centre. Work trips within the periphery are largely undertaken by car, and because of the radial nature of most public transport routes, the non-car user wishing to commute within the ring faces severe accessibility problems. Certainly, the use of the car for commuting has increased in all parts of the SMLA. A recent Planning Department report, for example, noted that, although the number of people leaving Southampton city centre during the evening rush hour has remained at roughly the same level since 1967, twice as many people now go home in cars as by public transport, compared with equal proportions in 1967 (Southern Evening Echo, 3.3.81).

The increase in population, households and employment has inevitably precipitated much new construction, of housing, factories, warehouses and offices, as well as of roads, shops, schools and other social infrastructure. Indeed, one observer commented in the mid-1970s that the overriding impression of South Hampshire is "of new building everywhere" (Gladstone, 1976, 59). A large proportion of this building activity not surprisingly has occurred outside the SMLA core (Chapter 8). For example, much of the new housing built between 1974 and 1980 was located in Eastleigh, Romsey, Totton and the Waterside Parishes while residential development in Southampton has been mainly confined to the Lordshill district, a new suburb just within the city's northern boundary (Fig.1.7). Consequently, although between 1961 and 1971 the dwelling stock increased by 40 per cent in Southampton and by 35 per cent elsewhere in the SMLA, the respective rates of growth between 1971 and 1978 were 8 and 22 per cent (Hampshire County Council, 1973 and 1979b). This new residential development has partly been accommodated by the processes of infilling and redevelopment within the existing built-up areas and partly by the grafting of housing estates onto formerly free-standing villages and hamlets located beyond the city boundary (Fig.1.8). Many of these former rural settlements close to Southampton are today little more than modern 'Wimpey-land' suburbs, with only the occasional thatched cottage and converted farm building surviving as remainders of a byegone age when such settlements

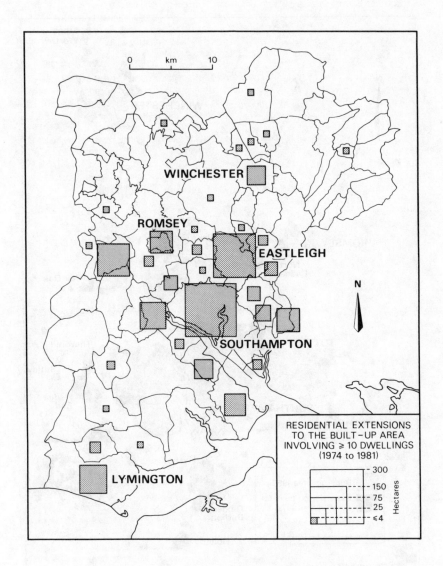

Figure 1.7 Residential extensions to the built-up area, 1974 – 81.

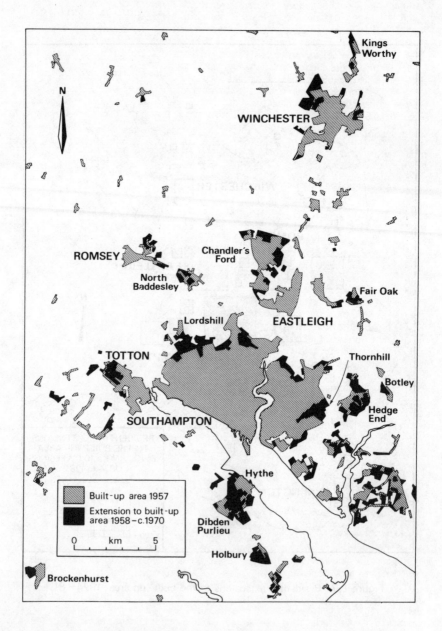

Figure 1.8   The growth of the built-up area from 1958 to circa 1970.

18

fulfilled a very different role. Even remoter villages well beyond the newly-spawned built-up areas have succombed to Southampton's influence through their increasing role as dormitory settlements for professional and managerial occupational groups. The small amount of new development in such villages often conceals the resultant and very real social stresses. For example, "within a village an old woman who has taught at the local school all her life and whose father may have been the rector of the parish may find herself living next door to an IBM executive who has lived in three different continents within the last five years" (Gladstone, 1976, 59). Likewise the larger historic towns, such as Romsey and Winchester, have also come under considerable threat and pressure from commercial developers.

One consequence of the expansion of the built-up area has been the disappearance under bricks and mortar of considerable tracts of agricultural land. Horticulture (especially the growing of straw-berries), concentrated in the south-east corner of the SMLA, has been particularly adversely affected by urban development, largely because horticultural areas were typically interspersed around and within the margins of the built-up area. But horticulture aside, it has been claimed that the agricultural land lost to urban development during the post-war period has not been of the highest quality (Buchanan, 1966). Nonetheless, urban growth has had some subtle effects upon farming. As Sinclair (1967) has argued from a theoretical standpoint, the expectation of urbanisation at some time in the relatively near future has inhibited farmers on the urban fringe from investing in their farms and prompted them instead to adopt less intensive farming practices with a resulting loss of visual attractiveness. For example, the grazing of horses and ponies for recreational use has become particularly widespread on agricultural land around the margins of Southampton (Hampshire County Council, 1980a). In addition, many farms close to the urban fringe either have become 'pick-your-own' enterprises concerned with the cultivation of fruit and vegetables or have adopted roadside selling practices in order to capitalise on their proximity to the urban market and to absorb the profits of the traditional wholesaler and retailer.

In contrast to the considerable development activity in the periphery of the SMLA during the past 20 years or so, the inner districts of Southampton have been characterised by under-investment in the housing stock and economic base. A large proportion of the housing in the inner city is now reaching the end of its economic life, having been built prior to the First World War; not surprisingly much is now suffering from physical deterioration and a lack of basic amenities. Current housing policy is attempting to prolong the life of such housing by making available grants for improvement in certain narrowly defined areas. To date that policy has met with only limited success and the problem of obsolescent and inadequate housing continues to confront the City Council (Chapter 7). There has also been a low level of investment in the manufacturing sector in inner Southampton. Here, as in other British cities, property companies have shown great reluctance to build industrial estates in inner-city areas, preferring instead to develop on greenfield sites in the periphery. The only substantial investment to be made in inner Southampton over the past two decades has been in office development, but this investment has been very much confined to the city centre, and to the neglect of the run-down areas of pre-1914 development located immediately outside the central business district.

So, despite the overall growth and prosperity of the Southampton SMLA during the past two decades, it is clear that spatial inequality has persisted, and arguably has increased. Resources have been attracted to the suburbs to create jobs and build homes, roads and social infrastructure for their affluent, car-owning middle-class residents and to the detriment of the inner city. Certainly, the symptoms of inner-city decline in Southampton are considerably less problematic than in many other British cities; nevertheless, it is sobering to note that a prosperous local economy and an expanding population has not prevented their eradication. Perhaps the one consolation is that, according to Donnison and Soto (1980), there is less inequality in a prosperous city than in a declining one.

URBAN GROWTH AND THE PHYSICAL ENVIRONMENT

Two strongly contrasting physical environments constitute the landscape of the Southampton city region (Fig.1.9). The northern part comprises a broad belt of mainly upland country, rising in places to 150 metres, and developed on the outcrop of the Chalk. To the south is a lower-lying area, rarely exceeding 80 metres, developed on outcrops of Tertiary sands, gravels and clays. Flowing south through the Chalk downlands and across the Tertiary lowlands are the two principal rivers, the Itchen and the Test, which converge to form Southampton Water. The shorter Beaulieu and Hamble rivers drain only Tertiary country. The Solent coastline is for the most part characterised by accretion, both through the development of shingle spits and as a result of the accumulation of widespread mudflats and salt marshes. However, there are some stretches of the Solent coast which suffer erosion, particularly where weaker Tertiary rocks have been fashioned into low cliffs, notably around Christchurch Bay (Small, 1964).

Opportunities

This physical landscape has offered a benign environment within which demographic and economic growth, together with the expansion of settlement, have proceeded relatively unfettered. For the most part, the relief of the area is gentle, thereby posing only the occasional developmental problem (Chapter 9). In addition, few parts of the area are subject to extreme natural hazard: river flooding and tidal inundation, for example, affect only a small number of localities (South Hampshire Plan Advisory Committee, 1969), while the most significant natural hazard, coastal erosion, is largely confined to Christchurch Bay where, despite extensive investment in cliff defences, a number of buildings have been lost and others are now in a precarious position following recent cliff slumping (Clark, Ricketts and Small, 1976).

Urban growth in the Southampton area has in fact been positively facilitated by the availability of local natural resources (Chapter 9). The Chalklands, because they are well-drained and easy to work, are of a high agricultural quality. They are classified by the Ministry of Agriculture as being of 'above' or 'well above' national average

20

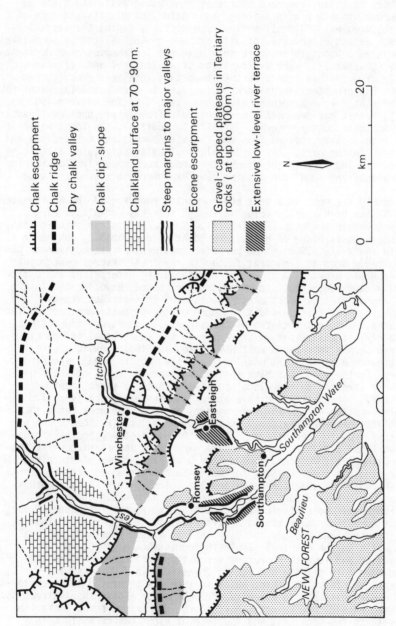

Chalk escarpment

Chalk ridge

Dry chalk valley

Chalk dip‑slope

Chalkland surface at 70–90 m.

Steep margins to major valleys

Eocene escarpment

Gravel‑capped plateaus in Tertiary rocks (at up to 100m.)

Extensive low‑level river terrace

N

0   km   20

Figure 1.9 The geomorphology of South West Hampshire
(after R.J.Small).

21

productivity and have promoted a thriving and efficient farming sector
(Tavener, 1964, 141; Buchanan, 1966). The Tertiary country, in
contrast, is generally of much less agricultural value, although there
are some pockets of Grade A land between Southampton and Fareham.
However, it is an important source of sand and gravel, and these
resources, together with sea-won aggregates, have satisfied much of
the requirements of local construction activity during the last 20
years. Recent discoveries of oil, gas and geothermal energy seem likely
to provide a boost to economic growth in the Southampton area during the
1980s (Chapter 12). The availability of a plentiful and reliable
supply of water has been a further important local resource. Urban
growth has prompted a considerable increase in the demand for water (by
47 per cent in the Hampshire River and Water Division between 1962 and
1977), but it has been met almost entirely from local supplies (Chapter
10; Hampshire County Council, 1979b). In addition, the local water is
of a high quality, coming from the Chalk at a constant temperature and
volume. In the past, this high quality of water stimulated a thriving
watercress industry in the Winchester area; more recently fish-farming
enterprises and syndicate fishing have exploited this same resource.

Possibly the most important environmental resource of the Southampton
area is its high amenity value, although this has not always been
appreciated in the past (Chapter 11). Southampton clearly falls within
the South Coast ridge of highest residential desirability in the UK
(Gould and White, 1968). The perceived residential attractiveness has
undoubtedly been an important factor in the SMLA's recent demographic
and economic growth. A number of manufacturing enterprises and offices,
in many cases decentralising from Greater London, have located in the
Southampton area at least partly because of this attractiveness
(Chapters 3 and 4). In addition, much of the population migration into
the area has been associated with residential amenity considerations.
Certainly, it has been a major factor in the substantial inflow of
retired people into South West Hampshire, and their pensions have
constituted a significant non-local addition to the area's spending
power. Furthermore, the high residential amenity value of the area,
which is stressed by many local employers in their recruitment
publicity, seems likely to have attracted many economically-active
people into the area. The high amenity value of the area has also
stimulated heavy recreational useage, both by local residents and by
visitors from further afield. The New Forest is the principal focus for
recreational activity, but there are many other important tourist and
recreational attractions, such as the historic centres of Winchester and
Romsey and the opportunities for water-based recreation offered around
the shores of Southampton Water and the Solent. The City of Southampton
is used by many visitors as a base from which to explore the many
environmental and historic attractions of the region, although it does
have a number of major tourist attractions in its own right. Indeed,
"next to York and Chester the City has the finest remaining medieval
town walls in the country" (Southern Tourist Board, 1980, 28).
Recreation and tourism represent a boost to local spending and have
stimulated both private and public investment in a variety of
recreational infrastructure, which in turn has generated local employment opportunities. In the City of Southampton alone, total direct and
indirect expenditure by staying visitors, day trippers and those 'in
transit' to the Continent and the Isle of Wight has recently been
estimated as being worth between £26 and £30 million, and provides

direct employment for well over 4000, mainly unskilled workers (Southern Tourist Board, 1980).

Constraints

The physical environment has on occasions and in certain localities played a restraining role in the pattern of urban growth (Chapter 9). There are some situations where development would clearly be imprudent, as for example along certain sections of the coast and in some river valleys where erosion and flooding respectively constitute real hazards; but the number of instances is very small compared with many other parts of the country. However, the pressure of development has been such as to warrant use on many occasions of less suitable sites, as for example marshy tracts. Generally speaking, the difficulties presented by such sites can be overcome by civil engineering, but not without incurring higher development costs.

Consequences

The relationship between urban growth and the physical environment is, of course, a reciprocal one, wherein just as the pattern of growth reacts to environmental constraints, so growth itself induces a range of environmental repercussions (Chapter 9). In some instances that environmental impact is essentially negative in character, as when the spread of the built-up area sterilises land resources under a blanket of bricks and mortar. In other cases, growth has visually intrusive effects, such as caused by the spoil banks thrown up by sand and gravel working, by the cutting of great swathes across the countryside for new arterial roads and by the construction of electricity transmission lines and high-rise buildings. Urban growth also has a detrimental impact on the environment by impinging upon specific components of the physical system - on water (both freshwater and marine), air and land resources.

Urban growth can affect the hydrological characteristics of the physical environment in a variety of ways (Park, 1981). Spread of the built-up area produces a modification of the runoff pattern of the drainage basin through increasing the amount of impervious surfaces and the speed with which water is transmitted into channel systems. This, in turn, tends to raise the volume of streamflow and intensify flood peaks. Sediment yields of streams are also increased, especially during the construction phase, whilst river water quality is adversely affected by the discharge of domestic and industrial effluents (Chapter 10). Fortunately, with the exception of local problems created by sporadic pollution from industrial effluents, the latter does not constitute a serious problem in the Southampton area, and only very small localised stretches of river are polluted severely enough to be classified as being of 'poor quality' (Hampshire County Council, 1977a). The coastal waters are perhaps rather more vulnerable as a result of their exposure to chemical pollution by industrial effluents, to thermal pollution by the cooling systems of the power stations and the possibility of oil spills at the Fawley refinery. However, to date the Esso refinery has maintained a relatively clean record regarding spillages, while one indicator of marine pollution levels, the concentration of heavy metals found in oysters, is low in the Solent compared with other British coastal waters (Department of the Environment, 1980).

The growth of housing, traffic, power generation and industry has inevitably raised levels of air pollution. Much of the industry in the Southampton area is categorised as 'clean', but the Fawley petro-chemical complex and the power stations at Marchwood and Fawley, all located along the western shore of Southampton Water, do pose a serious threat to atmospheric quality. Evidence provided by a government survey of air pollution during the period 1961 to 1971 suggested that pollution levels in and around Southampton were no higher than the average for the South East, the only exception being in the immediate vicinity of the Fawley oil refinery (Warren Springs Laboratory, 1972). City growth and the resultant increase in atmospheric emissions may be expected to have a climatic response in the form of an 'urban heat island'. Whether such a feature is well developed over Southampton has yet to be substantiated; the extent of water surfaces might be expected to dissipate the general effect, although there is evidence of a broad heat island being developed over Portsmouth (Harrison, 1976). However, the Fawley complex does generate an industrial haze and also a smell which can drift as far east as Portsmouth when the wind conditions are right (Warren Springs Laboratory, 1972).

Possibly the most significant impact of recent urban growth on the physical environment has stemmed from the greatly increased demand for countryside recreation. One indication of this enormous intensifica-tion of 'people pressure' on the Hampshire countryside is the fact that in 1979 there were over 2.5 million visitors to sites managed by the County Recreation Department, this representing an annual growth of 15 per cent since 1974 (Hampshire County Council, 1979b). Recreational pressure is most acute in the New Forest, a unique area representing the largest single tract of unenclosed, semi-natural vegetation now remaining in Lowland Britain. In addition, its diversity of flora and fauna, its range of habitats and its number of species now thought to be rare in Britain makes it a site of immense ecological significance (New Forest Steering Committee, 1970). Recreational problems were dismissed quite lightly in the report on the New Forest published soon after the Second World War (Forestry Commission, 1947); certainly there was no anticipation of the degree to which demands would increase. In 1977 some 6 million daytrippers and over 800,000 campers visited the New Forest; comparable figures in 1968 were 3.5 million and 400,000 (Hampshire County Council, 1977a; New Forest Steering Committee, 1970). Undoubtedly, this recreational pressure, which is most intense in the summer months, has resulted in a steady erosion of the Forest's intrinsic character, conflict with its other important interests (especially forestry and the grazing of livestock), disturbance of wildlife and ecological damage. But other parts of the Southampton area are under acute pressure, notably the coast and the in-shore waters. Here, although the demand for marinas and moorings appears to be insatiable and the proliferation of pleasure boats endless, capacities are fast reaching saturation point (Hampshire County Council, 1980a).

THE PLANNING RESPONSE

Planning policies in operation for approximately the first half of the period under consideration were essentially uncoordinated in the sense that until the preparation of the South Hampshire Structure Plan, the

SMLA was controlled by two separate and independent planning regimes. Development within the City of Southampton was guided by its own Development Plan (1956), while those areas in the remainder of the SMLA were controlled by the Hampshire Development Plan (1955). There was, in short, a lack of any overriding strategy for the city region in order to accommodate and direct the overspill pressures and spontaneous decentralisation which resulted from the general prosperity of the area and the particular shortage of land within the City of Southampton. Indeed, the imposition by the county of an 'unofficial' green belt around the city in 1958 was an attempt to prevent the emergence of "a continuous sprawl of urban development" (Smart, 1964, 156). The city did, nevertheless, succeed in obtaining one extension to its boundary in the early 1960s to allow the development of the Lordshill area for housing. The strict planning policies imposed around Southampton prompted a redirection of development pressures to settlements with existing Town Maps and others considered by the planners as capable of satisfactorily accommodating a measure of further growth and so exempted from the severe planning restrictions operative in the unapproved green belt (Smart, 1964).

Planning policies currently operating in the Southampton SMLA reflect the need to have more strategic planning, a need which became apparent as a direct result of the South East Study (1964). This document identified South Hampshire (subsequently delineated as embracing Southampton SMLA with the exception of the New Forest and Winchester MB and RD, together with the city of Portsmouth and its neighbouring authorities of Havant, Fareham and Gosport) as a self-generating growth area, and thus recommended its selection as one of the locations in South East England to which there might be large-scale planned migration from London. The planning consultants of Colin Buchanan and Partners were then commissioned to investigate the feasibility of accommodating there a total population increase of 300,000 by 1981, of whom 150,000 would represent planned in-migration. However, the striking revelation of their report (Buchanan, 1966) was that spontaneous net in-migration, being then at a level of about 6000 persons per annum and increasing, might well account for nearly all of the proposed intake of migrants. In the circumstances, it became readily evident that South Hampshire's potential contribution to the planned relief of London's overspill problem was likely to be extremely limited. In this regard, it is significant to note that in the plethora of planning documents which followed publication of the South Hampshire Study, there is scarcely reference to the area's role as a reception centre for London's overspill. However, the demise of this possible role for South Hampshire in no way invalidated the basic need at that time for a planning strategy to provide guidelines for the continuing growth and proper development of the area during the remainder of the 20th century (Hall et al., 1973).

In 1968 work began on the preparation of the required planning strategy. Not only was the eventual outcome to be one of the first 'structure plans' produced under the terms of the Town and Country Planning Act (1968), but following the Skeffington Report (1969) the South Hampshire Structure Plan was to be a pioneering venture in terms of positively encouraging public participation in the planning process. Although the first draft of the Plan was published in September 1972, it was not until March 1977 that the Secretary of State for the Environment finally gave official approval to a modified version of the draft plan. This unduly protracted delay possibly stands as an indictment of the procedures embodied in the current machinery of British planning. The delay in approval may well have had damaging effects upon the general economic buoyancy of South Hampshire, in as much that during those years with the fate of the Plan seemingly in the balance and the area held in a sort of planning limbo, there was an understandable reluctance on the part of local authorities to initiate major investment in infrastructure and services. The deleterious impact of the delay and its associated moratorium within the public sector would have been considerably worse had it not been for some makeshift planning by Hampshire County Council (1971 and 1972) and for a general easing of growth rates in the South East as a whole. The latter also prompted a review in 1976 of the Strategic Plan for the South East, which five years earlier had been endorsed by the Government as setting out regional planning policy (SEJPT, 1970 and 1976). Although it was the decline of population and employment in London which precipitated and dominated this reappraisal of the regional strategy, the case was argued that planning for expansion in South Hampshire was unlikely to exacerbate the reversal of the capital's fortunes.

The principal objectives of the South Hampshire Structure Plan (Hampshire County Council, 1977c) may be summarised as being (i) to permit, within defined limits, the continued economic and demographic growth of Southampton and Portsmouth, (ii) to concentrate much new urban growth in clearly defined 'growth sectors', originally six in number, with three located within the Southampton SMLA, and (iii) to conserve large tracts of countryside, especially the Downs and the river valleys, for agriculture, horticulture, recreation and amenity. The district plans for two of the SMLA's 'growth sectors', namely Totton and Chandler's Ford have now been adopted (Hampshire County Council, 1977d and 1980c). Although both areas were originally scheduled for expansion of the same order (a population increase of 8000 in each case), the agreed plans show that only the Totton expansion will proceed as initially suggested, with an addition of 3000 houses, 1400 industrial jobs and 500 office jobs being accommodated between 1981 and 1991. At Chandler's Ford, the expansion has been reduced to an expectation of 1700 houses, 650 industrial jobs and 800 office jobs during the same decade. The altogether larger 'growth sector' proposed for the Horton Heath area, lying to the east of Southampton, has been left somewhat in abeyance, but the County Council recently instigated a study aimed at identifying the opportunities for development in the Hedge End-West End area, although at a scale which would be far less than the 13,000 new dwellings proposed in the approved Structure Plan (Hampshire County Council, 1980a). This scaling down of two of the 'growth sectors' appears to be consistent with the most recent population projections for the plan area as a whole which indicate only an 8 per cent increase between 1981 and 1991, compared with the Structure Plan's projection of 15 per cent (Hampshire County Council, 1980a). These readjustments reflect the flexibility embodied in the 'growth sector' strategy, allowing development to be phased in accordance with changing circumstances.

However, by no means all of the Southampton SMLA is controlled by the provisions of the South Hampshire Structure Plan; parts are governed instead by policies of a rather different complexion. Although closely linked to South Hampshire, the Winchester area in fact falls within the remit of the Mid-Hampshire Structure Plan, which was submitted in 1978 and approved in 1980. Here the policy is one of 'selective restraint', with the conservation of "natural resources, productive capacity and historic features" being set alongside objectives such as the improvement of prosperity, social well-being and mobility (Hampshire County Council, 1978c, 13-14). The Winchester sub-area will receive some limited additional growth; only in the Borden and Andover areas, which lie outside the SMLA boundary, will new development in Mid-Hampshire be actively encouraged. As for the City of Winchester itself, three principal issues emerge, namely the need to maintain adequate access to the city centre, to provide more city-centre car parking for shoppers and tourists and to ensure that the fulfilment of these two requirements is accomplished without harming the historic character of the city centre (Hampshire County Council, 1978c, 94-95).

A policy of possibly even stronger restraint underlies the submitted South West Hampshire Structure Plan (Hampshire County Council, 1980d), which applies to those parts of the New Forest and Solent coast falling within the SMLA. Undoubtedly a prime objective of this draft structure plan is to protect and conserve the unique character of the New Forest and yet at the same time provide for a measure of growth in the towns peripheral to it. The general sensitivity and vulnerability of the Forest to the growth pressures which impinge upon it constitute the major planning issue. Diverse threats are posed by the growth of the Forest towns of Brockenhurst, Lyndhurst and Sway, by the ever-increasing volumes of day-trippers, campers and caravaners and by the efforts to pursue economically-viable forestry and sand and gravel industries. Individually or collectively, such developments could easily provoke irrevocable damage to the inimical character of the New Forest. At the present time, there is also much concern about possible oil exploration within its boundaries and the likely environmental consequences. To the south of the Forest provision will have to be made for some expansion in the Lymington-New Milton area, although the agricultural and landscape value of the Solent coastlands are recognised by their inclusion within a green belt in order to limit the spread of urban development.

At a smaller scale, the pressures on high amenity, natural and man-made environments stemming from the expansion of Southampton have resulted in the adoption of policies of containment and conservation both by local planning authorities and by national statutory bodies. Scenic rural areas have been protected by the creation of four Areas of Outstanding Natural Beauty lying partly or wholly within Hampshire. The creation of nature reserves, sites of special scientific interest and country parks each represent attempts to conserve areas which are important for their plant and animal life or the provision of rural recreation (although in some cases recreational usage is incidental). However, countryside policy in Hampshire has shifted in recent years from a concern simply for the protection of a few valued landscapes and habitats towards a broader approach for the management of all rural areas (Chapter 11). In the New Forest specific strategies have been adopted in an attempt to combat the problems created by 'people pressure'. All but a very small part of the conflict between recreational use and the steady erosion of its special character has been caused by the indiscriminate use of motor vehicles by the visiting

27

public, allowing them to penetrate and erode large areas which would otherwise remain undisturbed. Two main protective measures have been adopted, first the selection of a number of small sites throughout the area where the Forest's interests would not be materially affected and into which motorists could be channelled by the provision of car parks, and second by the creation of car-free areas to limit indiscriminate vehicle penetration (New Forest Joint Steering Committee, 1970).

Measures to protect, conserve and enhance the character of high amenity built environments have included the designation of 'listed' buildings and conservation areas, the latter being defined as areas of "special architectural or historical significance, the character or appearance of which it is desirable to preserve or enhance" (Hampshire County Council, 1980b, 39). Some 34 conservation areas have been designated within the Southampton SMLA, including villages, particular streets in Southampton and historic town centres, notably that of Winchester. Existing buildings in such areas are protected when alteration, demolition or extension is proposed, while new development will only be permitted if it is unobtrusive, sets a high design standard and is likely to make a positive and appropriate contribution to the appearance of the area. The pressures created by traffic have, in some cases, been reduced or eliminated by the provision of alternative car-parking areas and diversionary traffic routes.

For much of the past twenty years or so, therefore, the Southampton SMLA has lacked a continuous, comprehensive and clearly-defined macro-level planning strategy. Rather, when planning policy has not been in limbo, it has been successively restrictive, piecemeal and uncoordinated, and more recently short-term and pragmatic. Nevertheless, it seems incontrovertible that the Southampton area would still have been developed during the past two decades whether or not planning policies existed (Gladstone, 1976). But with the recent emergence of structure plans for the entire area, the guidelines for development are now clearly visible. However, it does seem likely that the division of the Southampton city region between three different planning regimes will only serve to heighten existing intra-SMLA contrasts. A middle belt of rapid expansion and pro-growth planning policies is surrounded on the one side by planning restraint in the periphery and on the other by inner-city decline in the core. In short, the prospect of a further polarisation of growth seems a likely scenario for the 1980s.

This overview of growth and change in the Southampton city region since around 1960 provides the scene for the following essays which look more closely at individual components of growth. The pervading image is one of an area still grappling with the pressures of growth whilst much of the country has been slipping deeper and deeper into decline. Consequently, its problems are predominantly, but not exclusively, the problems of success; nonetheless this does not render them any less pressing. Indeed, the lessons learnt may serve as a basis for the planning of other city regions in the event of the arrival of the economic recovery that has been promised by successive governments since the mid 1960s.

REFERENCES

ALEXANDER, I (1979), Employment in retailing: a case study of employment
          in suburban shopping centres, Geoforum, 10, 407-425.

BACON, R and ELTIS, W (1978), Britain's Economic Problem: Too Few
          Producers (London, Macmillan).

BARNARD, K C (1978), The Residential Geography of the Elderly: a
          Multiple-Scale Approach (Unpublished PhD thesis, University
          of Southampton).

BUCHANAN, C and Partners (1966), South Hampshire Study (London, HMSO).

CLARK, M J, RICKETTS, P and SMALL, R J (1976), Barton does not rule the
          waves, Geographical Magazine, 48, 580-587.

DREWETT, R, GODDARD, J and SPEAKE, N (1976), British Cities: Urban
          Population and Employment Trends, 1951-71 (London, Department
          of the Environment).

DEPARTMENT OF THE ENVIRONMENT (1980), Digest of Environmental Pollution
          and Water Statistics (London, HMSO), 3.

DONNISON, D and SOTO, P (1980), The Good City: a Study of Urban
          Development and Policy in Britain (London, Heinemann).

FORESTRY COMMISSION (1947), Report of the New Forest Committee (London,
          HMSO), cmmd 7245.

GLADSTONE, F (1976), The Politics of Planning (London, Temple Smith).

GOULD, P R and WHITE, R R (1968), The mental maps of British school
          leavers, Regional Studies, 2, 161-182.

HALL, P, GRACEY, H, DREWETT, R and THOMAS, R (1973), The Containment of
          Urban England (London, Allen and Unwin), vol.1, ch.9.

HALL, P (1980), Regional planning: directions for the 1980s, Town
          Planning Review, 51, 253-256.

HALL, P (1981), Issues for the Eighties, The Planner, 67, 4-5.

HAMPSHIRE COUNTY COUNCIL (1971), South Hampshire Interim Policy Plan,
          No.1 (Winchester, County Planning Department).

HAMPSHIRE COUNTY COUNCIL (1972), South Hampshire Interim Policy Plan,
          No.2 (Winchester, County Planning Department).

HAMPSHIRE COUNTY COUNCIL (1973), Hampshire Digest of Statistics 1961-
          1971 (Winchester, County Planning Department).

HAMPSHIRE COUNTY COUNCIL (1977a), Hampshire Facts and Figures
          (Winchester, County Planning Department).

HAMPSHIRE COUNTY COUNCIL (1977b), South East Hampshire employment study: employment structure and trends, County Planning Department Research and Intelligence Group, Working Paper 77/3.

HAMPSHIRE COUNTY COUNCIL (1977c), South Hampshire Structure Plan (Winchester, County Planning Department).

HAMPSHIRE COUNTY COUNCIL (1977d), Totton District Plan (Winchester, County Planning Department).

HAMPSHIRE COUNTY COUNCIL (1978a), Southampton Travel-to-Work Area (Winchester, County Chief Executive).

HAMPSHIRE COUNTY COUNCIL (1978b), Hampshire Strategic Monitoring Report (Winchester, County Planning Department).

HAMPSHIRE COUNTY COUNCIL (1978c), Mid-Hampshire Structure Plan (Winchester, County Planning Department).

HAMPSHIRE COUNTY COUNCIL (1979a), Small area population forecasts County Planning Department Research and Intelligence Group Technical Series, 79/1.

HAMPSHIRE COUNTY COUNCIL (1979b), Hampshire Facts and Figures (Winchester, County Planning Department).

HAMPSHIRE COUNTY COUNCIL (1980a), Hampshire Strategic Monitoring Report (Winchester, County Planning Department).

HAMPSHIRE COUNTY COUNCIL (1980b), Hampshire Facts and Figures (Winchester, County Planning Department).

HAMPSHIRE COUNTY COUNCIL (1980c), Chandler's Ford District Plan (Winchester, County Planning Department).

HAMPSHIRE COUNTY COUNCIL (1980d), South West Hampshire Structure Plan (Winchester, County Planning Department).

HAMPSHIRE COUNTY COUNCIL (1981), 1981 Census Newsletter, County Planning Department Research and Intelligence Group, 3.

HARRISON, S J (1976), Local climates of the Portsmouth area, in MOTTERSHEAD, D N and RILEY, R C (eds), Portsmouth Geographical Essays, 2, 51-65.

JONES, P N (1978), The distribution and diffusion of the coloured population in England and Wales 1961-71, Transactions, Institute of British Geographers, 3, 533-547.

LAW, C M and WARNES, A M (1976), The changing geography of the elderly in England and Wales, Transactions, Institute of British Geographers, 1, 453-471.

MONKHOUSE, F J (ed.)(1964), A Survey of Southampton and its Region (Southampton, British Association).

NEW FOREST JOINT STEERING COMMITTEE (1970), Conservation of the New Forest (Winchester, Hampshire County Council).

PARK, C C (1981), Man, river systems and environmental impacts, Progress in Physical Geography, 5, 1-31.

RILEY, R C and SMITH, J-L (1981), Industrialization in naval ports: the Portsmouth case, in HOYLE, B S and PINDER, D A (eds), Cityport Industrialization and Regional Development: Spatial Analysis and Planning Strategies (Oxford, Pergamon), 133-150.

SINCLAIR, R (1967), Van Thünen and urban sprawl, Annals of the Association of American Geographers, 57, 72-87.

SMALL, R J (1964), Geomorphology, in MONKHOUSE, F J (ed.), A Survey of Southampton and its Region (Southampton, British Association), 37-50.

SMART, A D G (1964), The Hampshire Development Plan, in MONKHOUSE, F J (ed.), A Survey of Southampton and its Region (Southampton, British Association), 152-168.

SOUTH EAST JOINT PLANNING TEAM (1970), Strategic Plan for the South East (London, HMSO).

SOUTH EAST JOINT PLANNING TEAM (1976), Strategy for the South East: 1976 Review (London, HMSO).

SOUTH HAMPSHIRE PLAN ADVISORY COMMITTEE (1969), Study Report A: Rural Conservation, 5 (Winchester, South Hampshire Plan Technical Unit).

SOUTHERN TOURIST BOARD (1980), Southampton Tourism Study 1979-1980 (Southampton, Southern Tourist Board/Southampton City Council).

SOUTHAMPTON CITY COUNCIL (1981), Office Policy and Employment (Southampton, City Planning Officer).

TAVENER, L E (1964), Land use and agriculture, in MONKHOUSE, F J (ed.), A Survey of Southampton and its Region (Southampton, British Association), 131-140.

WARREN SPRINGS LABORATORY (1972), National Survey of Air Pollution 1961-71 (London, HMSO), 1.

31

2 The Port and its Local Multiplier Effect
M E WITHERICK

Given Southampton's undoubted repute as a deep-sea port, it would be tempting to devote this essay to a thorough appraisal of its current ranking and status both within the national port hierarchy and at an international level(1). However, rather than pursue this particular line of investigation, attention will be directed instead towards the somewhat neglected matter of the strictly local repercussions of the port function. By identifying and calibrating the major functional links which stem from the docks and impinge upon the local area, an attempt will be made to determine what the port function really means to the economy of Southampton and to the city's immediate hinterland(2). Within this specific spatial framework, two key questions will be addressed. Has the port made a significant contribution to the overall growth experienced in the study area over the last two decades? To what extent have changes in the nature of Southampton's port traffic during the same period affected the degree of port-dependence in the local economy and the potency of the port's local multiplier effect? In order to set this whole investigation in context and to provide a perspective on significant developments of the recent past, some consideration will be given initially to the latter question.

PORT CHANGES

Traffic

As with so many major ports, the character of Southampton's maritime activity has undergone a fairly radical transformation during the last twenty years. The ocean-going passenger trade, on which Southampton's reputation as a port was so substantially built in the first half of the century, has declined considerably from over 370,000 passengers in 1960 to a total now half that figure (Fig.2.1). The make-up of that passenger traffic has also changed. In 1960 84 per cent were line-voyage passengers. However, with the virtual cessation of all regular services to the United States, South Africa, Australia and New Zealand, 80 per cent of the ocean-going traffic is now accounted for by cruise passengers. Although the popularisation of the cruise business has helped to soften the impact of a progressive withdrawal of line services, it has been the growth in cross-Channel passenger traffic which has really saved the day. The decision taken by British Railways in 1963 to withdraw the one cross-Channel ferry service operated from Southampton, that to Le Havre, was regarded at the time as a serious blow to the fortunes of the port. However, the apparently detrimental action was soon turned to advantage when, in the following year, Thoresen Ferries were permitted to take up the lapsed link and so inaugurated the first of Southampton's roll on/roll off (RO/RO) ferry services. Today, the two companies of P & O Normandy Ferries and Townsend Thoresen Car Ferries operate services to Le Havre and to Cherbourg and   Le Havre respectively, whilst the MacAndrews Shipping Company runs a weekly ferry to Bordeaux and Bilbao. There is now an annual throughput of over 900,000 passengers. In terms of vehicles, the RO/RO services reached a peak in 1973, when traffic amounted to almost 300,000 vehicles. The somewhat worrying contraction of that traffic which persisted throughout the remainder of the 1970s does now seem to have been halted, with throughput in 1980 recovering to 72 per cent of its 1973 volume.

Table 2.1

Cargo throughput, 1980.
(thousand tonnes)

	Import	Export	Total
Cereals (incl. flour)	98	75	173
Fruit and vegetables	392	-	392
Other foodstuffs	204	218	422
Timber	27	-	27
Non-ferrous ores	35	-	35
Other basic materials	73	37	110.
Vehicles	165	158	323
Machinery	228	337	565
Other manufactured goods	600	289	889
Petroleum (crude and refined)	13,396	5,905	19,301
Others	1,582	1,231	2,813
Total	16,800	8,250	25,050

Source: data communicated by BTDB, Southampton.

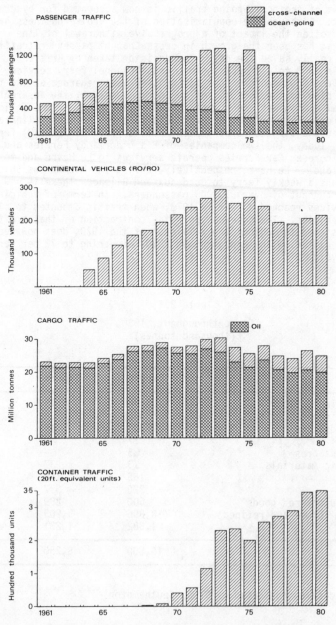

Figure 2.1 Southampton's port traffic, 1961–80.

Southampton's demise as an ocean-going passenger port has also been compensated by a marked increase in the handling of freight traffic (Fig.2.1). In the early post-war years, this involvement directly reflected the very substantial rise in crude-oil supply to the expanding Esso refinery at Fawley and the subsequent coastwise shipment of refined products. To a lesser extent, the expansion of cargo trade has been a response to increasing imports of commodities such as fruit and vegetables, cereals, machinery and motor vehicles, the last two products also figuring quite prominently in Southampton's export trade (Table 2.1). In 1969, the peak year for oil traffic, crude oil and refined oil-products accounted for about 95 per cent of Southampton's total freight trade by weight. During the 1970s, however, there was a general reduction in the proportional importance of oil, prompted by two quite separate developments. On the one hand, there was a fall in absolute terms of both crude-oil imports and refinery output (a direct consequence of the 'oil crisis'), whilst on the other there was a gradual rise in the handling of general freight boosted by the adoption of unitised cargo-handling techniques. Since 1968 Southampton has certainly risen to prominence as one of the country's leading container ports. But even with an annual throughput of some 350,000 containers, and despite handling about 5 million tonnes of non-oil freight, the cargo trade of Southampton today remains heavily dependent upon oil and its related products; in 1980 this reliance amounted to 77 per cent of total freight traffic.

A survey undertaken in 1978 (National Ports Council and Department of Transport, 1980) of the inland origins and destinations of Southampton's exports and imports (excluding fuels) has yielded data which enables some assessment to be made of the extent of, and the relative importance of areas within, the port's hinterland (Fig.2.2). Whilst it has always been assumed that the hinterland has a nationwide dimension, the survey demonstrates the dominant spatial component to be Greater London and the South East, in that this area accounted for 41 per cent of all exports and 30 per cent of all imports. Here at the heart of the hinterland, the volume of imports distributed far exceeds the volume of exports generated. In stark contrast, the trading balance is reversed in the peripheral areas of the North and Scotland, whilst in the middle-ground, a noteworthy feature is that the North West, despite the local availability of port facilities, contributes more to Southampton's trade than the land-locked West Midlands.

Thus, in terms of traffic, it may be said that during the 1960s the port of Southampton experienced a developmental phase characterised by significant change and a good measure of growth. However, in the following decade, the port gradually entered a phase with a rather different complexion, a phase exhibiting symptoms of consolidation possibly combined with more than a hint of stagnation. Certainly, the port seems to have fairly faithfully mirrored the stillstands and downward shifts in the British economy during the last decade (Hampshire County Council Planning Department, 1977) and perhaps this should serve as a warning to those who might advocate a deliberate nurturing of port-related industrialisation (Takel, 1974) or a further intensification of the degree of port-dependence in the local economy.

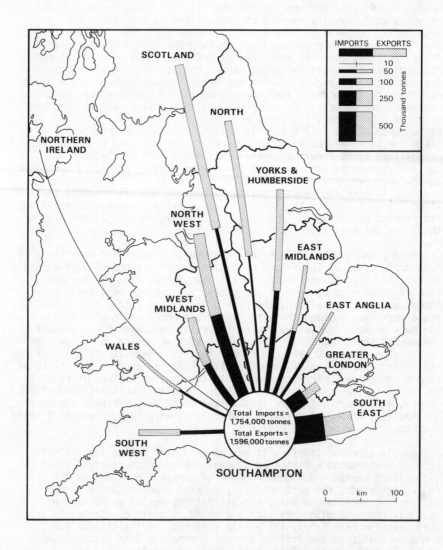

Figure 2.2 Inland origins and destinations of Southampton's
international trade, 1978.

Infrastructure

The limits of the port of Southampton are much more extensive than those
of the city proper; they include the whole of Southampton Water and
reach as far as the Solent and the Isle of Wight (Fig.2.3). Within
these limits, the port comprises a water area of approximately 65km^2 and
has a total foreshore length of just over 90km. In 1963 the British
Transport Docks Board (BTDB) took over ownership and operation of the
docks from the British Transport Commission, and five years later
harbour reorganisation led to the BTDB becoming the Port Authority,
thereby assuming responsibility for 'conservancy' functions such as the
maintenance, buoying and lighting of deep-water channels. The present
dock system comprises the Eastern and Western Docks and the Prince
Charles Container Port; in all there are some 10km of deep-water quays.

The post-war changes in port traffic have had concomitant effects
upon port infrastructure and layout. A large area on the western side
of Southampton Water has been developed by the Esso Petroleum Company as
the site for an oil refinery with a capacity of 19.5 million tonnes per
annum (Fig.2.3). The Marine Terminal at Fawley has five ocean berths
and a deep-water channel of 15m at low water springs, allowing tankers
of up to 180,000 deadweight tonnes to offload crude oil. Four berths on
the landward side of the Terminal are used by small coastal tankers
which distribute about 80 per cent of the refinery's output. On the
opposite shore, at Hamble, a Shell-BP distribution depot is equipped
with a single jetty and a 9.5m access channel. Both these oil
installations, although located within the port limits, are operated
independently of the BTDB. This unusual organisational arrangement
means that the Port Authority derives relatively little revenue from the
immense traffic in oil and related products.

Southampton's RO/RO ferry services to the Continent operate mainly out
of that part of the Eastern Docks along the River Itchen (Fig.2.3). The
provision of purpose-built berths and terminal facilities here at the
Princess Alexandra Dock has necessitated restructuring some 19th-century
quays. The process of redevelopment is continuing elsewhere in the
Eastern Docks, but with the object of providing increased open storage
and handling space for the transit of new motor vehicles. Along the
lower reaches of the Test estuary, the run of the Western Docks, from
the Ocean Terminal to the huge King George V graving dock, presents
something of a dilemma to the BTDB. The cessation of ocean-going
passenger lines and the reduction in hold-cargo services have resulted
in a marked decline in the use of this part of the port infrastructure,
with its 2440m of waterfront and its four large passenger and cargo
sheds. It is tempting to regard this part of the port system as
possibly being available for conversion to container handling, but the
cruise business and the shipment of non-unitised cargo, particularly of
cereals to the Rank Flour Mills, still require the availability of the
present terminal facilities, albeit at irregular and apparently
uneconomic intervals. There may be some scope for redirecting much of
the present traffic through the Eastern Docks; in which case, the
Western Docks would indeed be ripe for redevelopment.

Further up the Test estuary, 80ha of mudflat were reclaimed during the
1960s for the development of the Container Port. By 1981, about 48ha of
that land had been utilised to provide five berths with container

37

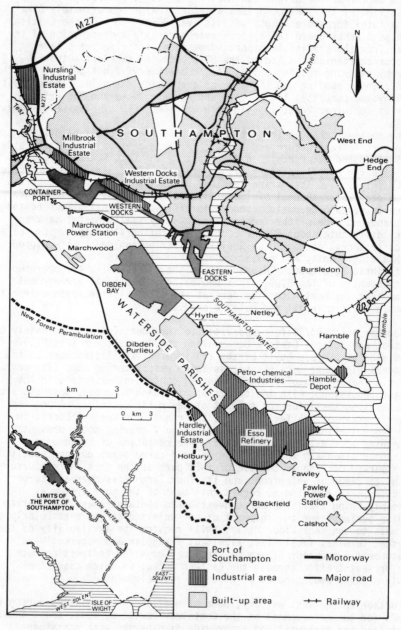

Figure 2.3 The port of Southampton.

cranes, a Freightliner depot for rail-borne traffic, road terminal
facilities and storage areas. It is this development which has received
the lion's share of the £40 million invested in the dock system over the
last decade. The investment certainly appears to have paid off in that
the Prince Charles Container Port is now reckoned to be one of the
country's principal deep-sea container ports(3). Long-term plans for
this aspect of port activity have designated a further 31ha of mudflat
upstream as being available for reclamation should the subsequent
expansion of the unitised cargo trade exceed the generous space
provision which has already been made.

PORT-CITY LINKAGES

Figure 2.4 attempts to represent schematically the principal ways in
which the port might be perceived as contributing to city growth through
the medium of employment. Port-city linkages clearly also involve
considerable flows of capital which, in their turn, ultimately generate
city growth, but for essentially pragmatic reasons of data availability
and relative ease of calibration, the ensuing discussion is centred upon
employment. Unless stated otherwise, the aggregated data refer to 1975
and have been derived indirectly from the annual census of employment
returns (Hampshire Careers Service, 1977), whilst figures relating to
the payrolls of individual firms have for the most part been directly
communicated.

Operational services

The running of the port itself is the most direct of the four main
linkages through which the port generates employment, involving such
activities as conservancy, customs and excise, pilotage and cargo-
handling (Fig.2.4). If the Minimum List Headings (MLHs) 705 and 706, as
used by the Central Statistical Office in its Standard Industrial
Classification, are taken to represent the full range of port
operational services, it means that over 10,000 people (or 9 per cent of
total city employment) are thus engaged in Southampton. Of these,
probably as many as one-half are actually employed in the merchant navy,
whilst the BTDB itself accounts for another 3300 jobs (approximately
1600 dockworkers plus a technical, clerical and managerial staff of
1700). Mechanisation of certain aspects of port operation have meant
that the BTDB has been able to reduce its labour force from a peak level
of 4100 in 1974.

Ancillary services

Outside the dock gates, the port has encouraged the establishment of a
wide range of essentially commercial undertakings which service the port
in diverse ways. These range from the shipping company offices to the
shipping broker, from the forwarding agent to firms of packers, from
naval outfitters to ship-chandlers. These disparate activities are
spread across a number of different MLHs in the Standard Industrial
Classification and many are not specifically enumerated in the annual
census of employment returns. For these reasons, it proves extremely
difficult to gauge their collective importance in the city's employment
structure. However, many of these services have over the years become
concentrated in a maritime quarter located between the Eastern Docks and

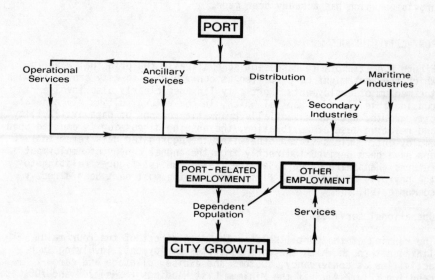

Figure 2.4 A model of port-city linkages.

the city's central business district (Witherick and Pinder, 1971), and a sample survey within that quarter has indicated that employment in these commercial services may well be in the order of 1750 jobs. The tentative nature of this estimate cannot be over-stressed, and it is to be regretted that the terms of the Statistics of Trade Act (1947) are such as to frustrate any attempt which might be made to achieve a reasonably accurate calibration of this little explored port-city linkage.

The decline in the number of ocean-going passengers passing through the port appears to have prompted the curtailment of some of the long-established ancillary services, such as those provided by caterers, shop-store merchants, launderers, and naval outfitters. Indeed, the empty premises and deteriorating fabric, which are much in evidence in the maritime quarter today, give the distinct impression of contraction and decline in certain aspects of this port-city linkage. It might also be argued that the cessation of regular deep-sea passenger services has had repercussions which reach beyond the strict confines of the maritime quarter. For example, the tradition of an overnight stop in the city immediately before departure and after disembarcation generated much business for local hotels and restaurants. However, today's cross-Channel passengers, who have succeeded the distinctly affluent ocean-going passengers of the past, tend to drive directly to and from the docks and without resort to the services of the city. Not only have hotels and restaurants felt the loss of a lucrative clientele, but possibly so too have central-city retailers.

The services considered so far have all been of a distinctly commercial calibre. There is, however, another dimension to this particular port-city linkage; this involves activities which may be categorised as being concerned very broadly with 'welfare' matters. The traditional benevolent institutions, such as the Missions to Seamen, the British Sailors' Society, the Merchant Navy Welfare Board, are still much in evidence, as indeed are the foreign consular offices. More recently, there have grown up the various organisations which represent the interests of the different groups involved in the day-to-day running of the port, from the National Union of Seamen and the Transport and General Workers Union to the National Dock Labour Board, the General Council of British Shipping and the Port Employers' Association. In all, these diverse 'welfare' activities are estimated as now employing around 500 people and thereby help to raise the significance of this overall linkage to at least 2250 jobs.

Distribution

A seemingly inevitable spinoff from port freight traffic is the development of a clearly-defined distributional and wholesaling function, whereby imported basic raw materials and manufactured goods are marketed at a national or regional level. At Southampton, some of this distribution is actually conducted through the city, as is well exemplified by the handling of fruit and vegetables. The shipment of fruit from South Africa and the import of vegetables from the Channel Islands have encouraged the agglomeration of wholesaling premises and the gradual emergence, close to the dock gates and the old Terminus Station, of a wholesaling quarter within Southampton's central business district (Witherick and Pinder, 1971). Some 5300 people are employed in wholesale distribution (MLHs 810, 811, 812), and probably about 80 per cent of these deal with commodities coming into Southampton by sea.

However, the increasing containerisation of fruit imports from South Africa may well prompt some decline in this particular activity, in that the use of refrigerated cargo units no longer requires the sort of intermediate step traditionally provided by the distributor in the cityport wholesaling quarter.

It is important to remember that the distribution of commodities also takes place directly from the docks and without recourse to the city proper. For example, the long-established imports of timber and building materials have always been dealt with in this manner. The same now applies to two relative newcomers to Southampton's cargo trade, wine and motor vehicles. The Martini Company, for example, has a large plant (seventy employees) in the Western Docks where wine from South Africa and member countries of the European Economic Community is blended and bottled before being distributed. Also in the Western Docks is the French company of Renault which has set up a servicing, distribution and spare-parts depot, this being one of two in Great Britain. The British Transport Docks Board is keen to encourage this traffic in vehicles, and other motor manufacturers (Alfa Romeo, Datsun, Fiat and Ford) are now also using Southampton as an import inlet. From the port's point of view the handling of motor vehicles represents a high revenue-producing traffic and one that requires only a small investment in infrastructure. On the other hand, the space requirements are high (mainly for storage/ parking) and, for the city, the generation of employment is of very modest proportions; the Renault depot in Southampton, for example, employs only about fifty people.

Outside the city, the employment figure for distribution is swollen by the considerable numbers of people engaged in the distribution of products from both the Esso refinery and its associated petrochemical complex. Furthermore, a recent survey of industrial estates in Eastleigh MB has revealed the setting up of firms specialising in such activities as continental road haulage and cold storage, and which are clearly related to the port distributional function.

Maritime industry

The amount and character of manufacturing industry located in British port cities can be fairly readily established by reference to published statistical sources, but assessment of the degree to which that industry, particularly in its location, relates directly or indirectly to the availability of port facilities involves formidable difficulties. In theory, the industrialist in search of an optimum site might perceive a port location as offering a range of opportunities and advantages. These might include the cost advantages of processing sea-borne raw materials at the break-of-bulk point or the benefits of the port's gateway role, whereby there is relatively ready access to overseas markets in the foreland (Robinson, 1970). On the basis of these and other conjectured advantages, it seems reasonable to define a broad category of maritime or port-related industry and to distinguish within that category between a) shipbuilding and other forms of marine engineering, which inevitably require a waterfront location, b) basic industries processing sea-borne imported raw materials, and c) indus- tries producing goods mainly for an export market.

(a) Applying this simple industrial classification to Southampton, it

42

is found that shipbuilding and marine engineering employ some 4900 persons. Strictly speaking, the distinction should be drawn between constructional and repair activity, with the latter perhaps more appropriately classified as an ancillary service. In practice, however, it is not possible to make the distinction in labour terms, and for this reason, all those enumerated under MLH 370 have been assigned as being involved in maritime industry. By far the largest firm is Vosper Shiprepairers Limited, which has premises in the port area. Whilst the prevailing tone in this realm of industrial activity has been one persistent decline, especially as regards the building and repair of large ocean-going ships, the post-war leisure boom and the harbour's renown as a sailing area have meant rising levels of business for the local manufacturers of yachts and small pleasure craft.

(b) Bearing in mind the composition of Southampton's freight traffic, it is hardly surprising that oil should figure prominently in the second category of maritime industry, the processing for sea-borne raw materials. Today the Esso refinery at Fawley processes about 13 million tonnes of crude oil a year (well below its capacity) and employs 2300 people. Automation has in fact meant that the labour requirements of the refinery have not increased commensurately with the expansion of refining capacity. However, the refinery has had a very considerable 'knock on' effect through its supply of refined products, such as ethylene and butadiene liquid gas, to a complex of 'secondary' petrochemical industries located immediately to the north (Fig.2.3). Here there are four major firms employing in all about 1300 people. Another local repercussion of the refinery is manifest in the two oil-fired electricity generating stations, one upstream at Marchwood and the other situated between Fawley and Calshot, which have a combined labour force of 900 employees.

All these oil-related industrial developments are located outside the boundaries of Southampton. Although there is some labour recruitment from within the city, undoubtedly the bulk of the labour force is now accommodated in residential developments concentrated in that corridor lying between Southampton Water and the eastern border of the New Forest, an area known as the Waterside Parishes (Pinder and Witherick, 1971) (Fig.2.3). As for the city itself, there are a few industrial firms, such as Calor Gas and British Oxygen, which have a raw material link with the Fawley petrochemical complex, whilst in another sector of the economy it is worth noting that some of the local petrochemical firms have set up administrative offices in Southampton; Esso Chemical Limited and the International Synthetic Rubber Company Limited are two such examples.

Oil is not the only imported basic material to be processed in and around Southampton. The Solent Flour Mills of Joseph Rank Limited are sited on the waterfront of the Western Docks and rely entirely on cereals brought by sea; furthermore, a significant proportion of the output of milled products is subsequently distributed by coasting vessels. Providing substantially more employment, of the order of 1350 jobs, is the British American Tobacco Company which relies almost exclusively on tobacco imported through the port.

(c) It is when one comes to consider the third category of maritime industry that problems of identification and measurement are really encountered. Certainly, Southampton has much manufacturing industry which is not embraced by the two preceding categories. In terms of employment, this hitherto unaccounted industry generates about 24,000 jobs and may be characterised as being of mainly post-war origin and principally concerned with various types of engineering. The question arises, how much of this industry has become established in Southampton because of the opportunities which exist for the ready export of finished goods? In response, one can readily point to firms such as the Ford Motor Company (3700 employees) and AC-Delco (1500 employees) which have a well-developed sea-borne export trade, and also to the Pirelli Cable Works (625 employees) and Standard Telephone and Cables (825 employees) which specialise in the production of sea-bed cables. But for many other firms the marketing patterns are much less clear-cut. Indeed, there is evidence which prompts the conclusion that much industrial development within and adjacent to Southampton may have been established for reasons having little or nothing to do with the port (Witherick, 1981, 123-124). Availability of sites and labour, together with good access to domestic markets, appear to have carried considerable weight in the location equation of many newly-established firms. Sample surveys conducted on the three industrial estates located within the city have indicated that possibly no more than 15 per cent of the previously unaccounted 24,000 industrial jobs in the city might ultimately be linked with the production of finished goods which are exported through the port. This category of 'export-oriented' maritime industry may therefore be evaluated as sustaining about 3600 jobs, or about one-third of all employment in port-related industry. At the same time, all three categories of port-related industrial activity, together with the spinoff of 'secondary' manufacturing, appear to account for a roughly similar proportion of all industrial jobs; this applies equally to the city proper and to the immediate hinterland (Table 2.2).

Table 2.2

Estimates of port-related employment, 1975.

	City of Southampton	Immediate Hinterland
Operational Services	10,000	100
Ancillary Services	2,250	250
Distribution	4,250	1,800
Maritime Industry		
a) Shipbuilding and marine engineering	4,900	900
b) Material-processing	2,100	3,800
c) Export-oriented	3,600	2,200
TOTAL PORT-RELATED EMPLOYMENT (P)	27,100	9,050
TOTAL EMPLOYMENT (T)	113,000	53,400
PORT-DEPENDENCE INDEX (P/T)	0.24	0.17

Assessment of port dependence

Table 2.2 summarises the calibration of port-city linkages which have been briefly justified in the foregoing discussion. A simple 'port-dependence index' can thus be readily derived by the formula P/T, where P is employment in port-related activities and T is total employment. The index value of 0.24 for the city indicates that nearly one-quarter of all the jobs in Southampton are linked in some way to the port function. If the same exercise is repeated for the area immediately outside the city, a lower index value of 0.15 is obtained. The significant difference between the two index values might at first sight appear surprising, bearing in mind that the latter value takes into account the Esso refinery at Fawley and its associated complex of 'secondary' petrochemical industries. However, the impact of this important port-related employment node is more than counter-balanced by a weak involvement in both operational and ancillary services and, to a lesser extent, by the presence of non-port activity, such as is to be found for example on the relatively new industrial estates at Hardley, Testwood, Eastleigh and Chandler's Ford.

At face value, the port-dependence indices might not suggest an intolerably high degree of reliance in the local economy on the port and its related activities. It needs to be borne in mind, however, that the significance and repercussions of the port are much greater than the derived values would indicate, for as Figure 2.4 seeks to demonstrate, the port-related employees both of the city and its immediate hinterland, together with their dependants, represent a substantial demand force. They have need of, and therefore help to sustain, a wide range of activities and services broadly falling within the tertiary and quaternary sectors; retailing, professional and social services, public transport and local government are but a few of the central-place functions thus supported.

No attempt has been made in this particular investigation to quantify the 'knock on' effect within the tertiary and quaternary sectors, but even by simple extrapolation, it is clear that in any city where almost 25 per cent of the labour force is related to one functional institution, those same workers are likely to account for a substantial proportion of service or 'nonbasic' employment. The BTDB recently estimated that, after tax, the annual wages of all those directly employed in the docks amounted to £40 million and that most of this money was spent within the local area. Bearing in mind that these workers represent only about 12 per cent of all port-related employees in the city, the possible dimensions of the port's multiplier effect within the local economy begin to assume considerable proportions. In addition, it is reasonable to suggest that a significant percentage of the earnings derived from port-related jobs located outside the city is also spent in Southampton, particularly on the higher-order services concentrated in its central business district. The spatial and hierarchical organisation of service activity means that the 'knock on' effect is unquestionably more keenly felt in the city's economy, as compared with its impact on the economy of Southampton's immediate hinterland.

Thus it may be said that of all the post-war changes in port traffic, the most significant for Southampton in terms of industrialisation has been the importation of crude oil, which now supports the Esso refinery and an appreciable amount of 'secondary' industry. However, these particular industrial developments cannot be viewed as anything more than medium-term prospects, for as the world's oil reserves gradually become exhausted, so inevitably such activities must decline. Apart from oil, the broad shift of emphasis from ocean-going passengers to containerised freight and cross-Channel ferry services appears to have remarkably little effect upon the industrial scene. Suffice also to say that the effect in employment terms of even those oil-related developments has been virtually cancelled out by a drastic cutback since 1960 of some 5000 jobs in shipbuilding and marine engineering alone, and not to mention the contraction of certain ancillary services. However, to evaluate port-city linkages solely in industrial terms is grossly to undervalue the significance of the port in the local economy. This investigation of Southampton clearly demonstrates that it may well be that ports directly generate as much, if not more, employment outside the industrial sector as they do within it, and that the collective multiplier effect of all port-related activity can provide a powerful stimulus to further growth within the tertiary and quaternary sectors.

Although employment statistics contained in the 1961 Census are not entirely compatible with the data used in the foregoing analysis, there is some indication of a decline in port-dependence during the last two decades. For Southampton itself, the port-dependence index possibly declined by as much as 10 per cent between 1961 and 1975. It is likely that a somewhat greater contraction was experienced in the immediate hinterland; this being brought about principally by a shrinkage in the labour requirements of the Fawley refinery and its 'secondary' industry and by a marked growth of non-port industry. But even allowing for this dilution of port-dependence, it is very evident that the port function and its diverse ramifications have made a significant contribution to the economic and demographic growth recorded in the Southampton SMLA during the last twenty years.

PORT PROSPECTS

Given the present situation in which about one in every four jobs in Southampton may be classified as being in port-related activity, some consideration may now be given to the future. What policy would the city be best advised to pursue in connection with the port? Should the city endeavour to capitalise still further on the port's local multiplier effect? Or should the policy be one of diversification, of seeking to reduce the degree of port-dependence in the local economy? Such questions need to be posed at a number of different spatial scales and against a backcloth which takes into account both current planning strategies and the trends and patterns of essentially spontaneous developments. The discussion also needs to recognise the fundamental organisational rift which completely divorces the planning of the port (the responsibility of the BTDB) from the more general planning of the city and its immediate hinterland (as undertaken by the Hampshire County Council).

Local and regional considerations

Any assessment of Southampton's future as a port and as a location for

46

further port-related development must at an early stage take into account competition from its near-neighbour and age-old rival, Portsmouth. With the gradual run-down of the Royal Naval establishment, Portsmouth City Council has taken positive steps to convert the port to a more commercial role. Portsmouth has already established RO/RO ferry links with Cherbourg and St Malo, and plans were elaborated in 1979 for the introduction of cross-Channel container services. On a number of important counts, Portsmouth would seem to have the edge over Southampton. For example, the Channel crossing from Portsmouth is appreciably shorter and permits the efficient operating schedule of four complete crossings every 24 hours, whereas from Southampton only three crossings can be achieved in the same period. Then the operational costs of the commercial port at Portsmouth are likely to be significantly less, due to the fact that the conservancy costs are borne by the Ministry of Defence. Thus Southampton may well have something to fear as regards the future of her RO/RO cross-Channel ferry services. Indeed, the levelling off in this particular traffic noted earlier (Fig. 2.1) may well reflect the pressure of competition from Portsmouth. On the other hand, however, Southampton still holds certain irrefutable advantages. For example, the port enjoys far superior deep-water access and berthing facilities. It also has in reserve, both at the head of the Test estuary and on the opposite shore at Dibden Bay, a large area of land ready to accommodate any possible expansion of port infrastructure and port-related industry. In these two specific contexts of deep-sea freight traffic and maritime industry, therefore, Southampton's local standing remains unchallenged.

The evolution of planning policies which currently operate locally and regionally has already been discussed in the general introduction to this collection of essays. In the present context, the point to be stressed is that the key document, the South Hampshire Structure Plan, gives scant attention to the two ports of Southampton and Portsmouth and to the parts which they might play in the future economic development of South Hampshire. This apparent neglect of the ports may possibly be traced back to the South Hampshire Study (1966), prepared by Colin Buchanan and Partners, and in which it was claimed: "The Port (of Southampton) and its urban hinterland appear to be largely independent of each other. Few local firms use the facilities offered by the Port. By corollary the Port does not rely, to any great extent, on traffic generated by local industry" (para.231). Whilst this may have been true for much of the more recent industrial development, the planning consultants were either unaware of, or preferred to ignore, the port's very significant multiplier effect in the various sectors of the local economy. Since then, there has perhaps persisted the view that, since the two ports are of a national and international rather than of a local significance, then they should be planned as it were outside the terms of the South Hampshire Structure Plan. No doubt the organisational arrangements of a separate planning of port and city have also encouraged this sort of divisive perception. In the event, the South Hampshire Structure Plan has only three proposals to make in the broad context of port development, and two of these relate specifically to Southampton.

The first proposal is to safeguard 365ha of reclaimed land at Dibden Bay, on the western side of Southampton Water, for possible long-term use for the development of maritime industry (Fig.2.3). Should

47

exploration for oil in the English Channel prove successful, then it could well be that this part of the BTDB estate would readily serve as a site for an oil-exploitation shore base. Indeed, it is possibly the only site with such potential along the whole of the south coast, and for this reason it should be regarded as a site of national significance. In the short term, there are pressures to release some of the land for immediate industrial development, but high infrastructural costs, especially as regards vehicular access, and the fact that much of the ground is still unstable, should ensure the preservation of the site until a more strategic use is found for it. The other proposal concerns an area of reclaimed land at Nursling in the Test Valley which the Plan has designated for possible development of a container depot and associated facilities. A recent review of this proposal has indicated a willingness to release some of the land for general industrial development, thereby relaxing the original restriction that 75 per cent of the site should be reserved for port-related developments.

National and international considerations

At the macro-scale, there is a need to comment briefly on Southampton's future gateway function and its international context. There is some indication that during the post-war period a gradual shift has occurred in the general distribution of port activity in Britain, whereby ports on the east and south coasts appear to have grown more than, and possibly at the expense of, ports located elsewhere. The United Kingdom's entry into the Common Market will undoubtedly have given further impetus to this shift, presumably by virtue of encouraging an increased volume of continental traffic. However, when one comes to consider which of the EEC's Channel and North Sea ports are most likely to stride ahead as the Community's principal gateways to overseas markets, it may well be that geographical conditions favour Continental rather than British ports. After all, ports like Antwerp, Le Havre and Rotterdam are much better situated with regard to the Community's centre of gravity. Furthermore, such ports have enjoyed a substantial head-start in terms of their integration and operation within the evolving commercial and industrial systems of the EEC from their inception. Considerable financial subsidies have also been forthcoming for Continental ports. In the absence of a Common Seaports Policy (Bird, 1978), and contrary to the basic principle of complete equality for the seaports of all member states (as set out in the Kapteyn Report, 1961), the possibility must now be countenanced that future rationalisation or 'harmonisation' of port activity within the Community might well exacerbate the emergence of a port hierarchy (Suykens, 1979). Such a hierarchy might be perceived as comprising a very limited number of 'super' and 'supranational' ports with extensive trading links outside the Community and with large-scale port industrialisation. Set below these, there is likely to be a more numerous order of essentially subordinate or feeder ports serving hinterlands of a national or regional scale, having forelands mainly confined to the Community and offering rather modest industrial potential. Should such a hierarchical arrangement eventually materialise, then it may well be that Southampton and other British ports will not achieve top-rank status. Admittedly, such a gloomy view of British port prospects is not universally shared (Takel, 1974, 213-215), but do the grounds for optimism really bear critical scrutiny?

CONCLUSION

This investigation of port-city relationships has demonstrated that the functional linkages thus forged directly and significantly impinge upon various sectors of the local economy, and that collectively these linkages, through the medium of employment, support a sizeable dependent population. In addition, this port-dependent population, in its turn, creates a multiplier effect within the tertiary and quaternary sectors whereby the demand for goods and services is intensified. Viewed in this way, the port must be seen as a major component in the local economy.

As regards the secondary sector, the conclusion may be drawn that the prospects of further port-related industrial development are not as bright as they were, especially when argued in terms of traditional location theory. Mechanisation of port operations, particularly the containerisation of cargo, appear to have reduced the incentive to establish manufacturing industry at ports for the simplistic reasons of ready access to overseas raw-material supplies and overseas markets and of convenient and economic processing at transshipment points. This is not to deny that some ports, especially those with good deep-water access, still offer a strong attraction to basic industries requiring large quantities of imported raw materials, the attraction being intensified where there is a high bulk-to-value ratio and a high weight-loss during processing. Undoubtedly some maritime industry, particularly the basic material-processing industries, can have an important propulsive effect by encouraging the growth of 'secondary' manufacturing. However, current planning policies being pursued both in Britain and in other member countries of the EEC (as exemplified by the implementation of MIDAs proposals) seem to be leading to an increasing concentration of large-scale port-related industrial development in a relatively small number of really large ports. In the event, and given the present downswing in the world economy (especially its depressing effect on levels of port traffic), it might seem consoling to suggest that cityports like Southampton need not be unduly perturbed by the contraction of port-related industry. Such reassurance applies particularly where the contraction is being matched by the creation of opportunities for the growth of non-port industry, and thereby serving to reduce the degree of port-dependence. As for the tertiary and quaternary sectors, it is sufficient to note that whilst changes in the character of Southampton's port traffic may have prompted the curtailment of some ancillary services, the port function still directly involves a wide spectrum of specialist commercial and welfare activities as well as a clearly defined distributional role. For many ports, it may well be that the number of port-related jobs within the tertiary and quaternary sectors does not fall far short of the number of such jobs created within the industrial sector.

So it would seem that the substantial throughput of passengers and vehicles on cross-Channel ferry services, the handling of increasing volumes of containerised cargo, the apparently spontaneous generation of non-port industry, the provision of high-order services for a large tributary area may all be interpreted as symptoms of Southampton's dual move towards a greater diversification of port activity and a general reduction in the degree of port-dependence. Such developments may thus be perceived as constituting prudent steps towards a sounder future.

NOTES

(1) This essay is a modified version of a paper originally published in
     HOYLE, B S and PINDER, D A (eds)(1981), <u>Cityport Industrialization</u>
     and Regional Development (London, Pergamon), 113-131.
(2) 'Immediate hinterland' is defined as constituting the labour
     exchange areas of Eastleigh, Hythe and Romsey.
(3) In 1979 Southampton was placed 26th in the world rankings, handling
     282,777 TEU; London ranked 20th (395,019 TEU) and Felixstowe 24th
     (301,024 TEU). (Containerisation International Yearbook, 1980
     (London, National Magazine Co.), Table 2.)

REFERENCES

BIRD, J H (1963), <u>The Major Seaports of the United Kingdom</u> (London,
     Hutchinson).

BIRD, J H (1971), <u>Seaports and Seaport Terminals</u> (London, Hutchinson).

BIRD, J H (1978), The future of seaports in the European Communities,
     <u>Geographical Journal</u>, 144, 23-48.

BUCHANAN, C and Partners (1966), <u>South Hampshire Study</u> (London, HMSO).

CONTAINERISATION INTERNATIONAL (1980), <u>Yearbook</u> (London, National
     Magazine Company).

HAMPSHIRE CAREERS SERVICE (1977), <u>Structure of Employment in City of
     Southampton and Travel to Work Areas</u> (Winchester, Hampshire
     County Council).

HAMPSHIRE COUNTY COUNCIL PLANNING DEPARTMENT (1977), <u>South-East
     Hampshire Employment Study - Part 1: Employment Structure and
     Trends</u> (Winchester, Hampshire County Council).

KAPTEYN, P J (1962), <u>Rapport fait au nom de la Commission des Transports
     sur les problèmes concernant la politique commune des
     transports dans le cadre de la Communaute economique</u> (European
     Parliamentary Assembly, Document 106).

MONKHOUSE, F J (ed.)(1964), <u>A Survey of Southampton and its Region</u>
     (Southampton, British Association).

NATIONAL PORTS COUNCIL and DEPARTMENT OF TRANSPORT (1980), <u>The Inland
     Origins and Destinations of the United Kingdom's
     International Trade</u> (London, National Ports Council).

PINDER, D A and WITHERICK, M E (1971), Urban expansion in the Waterside
     Parishes, <u>Field Studies in South Hampshire</u> (Southampton,
     Southampton Branch of the Geographical Association).

ROBINSON, R (1970), The hinterland-foreland continuum: concept and
     methodology, <u>Professional Geographer</u>, 22, 307-310.

SOUTH EAST JOINT PLANNING TEAM (1970), Strategic Plan for the South East (London, HMSO).

SOUTH HAMPSHIRE PLAN ADVISORY COMMITTEE (1972), South Hampshire Structure Plan (Winchester, Hampshire County Council).

SUKYENS, F (1979), European seaport policy, Ports and Harbours, 48(10), 11-17; 48(11), 16-19.

TAKEL, R E (1974), Industrial Port Development (Bristol, Scientechnica).

WITHERICK, M E and PINDER, D A (1971), Southampton's central business district, Field Studies in South Hampshire (Southampton, Southampton Branch of the Geographical Association).

WITHERICK, M E (1981), Port developments, port-city linkages and prospects for maritime industry; a case study of Southampton, HOYLE, B S and PINDER, D A (eds), Cityport Industrialization and Regional Development (London, Pergamon).

Acknowledgement   The assistance of the British Transport Docks Board at Southampton, in providing information and comments, is gratefully acknowledged.

3 Recent Trends in Manufacturing Employment

C M MASON

Under the twin pressures of increasing labour productivity and
deteriorating international competitiveness, manufacturing employment
has been declining in the United Kingdom for the past decade and a half.
Between 1966 and 1980, 1.7 million manufacturing jobs 'disappeared',
representing a 21 per cent decline. However, this loss of manufacturing
jobs has not occurred evenly across the UK space-economy. The
conurbations have borne the brunt of the 'de-industrialisation', while
sources of manufacturing employment growth have mainly been confined to
smaller towns and cities in less-urbanised and 'traditionally non-
industrialised' counties peripheral to the London-Liverpool axial belt,
notably in East Anglia, South West England and the Outer South East.
For the most part, these areas have a very favourable industrial
structure, and over the past twenty years or so have been recipients of
a large number of migrant firms. They have exhibited manufacturing
employment growth rates substantially in excess of that expected on the
basis of their industrial structure and volume of in-movement (Fothergill and Gudgin, 1979a; Keeble, 1976, 1980). The relatively few parts
of the economy which remain dynamic at this time, what might be termed
the British equivalents of the American 'Sunbelt Cities' (Hall, 1980),
are therefore found in the non-metropolitan counties of southern
England. Examples include Oxford, Cambridge, Reading, Exeter, Bristol
and Southampton. Generally speaking, these cities have populations
between one-quarter and half a million; they are free-standing and offer
a good residential environment. They have enjoyed the best rates of
job creation in recent years and, because of the spatial association
between industrial growth and high amenity, are in the most favoured
position to secure future employment growth. Admittedly, many of the
new jobs created in these cities and their hinterlands have been, and

52

will increasingly be, in the quaternary sector. Nevertheless, manufacturing industries, notably high-technology activities, have also been a major component in job creation and industrial expansion in such cities.

In the light of these spatial trends, it is regrettable that recent research should have focused almost exclusively on industrial decline in the conurbations. Such studies have established that manufacturing employment loss in metropolitan areas has been a function of very high levels of plant closure rather than of plant movement, but losses have been reinforced by labour shedding in surviving establishments. Sources of job creation, namely in situ expansion, new-firm creation and branch plant openings, have been able to offset only a fraction of the employment loss in the declining components of change (Dennis, 1978; Mason, 1980; Lloyd and Dicken, 1981). But what has been the relative importance of each of the components of change in the smaller free-standing cities of southern Britain? The evidence presented by Fothergill and Gudgin (1979a) suggests that in these areas employment growth is largely a product of the expansion of surviving establishments and of a high rate of new-firm formation. However, with the exception of a brief analysis of manufacturing change in Bristol (Lambert, 1978) and a more detailed investigation of Leicester (Fagg, 1973 and 1980; Gudgin, 1978), empirical confirmation is lacking. Consequently, this study of Southampton would seem to be both pertinent and timely, in that it is the first attempt to shed some light on the processes of manufacturing employment change in a prosperous, free-standing city in southern England.

DATA SOURCES

The main source of information on manufacturing industry in the Southampton SMLA is the South Hampshire Establishment Databank (SHEDB), which provides the following information on every manufacturing establishment present in 1979:

(i)   location - for confidentiality reasons and to facilitate mapping, this is available as an OS grid code;

(ii)   industry type - classified by minimum list heading (MLH) and order as defined in the Standard Industrial Classification (CSO, 1968);

(iii)   total number of employees - including the number of factory floor workers and the number of attached office staff;

(iv)   ownership status - using information from various business directories, notably Who Owns Whom, Kompass and Dun and Bradstreet's Guide to Key British Enterprises, plants have been classified according to whether they are locally- or externally-controlled.

Unfortunately, the establishment data are available only for one point in time, and for this reason it is impossible to undertake a full analysis of the components of change. However, using earlier editions of telephone and business directories (and when in doubt contacting firms directly), it has been possible to identify those members of the

53

1979 plant population which, during the 1971-79 period, (i) opened,
(ii) survived, and (iii) relocated within the SMLA. In addition, plant
openings have been further disaggregated in order to separately
identify independent firms and branch plants.

An indication of aggregate, structural and spatial manufacturing
employment change over time in the Southampton SMLA is provided by the
Department of Employment's unpublished ER11 data which are available for
each year between 1961 and 1977. The employment office areas (EOAs),
which collectively correspond most closely to the Southampton SMLA, are
those of Southampton-Woolston, Eastleigh, Winchester, Romsey, Hythe and
Lymington. Use of the Department of Employment data to indicate trends
over time is complicated because of changes in the Standard Industrial
Classification in 1968 and in the method of collating the statistics in
1971. Use of Fothergill and Gudgin's (1978) 'Composite Industrial
Classification', which involves the grouping of various MLHs, can
overcome the first difficulty. However, the change in data compilation
(Department of Employment, 1973) has resulted in "massive, widespread
and erratic" discontinuities at the local level (Allen and Yuill, 1978,
125). Hence analysis over time must adopt two distinct time-periods,
namely 1961-1971 and 1971-1977. The data for 1971 were collected on the
basis of both the former and current modes of compilation.

INDUSTRIAL DEVELOPMENT IN SOUTHAMPTON PRIOR TO 1961

A lack of coal and iron meant that Southampton failed to develop as a
major industrial centre during the 19th century. Rather, urban growth
was stimulated by commercial developments, notably the coming of the
railway in 1840 and the construction of the Outer Dock between 1836 and
1842. By 1914 Southampton was the leading passenger port in the
country; it was less important as a cargo port because of its distance
from the main industrial areas (Tavener, 1950). The only manufacturing
industry of any note was shipbuilding, but with the use of iron and
later steel for construction, this industry became progressively
concentrated on Clydeside and Tyneside (Coppock 1973). Consequently, on
the eve of the First World War, Southampton had only one major shipyard
(Patterson, 1975), but a considerable number of specialist small-boat
and yacht manufacturers,together with a ship-repair industry,associated
with its port function. The only significant source of manufacturing
employment outside Southampton was the London and South West Railway
Company's locomotive and carriage works at Eastleigh which had
relocated from London in two stages between 1890 and 1903.

The initial location and expansion of Pirelli General's electric cable
works in Southampton (opened 1913) and Eastleigh (opened 1921)
contributed to a widening of the city's industrial base before 1939.
Further diversification resulted from the development of some 'port-
reliant' industries, the most significant being food-processing
industries, which used imported raw materials, and the British American
Tobacco cigarette factory (1916), which exported its entire output. In
addition, the Southampton area emerged during the 1920s as an important
centre for aircraft manufacture, particularly of seaplanes (Ford, 1934;
Denton and Thomas, 1964). Yet, despite the expansion of these
alternative job opportunities, at the outbreak of the Second World War
Southampton still remained heavily dependent for employment on the

docks, shipping and port-related industries, particularly ship-repair. The fact that much of the employment in these three principal trades was either seasonal or casual added to the economic difficulties resulting from the city's narrow economic base.

In their plans to rebuild the war-damaged city, Southampton City Council placed considerable stress on the need to achieve a substantial diversification of the local economy in order to ensure its prosperity in the post-war period (Adshead and Cook, 1942; Ford and Thomas, 1950). Anticipation of government controls on industrial location, in order to assist the depressed industrial regions of northern Britain, was "a further reason why the Council should give consideration to a policy of industrial development for the future, and the introduction of new industries into Southampton" (Adshead and Cook, 1942, 15). As a move towards achieving this end, a number of sites were made available for industrial development in the early years of the post-war period (CB of Southampton, 1952). As Denton and Thomas (1964) show, there was both a widening and an expansion of Southampton's manufacturing base between 1945 and 1961. Shipbuilding and aircraft manufacture both contracted (the latter only in the late 1950s, following government-inspired mergers in the industry), but the resulting job losses were more than offset by the expansion of 'new' industries, notably electronics, motor vehicles, pharmaceuticals and oil-refining.

Although some of these new manufacturing jobs were created by the expansion of locally-based companies, the majority were the result of the migration of firms into the Southampton area. In many cases, the firms came from London and the Home Counties (Keeble, 1964), and this despite the existence of government controls on new industrial building in South East England. Furthermore, many of the new firms were British subsidiaries of American companies (Mason, 1981). The particular attractions of the Southampton area for migrant firms in the early post-war period were its proximity to London, the availability of labour (especially females, because of the area's then male-dominated employment structure) and the attractive residential environment which helped in the recruitment of labour, especially of highly-qualified staff for the science-based industries (Keeble, 1964; Denton and Thomas, 1964; Kirkbride, 1969). Whether the port was an important factor in the decision to locate in the Southampton area is less clear. Buchanan (1966) has concluded that the port of Southampton was not a major factor in accounting for new industrial development in the post-war period. On the other hand, British subsidiaries of American companies did show a preference for port locations, because many either relied on imports from their parent companies or were export-oriented (Dunning, 1958).

The current structure of manufacturing activity in the Southampton SMLA owes much to these industrial developments in the early post-war years. In particular, many of the largest employers (including ten of the top twenty) are firms which moved into the Southampton area in the period between 1945 and 1961. These include Fords, formerly Briggs Motor Bodies (commercial vehicles), A C Delco (motor vehicle components), Standard Telephones and Cables (submarine cables), Dreamland Electrical Appliances (electric blankets), Petters (diesels), Borden (chemicals), Mullard (electronics) and Warner-Lambert (pharmaceuticals). However, the most significant of all the new

industrial developments was Esso's massive expansion of a pre-existing
small oil refinery at Fawley, on the western banks of Southampton Water.
The transformation of the site began in 1951. By the early 1960s Fawley
had become a major petro-chemical complex, as a result of the coming 'on
stream' of two naptha cracking plants in 1958 and 1962, the opening of
new plants by three independent chemical companies between 1958 and 1960
to utilise part of the refinery's output, and by a fourth in 1961 to
provide industrial gases to the other plants (Chapman, 1970; Lester,
1973).

These industrial developments ensured that by 1961 the engineering and
electrical sector had become the major industry in the Southampton SMLA,
accounting for 33 per cent of manufacturing employment. This was
equivalent to almost as many jobs as had been jointly provided by the
formerly dominant industries of shipbuilding (15 per cent) and vehicle
manufacture (19 per cent), the latter including the manufacture of
aircraft and of railway locomotives and rolling stock. Chemicals and
allied industries (10 per cent) and food, drink and tobacco manufacture
(9 per cent) were the only other significant sources of manufacturing
employment at that time.

MANUFACTURING EMPLOYMENT TRENDS SINCE 1961

The early 1960s was a period of 'no-growth' in Southampton's
manufacturing sector, as shipbuilding, aircraft manufacture and
railway engineering underwent further contraction, thereby offsetting
job creation in other industries. However, manufacturing employment
growth resumed in the second half of the 1960s, and just over 4000 new
manufacturing jobs were created between 1967 and 1971 (+7.2 per cent) at
a time when the manufacturing workforce was shrinking both nationally
(-3.1 per cent) and in the South East (-4.4 per cent)(Fig.3.1A).
Between 1971 and 1976, there was again relatively little change in the
number of manufacturing jobs in Southampton, although employment
continued to decline both nationally and regionally; indeed it even
contracted in the ROSE area (that part of the South East Region lying
outside Greater London). The beginning of a brief economic recovery in
1976 from the recession of 1974 resulted in a slight reversal of both
national and regional manufacturing employment trends. However, the
economic upturn had a much greater effect on manufacturing employment in
Southampton, resulting in the creation of around 4000 additional jobs
(Fig.3.1B). So, when set against the national and regional yardsticks,
it is clear that Southampton has not followed the trend of 'de-
industrialisation', and in fact it had a larger manufacturing workforce
in 1977 than in 1966. But due to the substantial growth of non-
manufacturing jobs in Southampton during the same period, manufacturing's share of total employment shrank from 31.7 to 28.2 per cent.

Important changes in industrial composition accompanied the growth of
manufacturing in the Southampton SMLA (Table 3.1). Shipbuilding
continued to contract during the 1960s, but gained approximately 700
jobs between 1971 and 1977. Employment in vehicle manufacture exhibited
a similar trend. A loss of employment during the 1960s (mainly in
railway engineering, MLHs 384 and 385) was followed by an increase of
over 3000 jobs in the 1970s (largely in MLH 381, motor vehicle
manufacture). Employment in chemicals and allied industries contracted

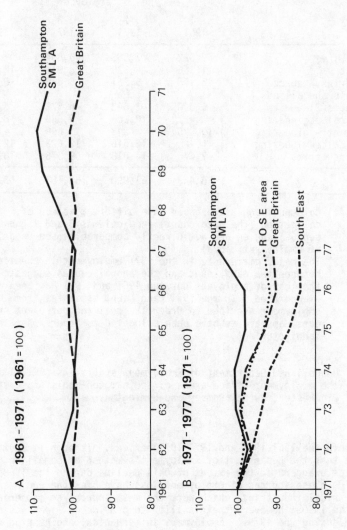

Figure 3.1 Manufacturing employment change, 1961–77.

Table 3.1

Manufacturing employment change in the Southampton SMLA, 1961-77.

Industry	No. of employees(1)			
	1 1961	2 1971	3 1971	4 1977
Shipbuilding	9,022	7,583	6,804	7,551
Vehicles	11,366	8,530	8,911	12,001
Food, drink, tobacco	5,155	5,251	5,848	5,185
Chemicals and allied products(2)	6,020	3,643	6,572	6,031
Mechanical engineering	)	10,206	9,350	8,090
Instrument engineering	) 19,225	243	699	519
Electrical engineering	)	12,516	12,623	12,866
Other industries	7,675	14,018	9,376	10,821
TOTAL	58,463	61,990	60,183	63,064

Notes: (1) Columns 1 and 2 are based on a different method of
            collection (the card count) from columns 3 and 4 (annual
            census) and so are not directly comparable (see Department
            of Employment, 1973).
        (2) The major difference in the 1971 employment in chemicals as
            between the card count and the annual census suggests that
            the loss of employees between 1961 and 1971 has been
            exaggerated. In the 1971 card count estimates, some of the
            employment ascribed to Order IV (coal and petroleum prod-
            ucts) appears to have been allocated to Order XIX (other
            manufacturing).

Source: Unpublished Department of Employment statistics (ER11s) for the
         the employment office areas of Southampton-Woolston, Eastleigh,
         Winchester, Hythe, Romsey and Lymington.

during both the 1961-1971 and 1971-1977 periods, although it seems
probable that the Department of Employment's method of compiling the
statistics exaggerated the extent of this decline during the 1960s.
Offsetting these sources of employment loss have been the engineering
and electrical industries, which were the main sources of job creation
during the 1960s; however, their ability to provide new jobs was not in
evidence during the 1970s. Employment in mechanical engineering contracted by some 1250 jobs between 1971 and 1977, while there was a
static workforce in the electrical engineering industry.

So, it is clear that between 1961 and 1977 some important changes
occurred in Southampton's industrial structure, although for the most
part the changes were observable at a MLH- rather than an order-level.
In particular, shipbuilding, aircraft manufacture, railway engineering
and oil refining were no longer as significant in terms of their

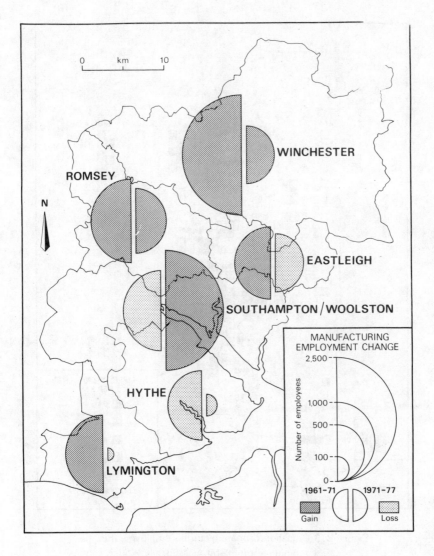

Figure 3.2 Manufacturing employment change by employment
office area, 1961–77.

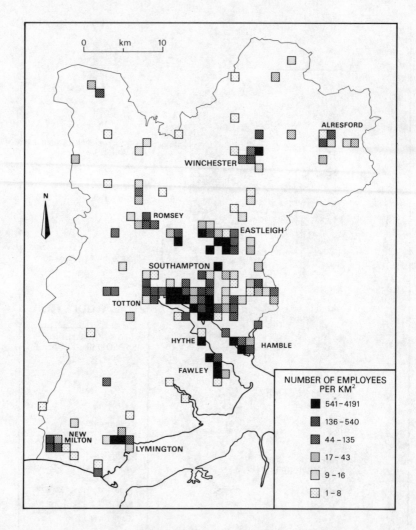

Figure 3.3 Location of manufacturing employment in the
Southampton SMLA, 1979.

proportion of total manufacturing employment in 1977 as in 1961, while motor-vehicle manufacture and electronics had increased in relative importance.

The distribution of manufacturing jobs within the SMLA has also changed since 1961. Although locational shifts in employment have not been great, the main trend has been the decentralisation of manufacturing activity. Between 1961 and 1971, the Southampton-Woolston EOA (which is only a very rough approximation of the SMLA 'core', because it includes suburban areas such as Totton, Hedge End and Hamble as well as the City of Southampton) lost over 1000 jobs (-3 per cent), while the 'periphery' gained an additional 4500 manufacturing employees (+19 per cent). However, between 1971 and 1977, the 'core' gained over 2000 jobs (+7 per cent), due largely to employment growth in Southampton's shipbuilding and vehicle industries, while the 'periphery' made a net gain of just 518 jobs (+2 per cent). Consequently, while the 'core' contained 59 per cent of total SMLA manufacturing in 1961, its share had only fallen to 55 per cent by 1977. Within the 'periphery', the major growth areas have been Romsey and Winchester which virtually doubled their share of total SMLA manufacturing employment from 6.7 to 13.1 per cent between 1961 and 1977. In contrast Hythe, with its high level of dependence on the petro-chemical industry, lost jobs during the 1960s and 1970s, and in both Eastleigh and Lymington manufacturing employment contracted between 1971 and 1977, following gains in the 1960s (Fig. 3.2).

The current distribution of manufacturing employment in the Southampton SMLA is thus still largely focused on Southampton itself, with the Eastleigh-Chandler's Ford area as an important secondary manufacturing centre (Fig.3.3). The only other significant employment nodes are at Fawley and Hamble, both of which contribute further to the industrialised character of Southampton Water. Some manufacturing employment is also found in the smaller urban centres of the 'periphery', notably in Lymington, New Milton, Winchester and, to a lesser extent, in Romsey and Alresford.

SOURCES OF MANUFACTURING EMPLOYMENT GROWTH

Individual industries have experienced differing national employment trends as a result of international competition and of changes in demand and in capital-labour substitution. One possible explanation for the fact that the manufacturing sector in the Southampton SMLA, as measured by employment, has outperformed both national and regional trends is therefore that it has a favourable industrial mix, specialising in nationally-expanding industries. Shift-share analysis can indicate the extent to which industrial structure might 'explain' rates of employment growth and decline. Although it is a widely-used technique, it does not lack critics. Fothergill and Gudgin (1979b) have however, recently defended its utility. Applying the shift-share technique to Southampton SMLA for the 1961-1971 period reveals that, if its total manufacturing workforce had changed at the same rate as total manufacturing employment in Great Britain, the area would have lost 1287 jobs (the national component)(Table 3.2). In fact, Southampton gained 3383 jobs, so the total shift, that is the difference in the performance of Southampton compared with Great Britain, was +4670 jobs.

Table 3.2

Shift-share analysis for the Southampton SMLA, 1961-77.

(a)	No. of jobs	% of 1961 employment
Change, 1961-1971(1)	+3,383	+5.79
National component	-1,287	
Total shift	+4,670	
Structural component	+21	+0.04
Differential component	+4,649	+7.95

(b)	No. of jobs	% of 1971 employment
Change, 1971-1977(2)	+2,881	+4.79
National component	-5,618	
Total shift	+8,499	
Structural component	+561	+0.93
Differential component	+7,938	+13.19

Notes: (1) Calculated for 99 industries.
(2) Calculated for 121 industries.

The structural component, the employment change resulting from the mix of industries in the area, was only +21 jobs. In other words, Southampton's industrial structure in 1961 had virtually a neutral influence on employment change over the whole decade. It accounted for only 0.4 per cent of the total shift, thereby leaving a 'residual' of an increase of 4649 jobs, the differential component, which cannot be explained by industrial structure. Shift-share analysis for the 1971-77 period reveals essentially similar results. On the basis of national trends, Southampton was 'expected' to lose 5618 jobs; in the event, it actually gained 2881 jobs, so the total shift was 8499 jobs. Certainly, Southampton's industrial structure was more favourable in the 1970s than in the 1960s; nevertheless the structural component only accounted for +561 jobs, or 6.6 per cent of the total shift, leaving a residual of an additional 7938 jobs which cannot be explained by industrial structure. So, as in many other parts of Great Britain, inherited industrial specialisation in the SMLA 'explains' little of the actual manufacturing employment change.

The differential component, representing the employment change in an area which cannot be attributed directly to industrial structure, reflects the addition of manufacturing jobs from two sources (Fothergill and Gudgin, 1979a):

(i)   the movement of industry into an area from elsewhere in the country or from overseas. This includes both transfers, where a firm or plant moves completely from one location to another, and new branches, where a firm opens an additional establishment in an area in which it was not previously manufacturing;

Table 3.3

In situ employment change in Southampton, 1966-79.

| | No. of plants | % | Employment change | |
			No.	%
In situ growth	46	34.8	+4741	+41.2
In situ decline	70	53.0	-4121	-43.6
Static employment	16	12.1	-	-
Net employment change			+620	+2.9

Sources: City of Southampton Planning Department Establishment File (1966) and SHEDB.

(ii) employment generated within an area through the superior performance of both its locally and non-locally owned firms and through a high rate of new-firm formation.

The relative importance of these sources of employment growth in the Southampton SMLA can be assessed by examining the two processes involved in job creation, namely in situ employment growth and plant openings.

Unfortunately, there is relatively little information available to assess the contribution of employment change in surviving plants. However, the use of a City Planning Department Establishment File for 1966 in conjunction with the Establishment Databank for 1979 at least provides an indication of in situ employment change in the City of Southampton (the SMLA's 'core'). Some 47 per cent of the 1979 plant population in the City of Southampton also existed in 1966, and in aggregate these establishments made a modest gain of 620 jobs (+2.9 per cent). Employment growth in expanding plants more than offset the job losses in declining plants, although the latter were of greater numerical significance (Table 3.3). Information on numbers of employees in individual plants in the Fawley complex (Lester, 1973) and in the borough of Eastleigh (Clark, 1968) similarly suggests that employment change since the mid 1960s amongst surviving establishments has involved a combination of in situ expansion and contraction, the one largely cancelling out the other. The tentative conclusion from this fragmentary evidence is, therefore, that for the SMLA as a whole in situ employment change is likely to have had a very minor impact on total employment change.

It is interesting to note that amongst those surviving plants in the City of Southampton which increased their workforce during the 1966- period, there were some which had been established in the city during the late 1940s and 1950s, either as transfers from other parts of the country or as branch plants. Their continued expansion many years after being opened, perhaps as a result of their youthful capital stock, reflects the fact that new plants have the potential to contribute to employment creation over a considerable length of time. Employment

Table 3.4

Survivors and plant openings in the Southampton SMLA, 1971-79.

Category	No. of plants in 1979	Employment in 1979	% of 1979 total	
			plants	employment
Survivors (including moves within SMLA)	530	50,915	69.8	93.2
Openings of which:	229	3,744	30.2	6.8
new firms	(143)	(1,435)	(18.8)	(2.6)
branch plants	(78)	(2,168)	(10.3)	(3.9)
transfers into SMLA	(8)	(141)	(1.1)	(0.3)
TOTAL	759	54,659		

Source: SHEDB.

growth in the 1960s and 1970s by firms which arrived in Southampton earlier in the post-war period can, therefore, help to explain the positive <u>differential components</u> revealed by the shift-share analysis (Mackay and Thomson, 1979)(Table 3.2).

During the 1960s, and particularly since 1971, relatively few new jobs have been created in the Southampton SMLA as a result of the in-migration of firms from elsewhere in the country or from abroad. Indeed, establishments which were in existence before 1971, either at the same location or elsewhere in the SMLA, contained 93 per cent of total manufacturing employment in 1979, although only accounting for 70 per cent of the plant population (Table 3.4). The remaining 3744 jobs were the result of plant openings after 1971. However, only 1163 of these jobs (31.1 per cent) were created by companies without a manufacturing presence in Southampton in 1971 (Table 3.5). The movement of industry into the Southampton SMLA between 1971 and 1979 has, therefore, been on a relatively minor scale. Most of the jobs created in new plants have been generated from within the area, in new firms (38.3 per cent of employment in openings), new branch plants of locally-headquartered companies (13.6 per cent) and new branches of companies with a manufacturing presence in Southampton in 1971 but headquartered elsewhere in the UK or overseas (17.0 per cent).

When plant openings are classified according to the location of ownership, it appears that local enterprises (companies based in Southampton and new firms) have been responsible for creating only just over half (51.9 per cent) of the jobs in new plants (Table 3.5). Although the majority of new plants were opened by local companies (86 per cent of all new establishments), they were, on average, much smaller than those resulting from investment by non-local enterprises, the mean sizes being 11.4 and 67.2 employees respectively.

Table 3.5

Branch plant openings in the Southampton SMLA, 1971-79.

Type	Plants	Employment
1. Openings by companies HQd in Southampton SMLA	27	510
2. Openings by non-local companies with plants in Southampton SMLA in 1971	18	636
(a) HQd in UK	(16)	(577)
(b) HQd overseas	(2)	(59)
3. Openings by non-local companies with no plants in Southampton SMLA in 1971	33	1,022
(a) HQd in UK	(27)	(846)
(b) HQd overseas	(6)	(176)
TOTAL	78	2,168

Source: SHEDB.

It is widely accepted that the most important type of plant opening is the new firm, that is entirely new enterprises which did not previously exist as manufacturing organisations. The popular view is that a high rate of new-firm creation is important for an area's industrial vitality and prosperity. This line of argument points out that new firms act as a seedbed from which some larger enterprises will emerge. Furthermore, they make an important contribution to the job creation process, as well as acting as a source of technical innovation, contributing to industrial diversification and helping the competitive position of larger enterprises by providing them with specialist supplies and services. In most cases, however, these assertions have not been tested by empirical research. Certainly, in the Southampton SMLA new firms started after 1971 and surviving as independent companies to 1979, by accounting for 38.3 per cent of total employment in plant openings, made an important contribution to the job-creation process. In numerical terms, new firms were even more significant, comprising close to two-thirds of all new plants. Furthermore, almost one in five of the 1979 plant population were new firms having been started since 1971. However, because the typical new firm was very small, the median size in 1979 was 4 employees, with 61 per cent of firms having less than 10 employees (88 per cent less than 20 employees), they accounted for only 2.6 per cent of total SMLA manufacturing employment. The real job creation impact of new firms only comes over a much longer time period. Samples of independent firms founded in the 1960s (n=26), 1950s (n=12) and between 1945 and 1950 (n=13) reveal median workforces in 1979 of 14, 38.5 and 67 employees respectively.

Southampton's new firms are restricted to a narrow range of industries (Table 3.6). Just four industries - metal goods, shipbuilding,

Table 3.6

Industrial variations in rates of new-firm creation
in the Southampton SMLA, 1971-79.

Order	No. of new firms	%	New firms per 1000 employees, 1979	Average size of all plants, 1979
Food, drink, tobacco	5	3.5	0.94	151.7
Coal and petroleum products	1	0.7	0.38	878.7
Chemicals and allied products	3	2.1	1.18	82.0
Metal industries	2	1.4	1.23	108.2
Mechanical engineering	22	15.4	4.35	38.3
Instrument engineering	3	2.1	7.58	30.5
Electrical engineering	14	9.8	1.32	157.9
Shipbuilding	23	16.1	3.31	103.7
Vehicles	3	2.1	0.32	394.8
Other metal goods	25	17.5	10.29	25.8
Textiles, leather, clothing	4	2.8	5.67	29.4
Bricks, pottery, glass	4	2.7	6.46	12.6
Timber, furniture	21	14.7	7.77	24.4
Paper, printing, publishing	1	0.7	0.39	45.3
Other manufacturing	12	8.4	10.95	28.8
TOTAL	143		2.62	72.0

Source: SHEDB.

mechanical engineering and timber - contain almost two-thirds of new
firms. If electronics (MLHs 364-369) and other manufacturing
(especially MLH 496, plastics) are also included, then over 80 per cent
of new firms are accounted for. But, to a certain extent, this
industrial distribution of new firms simply reflects the industrial
structure of Southampton. A more accurate picture of the industrial
distribution of new firms emerges when account is taken of the size of
each industry in the SMLA. Calculating the number of new firms per
1000 employees indicates that the industries with the highest start-up
rates are metal goods, other manufacturing, timber and furniture,
instrument engineering and bricks, pottery and glass. Industries with
the lowest rates are food, drink and tobacco, vehicles, electrical
engineering, chemicals and, surprisingly, paper, printing and
publishing. At this aggregate level, the main factor which can account
for industrial variations in the new-firm creation rate appears to be
the plant-size structure of each industry. The number of firms per
1000 employees is significantly associated with the average size of
plant in the industry ($r_S=0.85$, significant at $p=.01$). Industries with
a large average plant size, suggesting high barriers to entry, have
attracted very few new firms, while industries with a low average size
of plant have generated a considerable number of new firms, a
reflection of low barriers to entry and the fact that small plants

'spin-off' substantially more new firms than do large plants (Johnson and Cathcart, 1979). However, it is impossible to assess from aggregate data, even at the MLH level, the extent to which new firms in Southampton are either innovative or contributing to a widening of the local industrial base. This is because of the wide range of activities included within an individual industrial category. Clearly, any adequate appraisal of this situation would require survey-based research.

There is no national yardstick by which to gauge whether the rate of new-firm creation during the 1970s in Southampton has been high or low. However, Gudgin et al (1979) note that in the East Midlands, which they describe as a region with a high rate of new-firm creation, firms started during or after 1968 accounted for 4.2 per cent of regional employment in 1975. In comparison, firms started in Southampton since 1971 contained only 2.6 per cent of total employment in 1979. Alternatively, Gudgin et al.(1979) expressed the East Midland's new-firm creation rate as 2.9 firms per 1000 employees per year. By this measure, the rate in Southampton is 3.6, suggesting that it may, after all, compare favourably with other high-birthrate areas. But clearly, evidence is required from a wide range of sub-regions, and agreement is needed on the method or methods for measuring new-firm creation rates, before it is possible to accurately identify 'high' and 'low' rates of new-firm start-up.

Table 3.7

Location of new manufacturing firms in the Southampton SMLA.

Area	No. of new firms, 1971-79	No. of new firms per 1000 manufacturing employees, 1979	Av. no. of employees per plant, 1979	Employment in new firms as % of total manufacturing employment
Southampton	45	1.86	85.4	1.50
Eastleigh	30	2.17	93.3	3.20
Winchester	16	5.05	34.5	5.68
Romsey	12	5.33	46.9	4.98
New Forest	40	3.56	59.8	3.19
(a) Waterside Parishes	(4)	(0.70)	(174.4)	(0.59)
(b) Rest of New Forest	(36)	(6.55)	(35.5)	(5.73)
TOTAL	143	2.62	72.0	2.63

A relatively high rate of new-firm start-up in Southampton has occurred, despite the fact that large plants dominate the labour market; 53 per cent of manufacturing employment in 1979 was in plants with 500 or more employees. Large plants are generally considered to be detrimental to new-firm creation, because they fail to give their employees sufficient relevant experience for them to start up firms on their own account. Security of employment, company pension schemes and other benefits provided by large employers may also deter employees from setting up their own businesses (Gudgin et al, 1979).

Within the Southampton SMLA, the City of Southampton has gained most new firms, but new-firm start-up rates have been highest in the rural periphery, particularly in Romsey, Winchester and the New Forest (excluding the Waterside Parishes)(Table 3.7). Factors which can account for this include the smaller average size of plant in the periphery, the tendency for former long-distance commuters (especially management and professional workers living in the periphery and working in the city) to set up new firms close to their homes, and the greater availability of nursery units and small, cheap premises outside the city. However, offsetting these advantages for new-firm creation in the periphery, there have been the restrictive planning strategies adopted in Mid and South West Hampshire, which have made it difficult to obtain suitable premises either for starting or perhaps more crucially, for expansion.

CONCLUSION

In the 1930s Southampton could convincingly demonstrate that it had an 'employment problem', involving a narrow industrial base and a dependence on dock-related activities (shipping, ship-repair and dock work) which were subject to seasonal fluctuations and which were offered on an insecure, casual basis (Ford, 1934). Since then, Southampton's manufacturing base has expanded and diversified, and employment is currently provided by a wide range of industries, the most important being shipbuilding, electrical engineering, electronics and vehicle manufacture. But despite this, Southampton remains a commercial rather than an industrial city; in 1977 only 28.2 per cent of jobs were in manufacturing as compared with 32.3 per cent nationally.

Rather less satisfactory is the extent to which manufacturing employment in Southampton is currently concentrated in a relatively small number of establishments. Only 11 plants in the SMLA contained 1000 or more employees in 1979, but they accounted for 41.2 per cent of total manufacturing employment. One in four of the manufacturing workforce was employed in the five largest plants. In contrast, 81 per cent of plants had less than 50 employees, but they accounted for just 16 per cent of manufacturing jobs. This top-heavy plant-size structure is not a new feature; indeed it was equally observable twenty years ago (Denton and Thomas, 1964).

During the late 1940s and 1950s, the in-movement of firms from other parts of the country, notably from London and the Home Counties, as well as from overseas, played a major role in Southampton's post-war industrial expansion. However, the influx of firms into Southampton during the 1960s was much smaller, and has been even more restricted since 1971. Consequently, most of the new jobs created in the past decade have been generated internally as a result of new-firm creation and the expansion, through in situ growth and branch plant openings, of both locally and non-locally headquartered companies.

The current ownership characteristics of the manufacturing sector reflect the heavy reliance, until the 1960s, on non-local sources of investment. In 1979, plants which were owned by firms headquartered outside the Southampton SMLA contained 78.1 per cent of manufacturing employment, whilst 31.8 per cent of jobs were in foreign-owned companies. Interestingly, dependence on outside capital had also been a feature of Southampton's economy in the 19th and early 20th centuries. Major components in the local economy, notably the docks, railway, shipyards and shipping companies, were all developed by non-local enterprise. Writing in the 1930s Ford observed that:

> "at present the majority of the greater businesses are either non-local in origin or are non-locally controlled.... The town presents a sharp contrast to such a port as Newcastle, where many local men built-up large businesses and fortunes on exporting, shipping and manufacture" (Ford, 1934, 23).

Southampton has therefore always been in a position where economic decisions affecting its major employers have been made outside the city. Furthermore, there are very few examples of firms which were started on a small scale in Southampton and which are now nationally-known enterprises. Indeed, only one local, independent firm (Conder, a steel frame building manufacturer) has grown sufficiently large to be included in The Times Top 1000 Companies (Times, 1979). Rather, it appears that successful, expanding local firms are generally taken-over, while still quite small, by larger national and international organisations. For example, Ford (1934) noted that in the early years of the aircraft industry, many small firms started in Southampton by local entrepreneurs were soon acquired by outside interests. Coming up-to-date, a tentative conclusion from a survey of recent business directories is that thirty-three firms which started in Southampton before 1971 were acquired between 1971/72 and 1979/80 by non-local companies. They provided 2402 jobs in 1979, equivalent to over 5 per cent of employment in Southampton's externally-controlled sector. Almost three-quarters of these firms were small, with less than 100 employees in 1979. However four companies, each with between 200 and 300 employees, accounted for 40 per cent of the employment in acquired firms.

As a result of the takeover of successful local companies and the in-movement of firms, the largest employers in Southampton now belong to organisations which are headquartered elsewhere in the United Kingdom or abroad. None of the ten largest enterprises in 1979 (all with 1700 employees or more) were locally-controlled, but amongst the largest twenty-five employers (minimum size of 350 employees) were four local firms. However, as one of these was acquired at the end of 1979 and the other moved into Southampton from Essex in the late 1950s, only two of those twenty-five largest employers are currently locally-controlled and the result of local initiative. Five more locally-controlled companies were included amongst the employers ranked 26 to 50 (minimum of 145 employees).

A dependence on non-local companies brings both advantages and disadvantages. Any individual plant is generally only a minor element in the company's national or international operations. The development of externally-owned plants in Southampton, therefore, depends on events external to the SMLA, and decisions affecting the local economy are, for better or worse, made elsewhere in the country or even outside the United Kingdom, and hence with little regard for the local impact of any action. Consequently, on the negative side, local plants may be deprived of investment which is instead directed to plants elsewhere in the country or overseas. Chapman (1973), for example, noted that during the 1960s Esso chose to expand its plants in Western Europe rather than at Fawley, while trade unions at Mullards have claimed that recent redundancies are the result of the policy of Philips (its Dutch parent company) of transferring work to cheap labour areas of the Far East (Southern Evening Echo, 18.2.81). On the credit side, however, local plants have access to capital-rich parent companies to finance investment schemes or to subsidise a period of loss-making.

There is a tentative suggestion that the high level of external control in Southampton has been advantageous in the present economic recession. Anecdotal evidence indicates that a number of companies have cut back employment at their plants elsewhere in the country, but have created few if any redundancies in Southampton. In some cases, they have even transferred product lines to Southampton. There is, however, no guarantee that such trends will continue if the recession is prolonged. Although redundancies have recently occurred in Southampton, they have rarely been of sufficient size to make 'headline news'. Approximately 3000 redundancies in manufacturing were notified to the Department of Employment or covered by the local media between January 1978 and December 1980. The majority of redundancy announcements involved relatively few workers (less than 50) and only two firms (Vosper Shiprepairers and Petters Refrigeration) made more than 250 employees redundant. However, as the recession has deepened, so 2500 more redundancies were announced during the first half of 1981. These included the loss of another 580 jobs at Vosper Shiprepairers (Financial Times, 28.2.81) and 837 jobs (64 per cent of the workforce) at AC Delco (Financial Times, 8.5.81). Some redundancies have involved plants which decentralised from the London area in the post-war period, although probably to a lesser extent than elsewhere in southern England (Townsend, 1981).

It seems unlikely that manufacturing jobs lost in the present economic recession will be offset by the expansion of Southampton's major employers. New technology is largely labour-saving, hence investment is likely to result in the need for fewer workers. Some companies are facing difficult demand conditions and a number (including Ford, Esso and British Rail Engineering) are in the process of reducing, or are about to reduce, the numbers employed in their British operations, in order to maintain or improve international competitiveness. It seems improbable that their plants in Southampton will escape contraction through either enforced or voluntary redundancies. Furthermore, trends during the 1970s have indicated that, unlike in the 1950s, new manufacturing jobs will not be generated on a large scale in the foreseeable future by the in-movement of firms. Rather, jobs must be generated locally through new firm creation and the expansion of small firms.

Many of the conditions favouring a high rate of new-firm formation are found in the Southampton SMLA, such as a desirable residential environment to attract 'footloose' entrepreneurs and highly-qualified manpower. Other advantages include the presence of a well-educated population and a high proportion of managerial, professional and technical employees (occupations likely to yield the most successful entrepreneurs), as well as the existence of a substantial small-firm sector and an economic structure which contains a number of high technology industries. But against these attractions, there is the relative shortage of industrial premises of a suitable type and rent for small firms, particularly in Southampton itself. In parts of the 'periphery', there is also a shortage of small industrial premises, a result of the conflict over the relative merits of providing jobs and of preserving both the natural environment and the physical fabric of small towns and villages.

With the possible exception of the Department of Industry Small Firms Counselling Service, which operates on a relatively modest scale in Southampton, the small-company sector in the SMLA receives little or no help from either local authorities or independent industrial promotion organisations. In contrast, other cities with unemployment rates similar to that of Southampton are considerably more active in local economic development. For example, Nottingham has an active small workshop construction programme, involving the building of units of between 45 and 185m^2, a size range which is generally not provided by private developers (Moreton, 1978). In Bristol two economic development organisations, which give advice and assistance to potential and existing small firms, have recently been set up, one by the local authority and the other by the Chamber of Commerce in conjunction with seven local companies (Moreton, 1980). It appears that only very recently have local authorities in the Southampton SMLA recognised the need to encourage local business expansion, particularly by small firms. Some schemes to build council 'starter units' are now under way, and there is a proposal by BAT Industries, a major employer in Southampton, to finance a local enterprise agency which would offer free advice to small companies (Southern Evening Echo, 23.6.81). Nevertheless, considerably more could be done to encourage new-firm formation and small-firm expansion. The fact that a policy of encouraging new and small businesses involves a long payoff period, perhaps taking as much as a generation to provide substantive results, suggests that action must be taken now in order to secure Southampton's economic prosperity at the turn of the century.

REFERENCES

ADSHEAD, S H and COOK, H T (1942), The Replanning of Southampton
          (Southampton, CB of Southampton).

ALLEN, K and YUILL, D (1978), Small Area Employment Forecasting
          (Farnborough, Saxon House).

BUCHANAN, C and Partners (1966), South Hampshire Study: Report on the
          Feasibility of a Major Growth Area (London, HMSO).

CB of SOUTHAMPTON (1952), Development Plan: Written Analysis
          (Southampton).

CSO (1968), Standard Industrial Classification (London, HMSO).

CHAPMAN, K (1970), Oil-based industrial complexes in the United Kingdom, Tijdschrift voor Economische en Sociale Geografie, 61, 157-172.

CHAPMAN, K (1973), Agglomeration and linkage in the United Kingdom petro-chemical industry, Transactions, Institute of British Geographers, 60, 33-68.

CLARK, R W (1968), The New Industrial Structure of Eastleigh MB (BSc dissertation, Department of Geography, University of Southampton).

COPPOCK, J T (1973), The changing face of England, 1850-circa 1900, in DARBY, H C (ed.), A New Historical Geography of England after 1600 (London, Cambridge University Press), 595-673.

DENNIS, R (1978), The decline of manufacturing employment in Greater London, 1966-1974, Urban Studies, 15, 63-73.

DENTON, G R and THOMAS, C J (1964), Economic activity, in MONKHOUSE, F J (ed.) A Survey of Southampton and its Region (Southampton, British Association), 259-277.

DEPARTMENT OF EMPLOYMENT (1973), A new series of annual employment statistics, Department of Employment Gazette, 81, 5-7.

DUNNING, J H (1958), American Investment in British Manufacturing Industry (London, Allen and Unwin).

FAGG, J J (1973), Spatial changes in manufacturing employment in Greater Leicester, 1947-1970, East Midland Geographer, 5, 400-416.

FAGG, J J (1980), A re-examination of the incubator hypothesis: a case study of Greater Leicester, Urban Studies, 17, 35-44.

FORD, P (1934), Work and Wealth in a Modern Port (London, Allen and Unwin).

FORD, P and THOMAS, C J (1950), A Survey of the Industrial Prospects of the Southampton Region (London, Basil Blackwell).

FOTHERGILL, S and GUDGIN, G (1978), Regional employment statistics on a comparable basis 1952-1975, Centre for Environmental Studies, Occasional Paper, 5.

FOTHERGILL, S and GUDGIN, G (1979a), Regional employment change: a sub-regional explanation, Progress in Planning, 12, 155-220.

FOTHERGILL, S and GUDGIN, G (1979b), In defence of shift-share, Urban Studies, 16, 309-319.

GUDGIN, G (1978), Industrial Location Processes and Regional Employment Growth (Farnborough, Gower).

GUDGIN, G, BRUNSKILL, I and FOTHERGILL, S (1979), New manufacturing firms and regional employment growth, Centre for Environmental Studies, Research Series, 39.

HALL, P (1980), Regional planning: directions for the 1980s, Town Planning Review, 51, 253-256.

JOHNSON, P and CATHCART, D G (1979), The founders of new manufacturing firms: a note on the size of their 'incubator' plants, Journal of Industrial Economics, 28, 219-224.

KEEBLE, D E (1964), The migration of metropolitan industry into Wessex, 1945-1964, Wessex Geographer, 5, 52-60.

KEEBLE, D (1976), Industrial Location and Planning in the United Kingdom (London, Methuen).

KEEBLE, D (1980), Industrial decline, regional policy and the urban-rural manufacturing shift in the United Kingdom, Environment and Planning A, 12, 945-962.

KIRKBRIDE, D (1969), Factors affecting future location of employment in South Hampshire, South Hampshire Plan Technical Unit, Working Paper, 4.

LAMBERT, J (1978), Manufacturing Employment Change in the Bristol TTWA (Bristol, Department of Industry, South West Regional Office).

LESTER, R H (1973), Industrial development around the Esso refinery, Fawley, Geography, 58, 154-159.

LLOYD, P E and DICKEN, P (1981), The components of change in metropolitan areas: events in their corporate context, in GODDARD, J B (ed.), The Urban and Regional Transformation of Britain (London, Methuen).

MACKAY, R R and THOMSON, L (1979), Important trends in regional policy and regional employment - a modified interpretation, Scottish Journal of Political Economy, 26, 233-260.

MASON, C M (1980), Industrial decline in Greater Manchester, 1966-1975: a components of change approach, Urban Studies, 17, 173-184.

MASON, C M (1981), Foreign-owned manufacturing firms in the United Kingdom: some evidence from South Hampshire, Area, 13 (forthcoming).

MORETON, A (1978), The city slum becomes a small workshop, Financial Times, 10 November.

MORETON, A (1980), Business tries self help, Financial Times, 14 April.

PATTERSON, A T (1975), A History of Southampton 1700-1914: Volume 3 - Setbacks and Recoveries 1864-1914 (Southampton, Southampton University Press).

TAVENER, L E (1950), The port of Southampton, Economic Geography, 26, 260-273.

TIMES (1979), The Times 1000, 1979-80 (London, Times Books).

TOWNSEND, A R (1981), Geographical perspectives on major job losses in the United Kingdom, 1977-1980, Area, 13, 31-38.

Acknowledgements   The financial support of the SSRC (grant HR6796) and the research assistance of Colin Taylor are both gratefully acknowledged.

4 Service Sector Employment Change and Office Development

C M MASON

The two most significant labour market trends in the United Kingdom in
the post-war period have been sectoral shift and occupational change.
Sectoral shift, which involves a decline in manufacturing employment and
an expansion of the service sector, has been very considerable in recent
years. In 1977 the service sector (orders 22 to 27 of the Standard
Industrial Classification) accounted for 57 per cent of total employment
compared with only 48 per cent in 1966. Over this same period the
service sector increased by over 1.6 million jobs (+14.6 per cent)
while, at the same time, employment in manufacturing was declining. An
important component in service sector employment growth has been the
recruitment of females, frequently working on a part-time basis
(Mallier and Rosser, 1979; Manley and Sawbridge, 1980). Occupational
change, involving a decline in blue-collar or manual jobs and an
increase in white-collar employment, has been equally significant.
Throughout the national economy manual occupations have declined,
whereas clerical, administrative, technical and professional occupations
have grown substantially.

  Both sectoral and occupational change are, of course, linked. There
is a higher proportion of white-collar employees in the service sector
than in manufacturing, thus sectoral shift is partly responsible for
occupational change. Nevertheless, even in the manufacturing sector
there has been a shift from blue- to white-collar occupations.
Production jobs in manufacturing have been declining since the 1950s,
whereas administrative, technical and clerical jobs have increased and
in 1971 accounted for around 25 per cent of total manufacturing
employment (Gudgin, Crum and Bailey, 1979). In addition, within the
service sector there has been a relative, and in some cases an absolute,

75

decline in tertiary activities and an expansion of the quaternary sector. Tertiary activities comprise the provision of services such as retailing and transport, and employ mainly low-skilled and manual employees. Quaternary activities are those which control, administer and co-ordinate economic activity and provide high-order services, such as finance, research and education, and largely employ white-collar staff. This shift from blue- to white-collar employment in both the manufacturing and service sectors reflects the decreasing emphasis in the economy on production and the provision of material-handling services and an increased commitment to the collection, processing and transmission of information, activities which are primarily undertaken in offices. As a result, office employment has increased considerably in the United Kingdom, from 1 in 6 of the economically-active population in 1951 to 1 in 4 by 1971 (Goddard, 1975).

Expansion of the service sector has occurred throughout all parts of the United Kingdom, although some areas have enjoyed much faster rates of growth than others. In particular, service sector employment has grown most rapidly in medium- and smaller-sized cities in central and southern England, notably in the Outer South East, East Anglia, Avon and in parts of the West Midlands lying outside Birmingham (Fothergill and Gudgin, 1979). Similarly, the growth of office employment has been most rapid in small- and medium-sized cities in the South East (outside Greater London) and in East Anglia. In contrast, office employment growth in both the peripheral regions and the provincial conurbations has been on a much smaller scale (Goddard, 1979).

In the light of these spatial employment trends, it is somewhat surprising to note the absence of research which directly focuses on office activity in the expanding centres of the Outer South East. The major office location research themes have been biased towards metropolitan areas, involving investigations of office-location trends particularly in London and to a lesser extent in the provincial conurbations (e.g. Goddard, 1967, 1970, 1973; Hall, 1972; Daniels, 1977; Damesick, 1979a,b) and office decentralisation from London (e.g. Daniels, 1969; Rhodes and Kan, 1971; Goddard and Morris, 1976). This study, therefore, takes Southampton as an example of a medium-sized city in southern England in order to examine office location trends outside metropolitan areas. The essay is in three parts: first, there is an investigation of employment trends in the service sector; this is followed by an analysis of the characteristics of offices occupying modern premises in central Southampton, and finally by an assessment of likely future office employment trends.

SERVICE SECTOR EMPLOYMENT AND OFFICE ACTIVITY IN THE SOUTHAMPTON SMLA

In view of national spatial trends in service sector employment and in the light of Southampton's long importance as a port and commercial centre, it is not surprising to find that service industries are the most important component in its employment structure. In 1977, the latest date for which information is available, the service sector (orders 22 to 27) accounted for 62 per cent of total employment in the Southampton SMLA (compared with 57 per cent in Great Britain). The service sector in Southampton is vitally important as an employer of female labour; women fill almost half the jobs in the service sector and

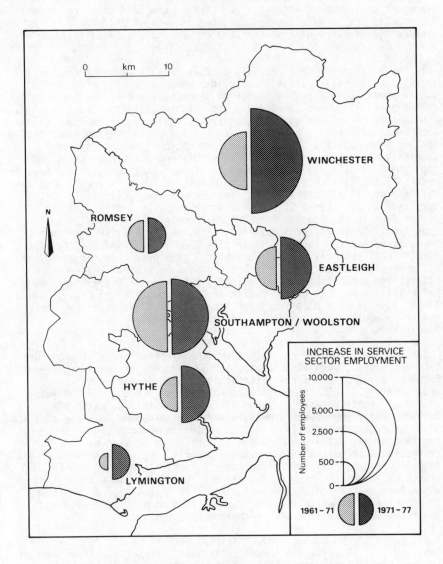

Figure 4.1 Service sector employment change in the Southampton
SMLA, 1961 – 77.

8 out of every 10 economically-active females work in service sector industries, compared with 52.6 per cent nationally. Professional and scientific services account for 28 per cent of service sector employment in Southampton, followed in order of importance by distribution (20 per cent), miscellaneous services (18 per cent) and transport and communications (17 per cent). Compared with the national distribution of service sector jobs, the only major difference is the greater significance of transport and communications in Southampton, an obvious consequence of its port function.

In the Southampton SMLA, as in any other city, a major portion of the service sector falls within the public domain, although, because the public sector cuts across a number of industries, it is difficult to define precisely where it ends and the private sector begins. However, a pragmatic definition would classify the public sector as comprising four broad categories: central government offices and establishments, local government, the health service and nationalised industries. Together, these groups accounted for nearly one-quarter of total SMLA employment in 1976 and one-third of service sector jobs (defined here as orders 21 to 27). Local government (Hampshire County Council, plus the district councils) is the largest employer in the public sector. In very approximate terms, it accounts for about 1 in 3 of all public sector jobs in the Southampton SMLA, with over half of such jobs in education. Nationalised industries, of which the British Transport Docks Board and the Central Electricity Generating Board are the most significant, probably account for about 1 in 5 public sector employees, while approximately 1 in 6 jobs are provided by central government offices and establishments, principally the Ordnance Survey and the University. The size of the public sector in Southampton thus under-lines its role as a major employer and emphasises that changing public sector expenditure priorities could have major labour market implications.

Service sector employment has grown considerably in the Southampton SMLA since 1961, when it accounted for 53 per cent of total employment. Between 1961 and 1971 service sector employment increased by approximately 11,000 jobs (+11.6 per cent) and by almost 22,000 jobs (+18.7 per cent) between 1971 and 1977. In comparison, rates of service sector employment growth in Great Britain were 10.2 per cent and 11.6 per cent respectively. Service sector employment growth in Southampton has largely been a function of the expansion of professional and scientific services, notably education and medical and dental services, but also, to a lesser extent, it has been due to the growth of insurance, banking and finance during the 1960s and miscellaneous services between 1971 and 1977 (Fig.4.1). In contrast, transport and communications and distribution made only modest contributions to service sector employment growth.

All parts of the SMLA gained additional service sector jobs between 1961 and 1977 (Fig.4.2), although particularly during the 1960s many of the additional jobs were created in the Southampton-Woolston area. Service employment in the periphery has also expanded, notably in Winchester, Eastleigh and Hythe. Indeed, 9000 additional service jobs were created in Winchester between 1971 and 1977, a 50 per cent increase. As a result, the proportion of total SMLA service sector employment located in the 'core' (Southampton-Woolston) fell from 70

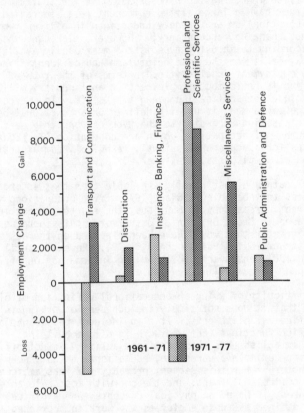

Figure 4.2   Employment change in service industry
in the Southampton SMLA , 1961 – 77.

per cent in 1961 to 61 per cent by 1977. Winchester, in contrast, increased its share from 14 to 20 per cent over the same period, as a result, in part at least, of becoming county town for the whole of Hampshire in the local government reorganisation of 1974. However, the size of its service sector workforce is artificially inflated by the inclusion of local government employees paid from Winchester but not necessarily working there (Hampshire County Council, 1979a).

The main service industries to have expanded in the Southampton SMLA since 1961 either have a large office component (e.g. education and health administration) or are largely undertaken in office premises (e.g. insurance, banking, accountancy). However, although employment classified according to industry type is the most easily available workforce data, it is not the most helpful method of identifying office jobs, because employment is classified in terms of the type of industry in which the job is performed. Employment in any industry will, therefore, include both office and non-office staff. To overcome this problem, office employment is usually defined on a functional basis, with workers classified according to the type of work they perform. There are a number of occupations which are conventionally regarded as office jobs, as for example professional, technical, administrative, managerial and clerical posts (Alexander, 1979).

Occupational data are most readily available from the Census. This source indicates that between 1966 and 1971 office occupations in the Southampton area increased by 10,550 jobs, the fourth largest increase of any urban area in Great Britain. Furthermore, this increase was substantially greater than would have been expected on the basis of its occupational structure in 1966 (Goddard, 1979). However, until the results of the 1981 Census are published, no information on office employment trends since 1971 is available.

A further difficulty of using an occupational definition of office employment is that it does not simply include people working in 'detached' office establishments. It also includes people who are performing office functions, but who work in office buildings 'attached' to establishments whose dominant activity is not office work, such as for example a warehouse, educational establishment, hospital or factory. For this reason, probably the least ambiguous definition of office employment, and the one with most relevance for planning purposes, is based on physical concepts, where office employment is defined as those employees who work in 'detached' or freestanding offices, that is, in physically separate establishments where office activities are conducted. But, of course, not all employees working in 'detached' offices actually perform office functions, since occupations such as cleaners, messengers and porters are likely to be included in the total office workforce.

Information provided by Hampshire County Council Planning Department for 1976 sheds some light on the amount of employment in the Southampton SMLA which is in 'detached' offices (Table 4.1). Two points emerge. First, only a relatively small proportion of the total workforce (just over 15 per cent) actually work in 'detached' offices, and even within the service sector only 1 in every 5 employees works in a 'detached' office (1 in 4 in the public services sector). Secondly, a large proportion (87 per cent) of employment in 'detached' offices is

Table 4.1

Employment by type of premises and by sector, Southampton SMLA, 1976.

Sector	TYPE OF PREMISES				
	Detached office and laboratory	Industrial site	Warehouse	Other	Total employment
Primary/extractive	409	110	0	3,252	3,771
Manufacturing	2,986	49,011	813	435	53,245
Construction	503	249	51	11,345	12,148
Private-sector services	15,343	2,569	7,816	59,275	85,003
Public-sector services	11,760	22	33	34,504	46,319
Inadequately described	4	11	0	14	29
Total employment	31,005	51,972	8,713	108,825	200,515

Source: Hampshire County Council Planning Department.

in the service sector. In contrast, only 5.6 per cent of 'detached' office jobs are in the manufacturing sector, suggesting that most office functions in manufacturing organisations are performed in premises where the main activity is either production or warehousing.

The Department of Environment floorspace data (1) provide an alternative indication of trends in office activity. They have many shortcomings (Daniels, 1975, 52-53) but can give a broad indication of increases over time in the size of the commercial office stock. However, analysis of the data is hindered because they are collected for local government areas. Changes in local authority boundaries in 1974 have, therefore, made difficult any analysis over time. Between 1967 and 1979, in a somewhat larger area than the SMLA incorporating the districts of Southampton, Eastleigh, Winchester, Test Valley and New Forest, the stock of commercial office floorspace increased by over 220,000m^2, a 93 per cent expansion. Over the same period the rate of increase in England and Wales was only 64 per cent. Some 120,000m^2 of new office floorspace was added to the office stock in the City of Southampton (whose boundaries were not altered by local government reorganisation), thus accounting for 54 per cent of the total increase in floorspace in the 'expanded SMLA' area. However, this was a smaller share than 'expected', given that in 1967 the City of Southampton contained two-thirds of total office floorspace in the five districts. But the City of Southampton did gain over 60 per cent of new commercial office floorspace in the 1974-79 period, exactly its 'expected' share.

So, despite the decentralisation trends which have affected most other types of economic activity, the City of Southampton has maintained a high level of commercial office development, although it should be pointed out that since 1974 Eastleigh has emerged as an important peripheral office centre.

Whether measured on an industrial, occupational or physical basis, it is clear that office activity in the Southampton SMLA has substantially increased over the past two decades. During this same period many private and public sector offices decentralised from London to towns and cities elsewhere in the South East. This inevitably raises the question, to what extent has decentralisation been a major element in the considerable growth of Southampton's office sector?

Here again, clear evidence is not available because of the lack of suitable data. Although information on the dispersal of government offices is reasonably comprehensive, this is not the case with private sector office decentralisation. The annual reports of the Location of Offices Bureau (which was disbanded in 1980) provide partial information on offices which decentralised from central London after 1963. However, the statistics are limited in their usefulness in that they relate only to moves from central London, they include only offices which contacted the LOB, and the employment totals are only estimates of the expected workforce at the new location. Hall (1972) has suggested that the LOB data covered approximately 75 per cent of the offices and 50 per cent of the jobs which decentralised from Central London.

Southampton has not been a major recipient of dispersed government offices during the past twenty years. For the most part, such offices have either been relocated to major cities in Assisted Areas, for example Cardiff, Glasgow and Liverpool, or to urban centres closer to London, for example Southend and Basingstoke. Between 1963 and 1972 Southampton received just two government decentralised offices, one belonging to the Inland Revenue and the other to the Ordnance Survey, following a decision to concentrate the latter's activities in Southampton. Together, these offices provided 947 jobs in 1972. A further 1730 jobs in the Ordnance Survey were the result of relocation prior to 1963 (Hardman, 1973; Hammond, 1967). There were no proposals in the post-1973 dispersal programme for Southampton to receive any additional government offices (Hardman, 1973).

From the limited data which are available, it appears that Southampton fared little better in attracting private sector offices decentralising from London. Daniels (1980) identified 16 private sector offices with 1132 employees which have decentralised to Southampton since 1963. Most were quite small, eleven having less than 50 employees. Office decentralisation from Central London exhibits a marked distance-decay pattern, with the majority of offices remaining within a 72km radius of the capital (Daniels, 1975), and for this reason alone Southampton would not seem to have been well placed geographically to attract many decentralising offices. Furthermore, for offices moving in a south-west direction from London, there are a number of 'intervening opportunities' (notably Basingstoke) before Southampton is reached. But although Southampton's relatively poor record in attracting decentralised offices can be excused, its neighbouring city, Portsmouth, has undoubtedly been considerably more successful, with decentralised offices creating about 2500 new jobs (LOB, 1977; Daniels, 1975; Riley and Smith, 1981).

OFFICE DEVELOPMENT IN THE CITY OF SOUTHAMPTON

The previous section has presented evidence to suggest that there has been a considerable expansion of office activity in the Southampton SMLA during the 1960s and 1970s, and that much of the new development has occurred within the City of Southampton rather than in peripheral locations. Between 1965 and 1979 an estimated 150,000m^2 of new office floorspace was constructed in the city, and this almost exclusively in the central area (Fig.4.3), thereby increasing the city's office stock by 59 per cent (2). Much of the new office development occurred between 1965 and 1975; there have been relatively few new schemes either given planning permission or completed during the second half of the 1970s (Southampton City Council, 1981).

Data on office activity collected by official agencies are limited and have many shortcomings, and so they can provide little more than an approximate indication of trends in commercial office floorspace and employment growth in Southampton. Consequently, a postal questionnaire was sent in mid-1981 to all firms occupying office premises constructed in central Southampton since 1964, in order to obtain a greater and more reliable understanding of the structure, characteristics and locational trends in its office sector (3). There was a response rate of 60 per cent, the completed returns providing information on a representative sample of 101 offices; they employed 4355 staff and occupied over 62,800m^2 of floorspace.

As in other cities, the majority of office developments constructed in Southampton have been speculative rather than custom-built schemes, being initiated either by property companies or financial institutions, notably insurance companies and pension funds who finance such schemes by investing their members life-policy premiums or pension contributions (Ambrose and Colenutt, 1975; Barras, 1979a). Consequently, the majority of firms occupying modern office premises in central Southampton are tenants; only eleven offices in the sample actually owned their premises.

The occupation of modern office premises is dominated by a minority of large offices. Just one office accounted for over one-quarter of total sample employment; seven offices (each with 100 or more employees) provided 60 per cent of the total employment in the sample. In contrast, 83.2 per cent of offices had less than 50 employees, but accounted for only 34.6 per cent of total sample employment. Similarly, just four offices occupied 35 per cent of total floorspace. The typical firm occupying modern office premises in central Southampton is, therefore, quite small; median employment is 18 staff and median size of premises is 279m^2.

Numerically, the most important group of offices occupying modern premises in central Southampton are in the financial sector (insurance, banking and credit houses). They account for just over one-third of all firms in the sample, and insurance offices comprise some 69 per

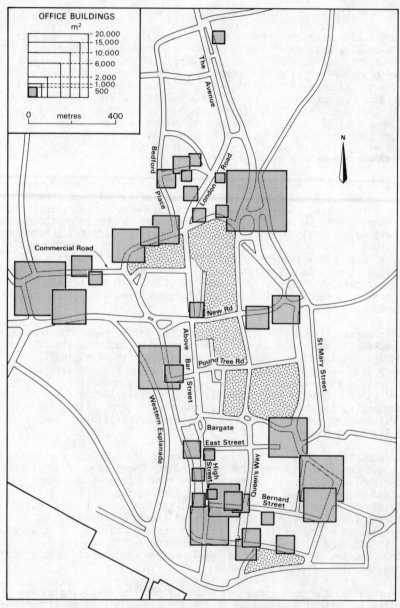

Figure 4.3 Location of new office developments
in Southampton, 1965 – 80.

Table 4.2

Staff structure in offices occupying modern premises.

Category	Female employees (%)	% OF EMPLOYMENT IN EACH OCCUPATIONAL GROUP				
		Administrators and managers	Professional and technical	Secretarial and clerical	Travellers and representatives	Others
Local government	49.5	11.6	54.7	28.4	0	5.3
Central government	59.1	10.8	5.4	81.0	0	2.8
Professional services	24.2	7.4	70.5	20.1	0.2	1.8
Manufacturing and primary	27.7	14.0	38.7	27.1	15.8	4.5
Finance	52.7	11.4	22.2	45.3	18.8	2.3
Business services	60.3	11.1	9.5	43.9	34.0	1.5
Shipping	45.0	14.9	23.1	58.2	0.6	3.2
Public utilities	50.0	9.8	20.9	64.0	0.9	4.3
Total	47.6	11.1	26.0	51.7	8.2	3.2

Source: Survey of Offices in Central Southampton, 1981.

cent of firms within the financial group. Professional services (e.g. accountants, architects and surveyors), business services (e.g. directory publishers and computer bureaux) and the offices of companies engaged in primary and manufacturing activities each account for between 12 and 14 per cent of the total sample. However, when measured in terms of employment and floorspace occupied, public service organisations (e.g. gas, water and rail) are the most significant office-based activities in central Southampton, accounting for 31 per cent of employment in the sample and 24 per cent of floorspace. In comparison, the financial sector accounts for only 24 per cent of employment and 22 per cent of floorspace. The third most important office group is shipping company offices, which contain 11 per cent of employment and occupy 10 per cent of floorspace in the sample. Professional and business services offices are, on average, quite small, and so these groups are less significant when measured by employment and floorspace than their numerical importance would suggest (Fig.4.4).

The public sector, comprising local authorities, central government and public utilities, is a major element in central Southampton's office sector, providing 42 per cent of total employment in the sample and occupying 41.5 per cent of floorspace (Fig.4.4). Other British cities reveal a similar picture; for example, in Manchester 36 per cent of new central area office space completed since 1960 has been taken up by the public sector (Catalano and Barras, 1980). One reason for this has been local government reorganisation, while another has been the movement by a number of public authority organisations into new headquarters during the 1970s. It seems likely that without public sector offices moving into new, mainly speculative office space during the 1960s and 1970s, the oversupply, which reached a peak of over 50,000m^2 in Southampton in 1976, would have been even greater (Barras, 1979a; Southampton City Council, 1981).

Because the office sector is an important source of employment in Southampton, it is important to identify more precisely what types of jobs are being created and for whom. In particular, there is a need to ascertain the extent to which new jobs are managerial, professional and technical rather than clerical, and whether they are predominantly filled by males or by females. Disaggregating total employment in the sample according to occupational structure indicates that just over half the workers were secretarial and clerical staff and a further quarter were professional and technical employees. Administrators and managers accounted for 11 per cent of office staff, travellers and representatives 8 per cent and the remaining 3 per cent were a miscellaneous occupational group which included porters, cleaners, messengers and security staff (Table 4.2). There are, however, considerable differences in the occupational structure of each office group. Secretarial and clerical staff, for example, form the largest occupational category in central government and public utility offices, but are the smallest group in professional and industrial offices. Travellers and representatives are a significant element in the employment structure of only three types of office, namely finance, business services and manufacturing. In each case, a major function of the offices is sales and sales support, with life insurance, pensions, credit, directory space and office equipment the main products being sold. A substantial proportion of employment in professional offices

86

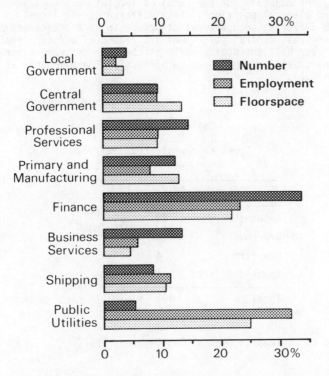

Figure 4.4   Characteristics of offices occupying modern premises
in central Southampton.

is accounted for by professional and technical staff, and they also comprise the largest component of employment in local government and industrial offices. Administrators and managers are most significant in shipping and industrial offices.

Almost 48 per cent of employees in the sampled offices were females, although again there were differences between the office groups. However, since the majority (82 per cent) of females were employed in secretarial and clerical positions, these differences are largely a product of the differing occupational structure in each office group. In business services, central government and financial offices females accounted for over half the staff, while at the other extreme comprised only around one-quarter of employees in professional and industrial offices (Table 4.2).

Table 4.3

Types of new offices.

	No.	%
Relocation	69	68.3
Branch	27	25.7
New firm	4	4.0
Rebuild in situ	1	1.0
Total	101	

Source: Survey of Offices in Central Southampton, 1981.

Demand for new office space in Southampton has primarily come from two sources, namely from organisations opening branch offices in the city and from firms undertaking short-distance relocation within the central area (Tables 4.3 and 4.4). Approximately one-quarter of firms occupying recently constructed premises were branch offices; 30 per cent of these were additional local offices opened by firms which were already operating in Southampton, while the remainder were new branches of organisations without a prior presence in the city. Just over two-thirds of offices had relocated. Typically, relocated offices were larger than new branches; respective median workforces were 19 and 14, and as a result of their larger size accounted for 79 per cent of employment in the sample. The majority of relocations were over short distances within central Southampton, and altogether 84 per cent of relocated offices had previous premises in the city. A further three relocated offices had dual origins, one in Southampton and the other elsewhere (London, Salisbury, Bournemouth). In contrast, only eight offices moved into Southampton, five having moved from London. However, only in two of these eight cases were the entire organisations moved to Southampton. The remaining offices were either partial moves, in which the companies only relocated some departments to Southampton, leaving other departments in the original location, or were relocations of South Coast branch offices.

Table 4.4

Origins of office relocations.

	No.	%
Central Southampton	48	69.6
Elsewhere in Southampton	10	14.5
Outside Southampton	8	11.6
Dual origins*	3	4.3
Total	69	

*Three firms each moved from two offices, one in Southampton and one outside, into one new office in Southampton.

Source: Survey of Offices in Central Southampton, 1981.

The majority of offices occupying new premises in central Southampton have, therefore, had local origins; indeed, only 31 per cent of total employment in the sample was a clear addition to the city's workforce, resulting from relocation into Southampton and from the opening of new firms and branch offices. In contrast, 57 per cent of offices, containing over two-thirds of jobs in the sample, simply moved from other premises in the city, although, of course, such moves into new premises may well have permitted firms to increase their employment. However, office development does have a displacement effect by attracting firms from the existing stock of floorspace and thereby creates vacancies which, depending on the age and location of the vacated premises, might prove very hard to relet.

Amongst relocated offices, by far the major reason for seeking new premises was expansion, being cited by two-thirds of firms as an important or very important factor, and so confirming the 'growth-movement' hypothesis established in the context of factory relocation (Keeble, 1971). Indeed, expansion appears to be the principal reason influencing offices to relocate in all cities regardless of size (Fernie, 1977). Desire for economy and company rationalisation or reorganisation were respectively the second and third most important reasons given for relocation, although in each case mention was by less than half the relocated offices. The main factors in office relocation were, therefore, the result of internal pressures on the firm (Table 4.5A). In contrast, external 'push' factors, such as shortages of

Table 4.5

Factors influencing office movement and location choice.

(A) <u>Reasons for movement</u> (n=69)	Score*
Expansion	57
Economy	27
Rationalisation/reorganisation	25
Traffic congestion/car-parking problems	15
Poor quality of accommodation	15
Expiry of lease	14
Staff recruitment problems	8
Rent review	7
Purchase of own premises	5
Move back to own site from temporary premises following its redevelopment	3
Demolition	3

(B) <u>Reasons for choosing present location</u> (n=101)	
Suitable office accommodation was available	79
Favourable rent and rate levels	51
Easy access to customers and clients	49
Availability of car-parking space	47
Ability to obtain or keep suitable staff	44
Good access to major road links	41
Proximity to other offices with which contact is made	32
Good access to rail links	27
Proximity to shopping facilities	13
Proximity to hotel and restaurant facilities	11
Access to the port of Southampton	10
Access to Southampton Airport	8
Prestige of premises	3

*Firms were asked to indicate whether each of the listed influences had been 'very important', 'important' or 'not important' in their relocation or location choice. Following Damesick (1979a), the 'scores' were obtained by multiplying the number of 'very important' responses by two, adding this to the number of 'important' responses and expressing the sum as a percentage of twice the total number of respondant firms.

Source: Survey of Offices in central Southampton, 1981.

labour, expiry of lease, demolition and rent review, were of fairly limited significance. However, one external factor, problems of car parking and traffic congestion, was acknowledged by one-quarter of companies as being a factor which prompted the relocation decision, although essentially as a supporting rather than a principle factor. It seems reasonable to suggest that offices where this was a very serious handicap would have moved to premises outside central Southampton, where traffic congestion is not as severe and car parking less restricted.

For offices moving into Southampton, the most frequently cited 'push' factor was the need for economy. Because office rents decline with distance from Central London, floorspace can be obtained relatively cheaply in Southampton; of 41 office centres in South East England only six currently have lower rents than in Southampton (Financial Times, 1981a). Prime office rents in Southampton are around one-sixth of those in the City of London and two-fifth of those in the London suburbs. These rent differentials are similar to those prevailing in the early 1970s. The difference in operating costs between Southampton and London is further increased when rates are considered; rates in Southampton are one-fifth of those in suburban London and one-tenth of those in the City (Debenham, Tewson and Chinnocks, 1981).

The search for a new office location can be regarded as a narrowing down process, involving first the selection of the urban area and then the finding of premises within that town or city. However, only twelve offices indicated that a location in another city had been seriously considered (frequently Bournemouth or Portsmouth). For the majority of new offices, which, after all, were either local branches or moves from other premises in Southampton, the search for new premises was restricted to the central area.

The single most important influence on the sampled offices in determining the choice of new location was, not surprisingly, the availability of suitable office accommodation (Table 4.5B). Favourable rent and rate levels and the availability of car-parking space, factors associated with the suitability of premises, were also important factors. A secondary consideration in the choice of new office premises related to their locational attributes; easy access to customers and clients was the third most important factor and an associated factor, good access to major road links, was ranked sixth. Proximity to 'linked' offices, on the other hand, was not such an important location factor. Firms taking up modern offices in central Southampton, therefore, appear to be more concerned with access from the city centre than with any agglomeration advantages deriving from a location within the central area. However, the ability to obtain or retain staff is an important advantage of a central location and was a major locational consideration. The central area is the focus of public transport routes and so has a large labour catchment, and proximity to city centre shops and other facilities is favoured by staff, making recruitment easier than in a suburban location. In addition, offices which moved within central Southampton minimised the likelihood of losing staff as a result of relocation. Offices moving into Southampton similarly stressed the availability of suitable accommodation and favourable rent and rate levels, but also emphasised the availability of good rail links.

Car parking is a major problem for offices in most city centres. In Southampton the desire for better car-parking provision was an important factor prompting firms to relocate, although it was rarely sufficient on its own to stimulate a move. On the other hand, over two-thirds of offices acknowledged that the availability of car-parking space was either an important or very important factor in their choice of new premises, although the majority of offices giving greatest weight to car-parking availability were small and, on average, obtained just three car-parking spaces at their new premises. The supply of car-parking spaces in central Southampton has been determined by the city council, which has adopted a standard of one space per 300m² of office floorspace in order to cater only for essential car users, to limit long-stay parking in the city centre and to encourage the use of public transport especially for journeys to work (Southampton City Council, 1981). Despite this, over six in every ten employees in the sampled offices travelled to work by car, and for every two car-parking spaces attached to the sampled offices, there were three essential car users, although in only 58 per cent of offices did the number of essential car users actually exceed their number of car-parking spaces. The general conclusion is, therefore, that car-parking difficulties are not a universal problem. There are many, mainly small offices with two or three car-parking spaces which can satisfactorily meet their essential car-user requirements, but there are also many other offices, both large and small, which are hampered by car-parking problems.

Table 4.6

Office status.

	No.	%
Headquarters office	5	5
Single, independent office	6	6
Branch office	90	89
Total	101	

Source: Survey of Offices in Central Southampton, 1981.

The majority of firms occupying modern premises in Southampton are branch offices, generally with their head office either in London or elsewhere in the South East (Tables 4.6 and 4.7). Only five of the firms are themselves head offices, of which two had decentralised from London since the mid-1960s. Southampton is not, therefore, a major 'control point' in the British urban system. This is confirmed by 'The Times 1000' list, which indicates that in the financial year 1979-80 only seven of the 1000 largest enterprises in Britain were headquartered in the Southampton SMLA, and only one of these occupied a 'detached' office in the city centre (Times, 1979). Rather, Southampton is a regional centre; the area of operations of just over half of the new offices in the central area covers southern England, that is Hampshire plus some or all of the five adjacent counties (Table 4.8). Professional and business-services offices, in particular, have a mainly regional sphere of operations. Public sector offices, in contrast, tend mainly to have local operations. Obviously, local authority offices are limited either to Southampton or Hampshire, but

Table 4.7

Branch offices: location of head office.

	No.	%
Southampton SMLA	5	5.6
Greater London	50	55.6
Elsewhere in South East England	22	24.4
Elsewhere in UK	9	10.0
Abroad	4	4.4
Total	90	

Source: Survey of Offices in Central Southampton, 1981.

Table 4.8

Area of operations.

	No.	%
Southampton	6	6.0
South Hampshire	7	6.9
Hampshire	15	14.9
Southern England*	52	51.5
South East and South West England and the Midlands	3	3.0
England and Wales	4	4.0
Great Britain	4	4.0
International	10	9.9
Total	101	

*Defined as Hampshire, West Sussex, Berkshire, Dorset, Wiltshire and Isle of Wight.

Source: Survey of Offices in Central Southampton, 1981.

in addition over half of the central government and public utility offices did not extend their operations beyond the county boundary. Those offices with national or international operations were almost

Table 4.9

Means of contact with clients and customers.

	Score*
Telephone/telex	84
Post	81
Staff visiting clients/customers	72
Customers/clients visiting office	47
Personal messenger	5
Passing trade (general public)	5

*See note for Table 4.5.

Source: Survey of Offices in Central Southampton, 1981.

exclusively either offices of shipping companies or of industrial organisations.

Branch offices generally perform routine, structured and standardised activities for which the most appropriate communication media are non-personal, notably post and telephone. As a result, they generate few face-to-face contacts with linked businesses and so have little need for physical proximity. In contrast, complex and non-structured activities, such as high-level decision-making, control, co-ordination and planning, which are generally undertaken by head offices, rely much more on face-to-face contacts, and so place a high value on physical proximity to linked businesses. Given that the majority of new offices in Southampton perform branch functions, it is not surprising, therefore, to find that they have relatively few essential contacts with local businesses. Those essential local linkages which do take place are mainly with banking and business services. For the majority of offices in the sample, essential business contacts cover a much wider area than central Southampton, generally extending throughout Hampshire or southern England. A number of offices also have essential links with London-based organisations. The importance of telephone, telex and post as the main communication media used by Southampton offices is also confirmed (Table 4.9). In so far as personal contacts do occur, it is more often at the client's premises, a reflection of the marketing, sales and sales support functions of many of the sampled offices (e.g. insurance, manufacturing). Many of the functions of professional services offices also involve visiting the client (e.g. accountancy, civil engineering design).

PROSPECTS

Office development in British cities is subject to a development cycle.

This is a result of variations in the profitability of commercial office development which, in turn, is explained by the changing balance between the demands for, and the supply of new floorspace, and compounded by the average four year delay between the start of a scheme and its final letting (Catalano and Barras, 1980). The stock of office floorspace has increased considerably in Southampton since the mid-1960s, although its main office development boom occurred in the first half of the 1970s. Demand for new office floorspace in central Southampton has come primarily from the financial and public sectors, which together occupied almost two-thirds of floorspace constructed between 1965 and 1980. Furthermore, much of the demand has been local in the sense that new floorspace has mainly been occupied by offices relocating from other premises in the city, either because of expansion, reorganisation or the upgrading of their accommodation, or through the opening of additional branch offices by organisations already operating in the city. Only a small number of offices actually moved <u>into</u> Southampton.

Barras (1979b) suggests that a new office development boom in Britain is just beginning. Certainly, there are signs that a further phase of office development is likely in Southampton during the early 1980s. The stock of vacant office accommodation, which existed throughout the second half of the 1970s, has now been considerably eroded as recently constructed floorspace has been let, falling from $50,000m^2$ in 1976 (approximately one-eighth of the city's entire stock of office floorspace) to less than $16,000m^2$ in early 1981 (under 5 per cent of the total office stock). Furthermore, there are no new schemes under construction (4). Office rents are not yet high enough to justify new speculative development (Vail, 1980), although the expectation of future shortages of office accommodation in the city has led to a belief amongst local estate agents that there will soon be a sharp upturn in rents, thereby providing developers with an economic incentive to initiate new schemes (Southern Evening Echo, 24.4.81).

Unlike the last main phase of office development, which was characterised by severe over-supply, office development in the 1980s is likely to see supply and demand much more closely aligned. One reason for this is that office developers seem likely to be much more cautious, having learnt some painful lessons from the property collapse which followed the last boom in 1974. In addition, the financial institutions have become much more influential in development and take a much more cautious attitude than the entrepreneurially-run property companies, which dominated development in the 1960s and early 1970s. Another factor is that planning authorities now operate restrictive policies towards new office development. Current office policy in the City of Southampton allows office development only if certain criteria are met. The specified conditions are that the development should be for occupation by concerns who are providing a service primarily to the local community, or that it is essential to their efficient operation that they should be accommodated in Southampton rather than elsewhere, or that the development will contribute to the solution of local employment problems, or that an office element is an essential component of a comprehensive scheme. In addition, the development should be satisfactory in transportation terms, should result in a more appropriate use of land and achieve a positive improvement in the quality of the local environment (Southampton City Council, 1981). The

South Hampshire Structure Plan also proposes to control strictly office development in the city centre in order to avoid serious traffic congestion and to channel new developments to growth sectors outside the city. However, despite these planning restrictions on new office development in central Southampton, schemes containing over 9500m^2 of office floorspace already have planning permission but have not yet been started, and the plan to redevelop part of the city centre (the Western Esplanade Development) proposes the creation of 23,000m^2 of new office floorspace.

But will there be sufficient demand in the 1980s for new office floorspace in Southampton? A recent study of future office developments has forecast that office floorspace in England and Wales will increase during the 1980s as a result of the expected increase in the service sector over the next ten years (Coopers and Lybrand, 1980). Hampshire County Council has also forecast that private sector service employment will increase during the 1980s, both nationally and in Hampshire, although it expects only a modest increase in public sector service employment (Hampshire County Council, 1979b). If confirmed, this should lead to a demand for additional office space. However, during the 1960s and 1970s the public sector was a substantial source of demand for new office floorspace, especially for larger units. This is unlikely to be repeated during the 1980s, principally because of public-expenditure cuts which will prevent an increase in public sector employment, but also because of the absence of 'one-off' events, such as local government reorganisation, to stimulate the demand for additional floorspace. Rather, demand for new office floorspace in Southampton will continue to come mainly from professional firms and from branch offices of large organisations requiring small and medium-sized offices. But, as past experience has shown, office development has a displacement effect resulting from firms moving into new offices from older premises. Often, the vacated premises have been built to less exacting standards and may not be appropriate in architecture, structure or layout for modern office operations; for these reasons they may prove difficult to relet. This has led some observers to suggest that the 1980s will see a considerable emphasis on the refurbishment and upgrading of older office premises in an attempt by owners to protect the value of their investments.

Further office decentralisation from London during the 1980s seems likely and this in its turn should create demand for office floorspace in other parts of the South East; but it seems unlikely that Southampton will benefit to any greater extent than in the 1960s and 1970s. Many rent reviews are due to take place during the early 1980s, in some cases affecting tenants whose rents were fixed seven, fourteen, or even more than twenty years ago and who will be forced to accept very sharp increases in rent. This seems likely to promote a surge of office relocation (Financial Times, 1978). In addition, the recently elected, Labour-controlled Greater London Council is proposing a very restrictive office development policy, which will only permit schemes which stimulate additional manufacturing jobs or provide other benefits to the community. The results of such a policy are likely to be similar to those which followed the introduction of Office Development Permits in the mid-1960s, notably an increase in office rents in London and a diversion of development activity to centres elsewhere in the South East (Financial Times, 1981c). However, because of their

proximity to London, centres such as Reading, Newbury, Basingstoke and
Milton Keynes, seem more likely than Southampton to benefit from such
trends in office location and development activity.

The effect of micro-electronics technology on office activity will
also influence demands for office floorspace in the 1980s. Although
there is considerable debate on possible consequences, it seems likely
that the main impact, at least in the short term, of electronic word-
processing machines and data-processing computers will be to reduce the
need for secretarial and clerical staff, so prompting a demand for
smaller office premises. However, micro-electronics are also creating
new types of occupations within existing office organisations and new
office industries, as for example computer bureaux, data-processing
agencies and office-equipment sales and sales support. Micro-
electronics might also be expected to help accelerate the trend of
increasing amounts of floorspace per employee because they are likely to
increase the proportion of administrative and professional staff in
offices, that is of grades with higher space standards. The implication
is, therefore, that the construction of new office floorspace will
create fewer jobs than in the past. The widespread adoption of micro-
electronics in the office will also prompt a reassessment of space
requirements which may, in turn, result in relocation from older office
premises ill-suited to the use of the new technology.

There are grounds for believing that, at least in the short term,
Southampton's office sector will not be particularly affected by the
new technology. Certainly, secretarial and clerical jobs, which are
most 'at risk' to displacement, comprise by far the largest category of
office staff in Southampton and provide a very high proportion of female
employment opportunities. However, it has been suggested that
displacement will be greatest in offices where there are large typing
pools. Smaller offices, which are typical of Southampton's office
sector, will be less affected, because the volume and type of work are
not appropriate to justify the introduction of machines (Green, Coombs
and Holroyd, 1980). Indeed, only two of the surveyed offices (both
insurance offices) indicated that they expected a decline in their
employment over the next two or three years as a result of the
introduction of micro-electronic equipment. Offices which are part of
a larger information network (like the branch of a bank) are also likely
candidates for the application of new electronic equipment, because the
interface between the branch and the main office can easily be converted
into an electronic system (Green et al, 1980). Because many offices in
Southampton, particularly in the banking, insurance and finance
industries, are branches of large organisations, it might be amongst
these firms that the introduction of new technology will be most
widespread and most strongly felt.

Although future development will, in the final analysis, be heavily
influenced by the prevailing economic climate, it does seem likely that
the service industries in general, and office activity in particular,
will remain the principal growth element in the Southampton economy
during the 1980s, thereby increasing their already considerable
significance as a source of employment. However, it is not expected
that they will generate sufficient new jobs to offset the recent and
expected future job losses in manufacturing and to provide employment
for the expanding labour force. Furthermore, those jobs which are

created by new office development will increasingly be for qualified white-collar staff, and will not, therefore, be appropriate for the many school-leavers, married women and former manufacturing employees in the labour market who in general are seeking unskilled, manual or clerical employment.

NOTES

(1) Published by the Department of the Environment (1972 and 1980).
(2) This information is based on local authority estimates of office floorspace in Southampton. The DoE floorspace data, based on Inland Revenue estimates, suggests that the rate of office-floorspace growth has been much greater, increasing by nearly $121,000m^2$, a 76 per cent increase.
(3) A list of post-1964 office schemes in Southampton was obtained from the City Planning Department. Only schemes with $464m^2$ ($5000ft^2$) or more of office space were considered in order to exclude small 'one-off' developments. Current occupiers were identified by field survey.
(4) The recent lack of new office development in Southampton has prompted considerable activity in refurbishing older property for office use (Financial Times, 1981b). Small, self-contained premises on the fringes of the central area have generally been favoured. An added advantage is that outside the central area, planning department car-parking restrictions are less severe.

REFERENCES

ALEXANDER, I (1979), Office Location and Public Policy (London, Longman).

AMBROSE, P and COLENUTT, B (1975), The Property Machine (Harmondsworth, Penguin).

BARRAS, R (1979a), The returns from office development and investment, Centre for Environmental Studies, RS 35.

BARRAS, R (1979b), The development cycle in the City of London, Centre for Environmental Studies RS 36.

CATALANO, A and BARRAS, R (1980), Office development in central Manchester, Centre for Environmental Studies, RS 37.

COOPERS and LYBRAND Ltd (1980), Office Market Survey (London).

DAMESICK, P (1979a), Office location and planning in the Manchester conurbation, Town Planning Review, 50, 346-366.

DAMESICK, P (1979b), Offices and inner-area regeneration, Area, 11, 41-47.

DANIELS, P (1969), Office decentralisation from London - policy and practice, Regional Studies, 3, 171-178.

DANIELS, P (1975), Office Location: An Urban and Regional Study (London, Bell).

DANIELS, P (1977), Office location in the British conurbations: trends and strategies, Urban Studies, 14, 261-274.

DANIELS, P (1980), Office Location and the Journey to Work (Farnborough, Gower).

DEBENHAM, TEWSON and CHINNOCKS (1981), Office Rents and Rates 1973-1981 (London).

DEPARTMENT OF THE ENVIRONMENT (1972), Statistics for Town and Country Planning, Series II: Floorspace - 2 (London, HMSO).

DEPARTMENT OF THE ENVIRONMENT (1980), Commercial and Industrial Floorspace Statistics, England and Wales - 8 (London, HMSO).

FERNIE, J (1977), Office linkages and location, Town Planning Review, 48, 78-89.

FINANCIAL TIMES (1978), Office Relocation, 20th October.

FINANCIAL TIMES (1981a), Office Property, 20th March.

FINANCIAL TIMES (1981b), Property Refurbishment, 18th May.

FINANCIAL TIMES (1981c), The GLC stuns the property market, 17th July.

FOTHERGILL, S and GUDGIN, G (1979), Regional employment change: a sub-regional explanation, Progress in Planning, 12, part 3.

GODDARD, J (1967), Changing office location patterns within central London, Urban Studies, 4, 276-284.

GODDARD, J (1970), Functional regions within the city centre: a study by factor analysis of taxi flows in central London, Transactions, Institute of British Geographers, 49, 161-182.

GODDARD, J (1973), Office linkage and location: a study of communications and spatial patterns in central London, Progress in Planning, 1, part 2.

GODDARD, J (1975), Office Location in Urban and Regional Development (London, Oxford UP).

GODDARD, J (1979), Office development and urban and regional development in Britain, in DANIELS, P (ed.), Spatial Patterns of Office Growth and Location (Chichester, Wiley), 29-60.

GODDARD, J and MORRIS, D (1976), The communications factor in office decentralisation, Progress in Planning, 6, part 1.

GREEN, K, COOMBS, R and HOLROYD, K (1980), The Effects of Micro-Electronic Technologies of Employment Prospects: a Case Study of Tameside (Farnborough, Gower).

GUDGIN, G, CRUM, R and BAILEY, S (1979), White-collar employment in UK manufacturing industry, in DANIELS, P (ed.), Spatial Patterns of Office Growth and Location (Chichester, Wiley), 127-158.

HALL, R (1972), The movement of offices from central London, Regional Studies, 6, 385-392.

HAMMOND, E (1967), Dispersal of government offices: a survey, Urban Studies, 4, 258-275.

HAMPSHIRE COUNTY COUNCIL (1979a), Hampshire Facts and Figures (Winchester, Planning Department).

HAMPSHIRE COUNTY COUNCIL (1979b), Hampshire Strategic Monitoring Report 1979 (Winchester, Planning Department).

HARDMAN, H (1973), The Dispersal of Government Work from London (London, HMSO), cmmd 5322.

KEEBLE, D (1971), Employment mobility in Britain, in CHISHOLM, M and MANNERS, G (eds), Spatial Policy Problems of the British Economy (London, Cambridge UP), 24-68.

LOCATION OF OFFICES BUREAU (1977), Annual Report 1976-77 (London, LOB).

MALLIER, T and ROSSER, M (1979), The changing role of women in the British economy, National Westminster Bank Quarterly Review, November, 54-65.

MANLEY, P and SAWBRIDGE, D (1980), Women at work, Lloyds Bank Review, 135, 29-40.

RHODES, J and KAN, A (1971), Office Dispersal and Regional Policy (London, Cambridge UP).

RILEY, R C and SMITH, J-L (1981), Industrialisation and naval ports: the Portsmouth case, in HOYLE, B S and PINDER, D A (eds), Cityport Industrialisation and Regional Development: Spatial Analysis and Planning Strategies (Oxford, Pergamon).

SOUTHAMPTON CITY COUNCIL (1981), Office Policy and Employment (Southampton, Planning Department).

TIMES (1979), The Times 1000, 1979-80 (London, Times Books).

VAIL, L S and Son (1980), An Annual Report on the Property Market in Hampshire (Fareham).

5 Structural and Spatial Changes in Retailing

M S HUSAIN

The last twenty years have been a period of rapid transition in retail
distribution. Far-reaching changes, involving not only the physical
characteristics of shopping areas but also the organisation of retailing
and consumer behaviour, have brought about a substantial modification of
traditional patterns. The corner shop at the end of the terrace has
been succeeded by the shopping precinct. The family business has been
replaced by the multiple firm. The daily walk to the shops is giving
way to the monthly expedition by car, and the simplicity of sticky price
labels has been overtaken by the high technology of bar-codes, light-
pens and computers. The changes that have taken place result from a
complex interaction of socio-economic processes, technological
developments and political trends which have been manifest at national
and, to a certain extent, international levels. Nevertheless, to
understand fully the developments in any specific area, it is essential
to recognise that local circumstances exert a significant effect on
resultant patterns. This essay examines those processes, discernible
across the country, which have provided the 'underlying current' for
change in retail structures, and relates them to developments in the
Southampton area. Attention is focused in particular on the city
centre, but this cannot be examined independently and consideration is
necessarily also given to developments in suburban areas. After a
brief summary of the situation at the beginning of the period under study,
changes affecting retail structures are examined under the three broad
headings of consumer behaviour and attitudes, decisions by retailers and
retail organisations, and development and planning policies.

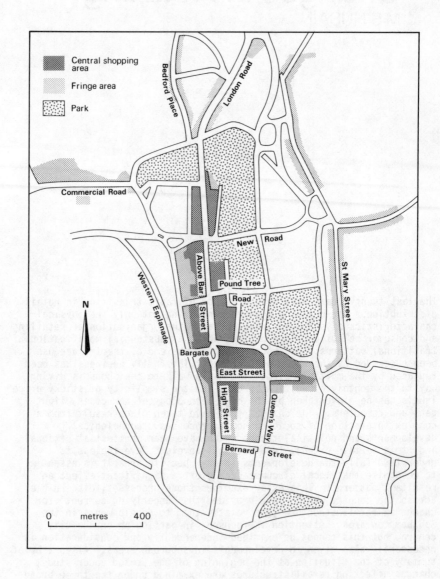

Figure 5.1 Southampton's central shopping area, circa 1960.

THE RETAIL STRUCTURE IN SOUTHAMPTON IN 1960

After a period of post-war reconstruction Southampton had by 1960 gradually been re-established as a regional shopping centre. Although rebuilding was incomplete, priority had been given to the devastated central area and the opportunity was used to create a new shopping district with a modern design. Despite these radical changes, the morphology of the shopping area remained largely unchanged. Parkland to the east and lack of available land to the west of Above Bar precluded the broadening of the retail spine and resulted in the perpetuation of the unusual linearity of the main shopping area which stretched 800 metres from north to south (Fig.5.1). Of the streets adjoining the main axis, only East Street, at the southern end, had a significant number of retail outlets, but its status was much lower with mean rateable values per metre of frontage only one-sixth that in Above Bar (Robinson, 1964). Other secondary shopping streets, Bedford Place, London Road and St Mary Street, were separated from Above Bar by parkland and there was therefore no gradual transition from central area to fringe. This also meant that space for expansion in the central area was strictly limited.

The design of the shopping centre reflected post-war constraints as well as contemporary architectural thought. Although each shopping block was designed as a unified structural unit, construction was limited to two storeys partly because of a shortage of building materials (Berger, 1964). Individual shops, notably those of multiples, were designed to accommodate the anticipated future expansion of trade. Marks and Spencer, C and A and British Home Stores all incorporated at least 2000m^2 of sales floorspace, while the Edwin Jones department store claimed to be the largest in the south of England when it re-opened in 1959. The Boots branch was described as "one of the most outstanding modern shops in Britain" (Southern Evening Echo, 1955). In general, though, the need to accommodate many of the firms previously displaced without any substantial spatial expansion resulted in most shops having a sales area of less than 200m^2.

With attention focused on the central area, post-war development in suburban neighbourhoods had been less spectacular. Local needs continued to be served by established district centres at Bitterne, Portswood, Shirley and Woolston, supplemented by the many shops on corner sites or in small parades outside the recognised foci. Despite the recognised need for additional service centres, priority had been given to the reconstruction and improvement of existing shopping areas and there had been no major new developments in the early post-war period.

CONSUMER BEHAVIOUR AND ATTITUDES

The behaviour and attitudes of individuals when shopping may be seen as a function of their social and economic environment. Within this broad compass four trends may be identified as having been particularly relevant over the period since 1960. First, and perhaps most important, has been the increase in car-ownership rates. Although this is a process that has been continuing steadily throughout the post-war years, registration of vehicles accelerated to unprecedented levels during the 1960s. Whereas in 1961 only 31 per cent of households in Britain had regular access to a car, this had risen to 52 per cent by 1971 and 58 per cent by 1979. Secondly, there has been a pronounced residential dispersal of the population away from major urban centres towards sub-urban and rural locations, effectively increasing travel times to central districts and transferring demand for services away from inner areas. Thirdly, there has been a significant increase in female activity rates. Although only accounting for 32 per cent of the labour force in 1961, women accounted for 37 per cent by 1971 and 39 per cent by 1979. This rise has been almost wholly due to the increased number of married women in the labour force. The consequence is that opportunities for other activities, including shopping, have become more restricted. Finally, there has been a steady rise in real personal disposable incomes, amounting to 67 per cent from 1960 to 1979. Whilst this was not matched by a commensurate increase in real consumer expenditure, the volume of retail sales rose nationally by approximately 45 per cent over the same period.

With slight variations, these trends are discernible in data covering the Southampton area. As far as car ownership is concerned, the process has continued further than in the country as a whole. By 1978 only 32 per cent of households were without the regular use of a car. The outward redistribution of population has been evident in the relatively rapid increases in outer-city ward totals and more recently in adjoining local authority districts, while inner-area populations have declined absolutely. The proportion of women in the labour force in Southampton has also risen steadily, although it has remained below the national figure and reached only 37 per cent in 1977. Finally, total personal income in the Outer South East region has risen faster than elsewhere to account for 19 per cent of the United Kingdom total in 1979 compared with only 14 per cent in 1960.

The interaction of these circumstantial changes has had noticeable repercussions on consumer behaviour and attitudes. The increase in car ownership has not surprisingly been accompanied by more extensive use of private vehicles for shopping trips. Estimates of the proportion of car-borne shoppers vary greatly, partly reflecting the composition of the shopper group or the function of their trip. A survey in 1969 of over 10,000 shoppers in city and district centres in South Hampshire revealed that 34 per cent had travelled by car, while a further 29 per cent came by bus and 33 per cent on foot (Hall, 1969). Other studies, however, have distinguished between main convenience-goods shopping and comparison-goods shopping at major centres for which cars are used relatively frequently, and minor grocery shopping for which many journeys are still made on foot (Daws and Bruce, 1971; Bradley and Fenwick, 1975). Indirect evidence for this distinction may also be found in the South Hampshire survey. Of the 2028 respondents in Southampton city centre, 38 per cent had arrived by car and only 15 per cent on foot, but in the district centres of Shirley, Portswood, Bitterne and Woolston over 41 per cent of trips were on foot; only in Bitterne did the car-borne contingent exceed 30 per cent.

The mobility provided by the car has improved access to shopping areas previously difficult to reach, thereby reducing reliance on local centres and central-area shops to which public transport is usually aligned. The consumer has used this flexibility to shop at locations where his requirements are best satisfied. An initial consideration has

104

inevitably become the availability of convenient parking space. This has become important not just for providing access to the shopping area but, as consumers are tending to make fewer and larger shopping excursions, to facilitate the transport home of increasingly bulky purchases. This tendency is of course partly a function of the additional carrying capacity that a car brings, but is also linked to the restricted time available to many people for shopping, their desire to minimise travel costs and the availability of more money to spend at any particular moment. Perhaps equally significant for food purchases has been the improvement in food-storage facilities brought about by wider ownership of refrigerators and freezers. The desire to minimise the number of shopping trips has led to the search for locations offering a comprehensive range of shopping facilities and a demand for 'one-stop' shopping.

Shop opening hours have also come to play a role in destination selection. For households in which the car is used daily for commuting or where both husband and wife are in employment, shopping trips have to be made outside normal working hours. The preference for Saturday or, in particular, weekday evening shopping has clearly brought custom to outlets offering extended opening hours. Moreover, from being an almost wholly female occupation, shopping has necessarily become much more a family activity. Behavioural patterns have also been influenced by the quality of shopping at alternative locations. The increased choice afforded by the motor car has made the consumer more aware of differences in the price or range of goods, quality of service and shopping environment, and has led to much greater discrimination on these grounds.

Spatial and temporal adjustments in shopping patterns have been accompanied by shifts in the pattern of consumer expenditure. As real incomes have risen, so too has the proportion of expenditure used to purchase non-essential items, a development which has had two main consequences. First, the demand for food has expanded relatively slowly; from 1960 to 1978 the volume of food sales in Britain increased by less than 10 per cent, while sales of clothing and durable goods rose by 53 and 113 per cent respectively. In the South East region, including the Southampton area, the proportion of household expenditure spent on food fell from 27 to 23 per cent from 1963 to 1977. Secondly, relatively less money is being spent on personal acquisitions. In 1960 64 per cent of consumer expenditure was for retail purchases, but by 1978 this had fallen to only 59 per cent. Simultaneously, demand had developed for non-retail services such as travel agents, insurance brokers and building societies (Fernie and Carrick, 1981).

DECISIONS BY RETAILERS AND RETAIL ORGANISATION

The changes in consumer behaviour have had a varied impact on retail traders. Certainly retail turnover has increased in real terms, but it has not kept pace with real incomes, and certain sectors, notably food, have experienced negligible growth. This limited expansion has served to heighten competition within the market as traders have sought ways to enlarge their market share and lift profits. Their response has had marked consequences on the organisation and location of retail activities. Discount pricing has been the main weapon in this contest, especially following the abolition in 1964 of resale price maintenance, which until then had covered one-third of consumer expenditure (Pickering, 1964). With this emphasis on prices has come a sharpened awareness of the need to reduce costs and this has been achieved in several ways. The introduction of self-service techniques enabled more efficient use to be made of retail floorspace and employed labour, an important consideration following the introduction of Selective Employment Tax in 1966 (Atkinson, Tulloch and Robinson, 1974). Economies of scale have been sought by operating larger outlets and placing larger orders. Centralised warehousing and computerised stock control have been used to reduce the need for local distribution centres or in-store storage space. But as well as price reduction, other techniques have been exploited to capture custom. Product diversification has been seen as a means of increasing turnover, especially once growth potential in an initial product range became limited. Obvious exemplifications of this trend in Southampton may be seen in the introduction of non-food items in J Sainsbury, non-clothing items in Marks and Spencer, variety goods in Boots and a travel agency in W H Smith. The process is continuing less conspicuously at a variety of levels. In addition, extended opening hours, the provision of parking space and improved customer service all represent attempts to capitalise on recent trends in consumer behaviour.

The same considerations account for retailer interest in the establishment of large new retail outlets in decentralised locations often outside or on the fringe of existing shopping centres. Given good road connections, the higher levels of car ownership and suburbanisation of the population, such sites may now be more easily reached than congested central-city areas. For the retailer they offer the advantages of low development and operational costs and space for larger stores and parking, with resultant scale economies and lower prices. Several types of retailer have utilised 'out-of-centre' premises. These include 'discount warehouses' selling specialised branded products (such as electrical goods), which are dependent on widely advertised low prices to attract custom, as well as retailers whose prime requirement is spacious accommodation for the display of bulky goods (notably furniture, carpets and D-I-Y equipment). Both these groups have been able to accept a wide range of sites. In Southampton, premises on the fringe of the main shopping area have been occupied in Commercial Road (Ukay Furnishing), St Mary's Road (MFI) and Back-of-the-Walls (Supreme Discount). Outside the city centre, units on trading estates have been taken over at Millbrook (B&Q) and Chickenhall Lane, Eastleigh (Comet). Vacated industrial buildings have been adopted, for example at Eastleigh (Peter Green), although this is less common than in more industrialised cities. A third group of users are the large, single-level, self-service superstores, normally with over 2500m^2 of sales area (often termed hypermarkets when over 5000m^2). Such outlets are usually to be found on 'green-field' sites or in district centres, but a wide range of other locations have been developed. To be successful they must generate a high volume of sales, and this in turn depends on drawing custom from a large population. One estimate suggests a catchment of 50,000 people within ten minutes drive may be necessary (Wade, 1976). Competitive pricing is also essential and high sales volumes enable goods to be ordered at a discount direct from manufacturers. A wide product range, extended opening hours and convenient parking all enhance the attraction of such stores.

These large retail units appeared relatively late in Britain compared to neighbouring continental countries but, since the first opened in 1965, they have proliferated rapidly and by 1977 210 were open or under construction (Jones, 1978). One of the earliest freestanding hypermarkets was the Carrefour store at Eastleigh, the first venture in this country by this French firm, and its characteristics typify this type of development. Constructed on a 5 ha site to the north of Southampton and with $11,400m^2$ of floorspace (subsequently extended), turnover in the first year of operation (1974-75) was approximately £10 million (Department of the Environment, 1976). Convenience-goods sales have subsequently contributed 70-80 per cent of turnover, although the majority of floorspace was allocated to durable and other non-food products. The growing significance of superstores in the retail scene has attracted the involvement of the store chains more traditionally associated with outlets in shopping centres, particularly food supermarkets. In 1977 J Sainsbury opened one of their largest stores covering $5000m^2$ at Lordshill, and this was followed in 1981 by the Tesco store at Bursledon with $6000m^2$ of floorspace. Both these groups have closed their central-area food supermarkets in Southampton, an indication of the extent to which this radical reorientation has progressed. At the same time, the largest British hypermarket group, Asda, are extending their network southwards and plan a $6000m^2$ store in Totton. In contrast to the Carrefour and Tesco developments, both the J Sainsbury and Asda stores have been planned as part of larger district centres. However, the presence of the superstore, which for example in Lordshill accounts for 60 per cent of the total floorspace, will be the principle attraction to non-local custom. All the superstores are strongly oriented to the car-borne shopper. Each site enjoys good road connections and offers 500-1200 parking spaces. A survey in 1977 revealed that 91 per cent of customers at Carrefour arrived by car (Department of the Environment and Transport, 1978). They also travelled there from a wide area; approximately 20 per cent of visitors lived beyond a twenty-minutes drive. In view of the travel costs involved, it seems likely that the availability of cheap petrol at Carrefour and Lordshill must be a major consideration among potential customers.

Not all retailers have been able to respond successfully to the changes. Indeed the total number of shops in Britain declined from over 500,000 in 1961 to 350,000 in 1978. Small independent retailers in particular have experienced difficulty in adapting to the new situation. Unable to benefit from economies of scale and without resources to expand, small-shop proprietors have been faced with a steady drift of custom to the competitive multiples and many have gone out of business. Prime sites in town centres have come to be dominated by branches of chain stores. Redevelopment schemes that removed as many as 55,000 independent retail shops from clearance areas between 1961 and 1971 added to this loss (Bechhofer, Elliott and Rushforth, 1971). New development has tended to include fewer, larger and more expensive units, often beyond the resources of the small independent shopkeeper. The multiple chains and co-operative stores have also undertaken widespread closures, often as part of rationalisation programmes. For this reason, the proportion of shops classified as independents only declined slightly from 81 to 79 per cent from 1961 to 1978, while multiples increased their relatively small share from 13 to 18 per cent, largely at the expense of co-operatives(1). These figures are, however,

deceptive and conceal the true problems of the independents, for during
the same period, the share of turnover claimed by the multiples climbed
from 31 to 47 per cent. The grocery sector, traditionally characterised
by a large number of small independents, has been most severely
affected. Firms in this sector with fewer than ten branches controlled
89 per cent of outlets in 1978, but could only attract 31 per cent of
turnover. Confronted with these difficulties, many independents have
joined voluntary groups (such as Spar, VG and Mace). These allow the
small retailer to become part of a large buying organisation, thereby
gaining some of the advantages of the multiple, and members of such
groups have performed appreciably better than unaffiliated independents
(Berry, 1977).

At first sight, the limited data covering the Southampton area from
the Census of Distribution appear to contradict these statements. The
total number of retail outlets in the city did decline between 1961 and
1971, albeit only by 4 per cent (Table 5.1). Surprisingly, though, the
number of independent traders apparently increased, while the combined
share of co-operatives and multiples declined from 30 to 23 per cent.
The data is however misleading; whereas in 1961 multiples were defined
as firms with a minimum of five branches, in 1971 the lower limit was
raised to ten. Given this more restrictive definition and the
contraction of the small co-operative sector, one may conclude that the
pattern in Southampton was comparable to the national trend. The
dominant and strengthening position of the multiples was more clearly
demonstrated by the fact that the multiples (together with a very small
co-operative group) fractionally increased their share of turnover to 65
per cent and in 1971 controlled 60 per cent of retail floorspace.

The small net decrease in establishments was actually the outcome of a
large number of openings and closures, frequently involving a change of
shop use. The resultant structural changes reflect the rationalisation
process that has taken place in the food sector vis a vis the relative
expansion in non-food markets. Table 5.1 shows that food shops
(grocers, provision dealers, other food retailers) decreased in number
by 28 per cent from 1961 to 1971, while non-food outlets (clothing,
footwear, other non-food retailers) increased by 27 per cent, with
similar trends evident in turnover. Data on more recent changes and
their location are scarce, but records from the city's Environmental
Health Department show that at least 260 food shops closed during the
period 1971 to 1981(2). The list of closures includes units of varying
size and with a wide distribution. At one extreme are the large
branches of supermarket chains which were in the city centre and have
either been relocated or closed completely. The great majority, however,
were very small shops with less than 100m^2 of gross floorspace,
belonging to independent traders and with few employees. Only 17 per
cent of the closures were in the main centres, being fairly equally
distributed between the city centre, Bitterne, Portswood, Shirley and
Woolston. A further 39 per cent were located in local convenience
centres, while the largest group, comprising 44 per cent of closures,
were individual shops in relatively isolated situations and included a
high proportion on corner sites (Fig.5.2). These latter two groups were
dispersed throughout the built-up area, excepting the northern suburbs
of Lordshill and Bassett, with the greatest concentration in the
southward extensions of Shirley district centre in Shirley Road and
Freemantle. The diverse character of closed outlets is matched by the

108

Table 5.1

Changes in the number and turnover of retail establishments in Southampton, 1961-71

	Establishments				Turnover			
	1961		1971		1961		1971	
	No.	%	No.	%	£,000	%	£,000	%
By retail sector:								
Co-operatives	72	4.0			2,609	5.7		
Multiples	470	26.1	398	23.0	27,259	59.6	58,922	65.1
Independents	1256	69.9	1334	77.0	15,850	34.7	31,622	34.9
TOTAL	1798	100.0	1732	100.0	45,718	100.0	90,544	100.0
By business type:								
Grocers, provision dealers	469	26.1	324	18.7	9,465	20.7	18,226	20.1
Other food retailers	399	22.2	305	17.6	8,458	18.5	11,973	13.2
Confectioners, tobacconists, newsagents	224	12.5	216	12.5	3,261	7.1	6,809	7.5
Clothing, footwear	233	13.0	278	16.1	7,154	15.6	16,076	17.8
Household goods	255	14.2	321	18.5	4,797	10.5	10,749	11.9
Other non-food	196	10.9	267	15.4	3,620	7.1	8,618	9.5
General	22	1.2	21	1.2	9,322	20.4	18,092	20.0
TOTAL	1798	100.0	1732	100.0	45,717	100.0	90,543	100.0

Notes: 'Multiples' included non-co-operatives with a minimum of five branches in 1961 but ten branches in 1971.

In 1971 the co-operative sector was extremely small and not tabulated separately.

Source: Census of Distribution.

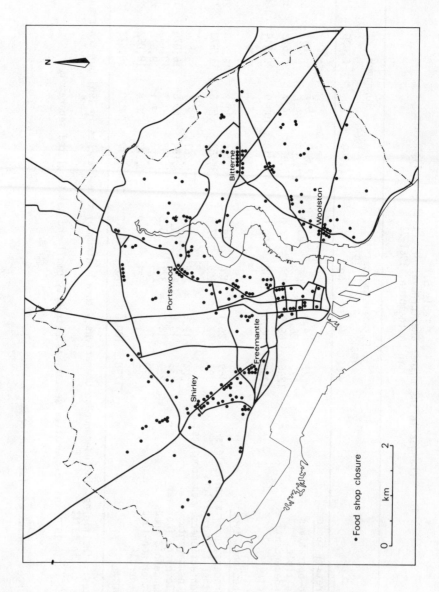

Figure 5.2 Food shop closures in Southampton, 1971–81.

varied reasons for their closure. Relocation from the city centre has already been mentioned, but this was only applicable in a small number of cases. Demolition as a result of road construction or urban redevelopment schemes has also taken its toll, for example in the Dorset Street link and Bevois Estate area improvement projects. Even where this has not led to physical removal of shops, it has contributed to the more general problem of unprofitability by reducing residential densities in retail catchments.

Although closure has meant the complete disappearance of some shops, in many cases there has been a subsequent re-opening as a different kind of business. The changes from food to non-food retailing and from independent to multiple store in the city centre are obvious manifestations of this, but more subtle shifts have accompanied changes in the character of an area. In addition, with increased consumer expenditure being directed to non-retailing activities, these have begun to compete strongly for premises and in some areas have replaced retailing as the dominant business activity. Figure 5.3 shows that these trends have been particularly noticeable on the fringe of the central shopping area. In Bedford Place, formerly an important local centre, the small old properties have attracted a variety of specialised retailers, characterised by the car radio, photographic equipment and stamp dealers, as well as service functions. Prominent among the latter are a cosmopolitan range of catering establishments. Northam Road, in an area which has experienced a degree of degradation, now offers a variety of secondhand, antique and junk shops. In contrast, London Road with its generally better-quality physical environment and larger units has been favoured by estate agents and building societies, the latter having also made incursions in Hanover Buildings and High Street. In the district centres, retailing continues to dominate floorspace use, but a relative decline in convenience goods may also be identified here. Nevertheless, despite the overall decrease in shop numbers and the expansion of non-retailing activities, the data depicted in Figure 5.3 show that the absolute area occupied by convenience goods actually increased by 2 per cent and that of durable goods by 11 per cent. This, however, contrasts sharply with the 55 per cent rise registered for office uses and is indicative of prevailing trends.

DEVELOPMENT AND PLANNING

Whilst the evolving relationship between consumer and retailer may have encouraged modification of shopping habits, retail methods and retail organisation, the initiative for more fundamental changes has often come from other sources. Indeed, during the post-war period the roles of the property development company and local planning authority have been crucial to the reshaping of shopping areas, although ultimate responsibility for regulating change lies squarely with the latter. The attitudes of planners have been influenced by their more general concerns for the protection of the environment and the provision of adequate facilities for the local population. But within this broad framework, there may be recognised three specific principles which have influenced policy. First, there has been a commitment to the concept of the shopping centre, expressed in support for existing centres and the spatial concentration of new facilities. This has protected the existing investment of the community in basic infrastructure and allowed

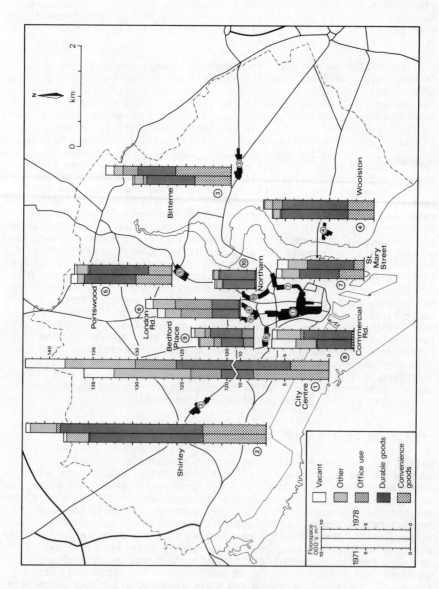

Figure 5.3 Floorspace used in Southampton's main
shopping centres, 1971 and 1978.

economies of scale in new construction in the form of lower infrastructure costs and less land loss. Moreover, for the population dependent on public transport, such centralised facilities have remained the most accessible. Secondly, policies have been directed to the provision of an optimal level of shopping facilities, incorporating a satisfactory range of services but avoiding overcapacity, with its unnecessary land and infrastructural costs and its potentially adverse effects on established centres. Thirdly, it has been accepted that shops should be available close to the population so far as this could be reconciled with the spatial concentration and minimum threshold considerations of individual businesses. This has led to the almost ubiquitous adoption of the concept of a nested hierarchy of centres, presupposing the dominance of the city centre and allowing for successive lower tiers to provide lower-order functions in decentralised locations.

These attitudes have resulted in the enhancement of town and district centre shopping facilities. Local authorities have in many instances produced plans themselves for the extension of shopping areas, the redevelopment of existing sites or the improvement of the shopping environment, while proposals from private developers and retailers have been treated sympathetically. The form of development favoured by both private and public developers has been the multi-unit pedestrian precinct; over 460 were opened from 1953-73 in British town and suburban centres (Economist Intelligence Unit, 1973). Space within such precincts is often only leased from the developer, who therefore remains interested in the continued success of the project. With the precinct, design measures can be taken to encourage this. The range of facilities may be carefully balanced and a pleasant shopping environment provided. A unified public image may be fostered and the precinct conveniently and effectively controlled by a single management. In contrast to this positive approach to development in centres, it has been argued that reaction to proposals for more radical development has been far from enthusiastic (Guy, 1980). Firms seeking to develop out-of-centre facilities, largely for the car-borne shopper, have experienced considerable opposition. Thus, decentralisation of services has proceeded slower in Britain than in neighbouring West European or North American countries.

Statements relating to retail planning in Southampton have until recently been extremely brief and scarce. The 1952 Development Plan, as amended by the Comprehensive Development Area Map, provided a programme for the period to 1971, and it was during these years that basic features of the present retail system were fashioned. As indicated earlier, the plans envisaged reconstruction of the central area and retention of the suburban district centres. Guy (1980) has been sharply critical of the general acceptance by planners that the shopping pattern that existed in 1939 should automatically form the basis for the post-war system; Northern and Haskell (1977) have voiced similar sentiments explicitly about Southampton. Considering the circumstances, however, it is difficult to envisage how radical alternatives could have been introduced at this time. Moreover, these early developments did show an awareness of the various new influences that were already beginning to affect retail structures. The increasing importance of private vehicular traffic was recognised in the provision of basement parking; spaces for 100 cars were provided in the Hanover Buildings-Pound Tree

Road block alone. The problem of traffic congestion was tackled by segregating through traffic, widening main roads and providing rear access for loading to all properties in the central area. Demand for additional floorspace was anticipated with more efficient use of exist-ing areas and removal of non-essential activities; in the street block identified nearly 4000m^2 of sales floorspace was added. Indeed, outside the central area the pre-existing pattern was not unquestioningly accepted. It was recognised that disparities in levels of service between different parts of the city needed to be rectified and new suburban shopping centres were planned, including the recently-completed Lordshill district centre.

The Plan was very much in accordance with the general principles outlined above, and these have also been evident in subsequent actions of the local authority, especially with respect to support for the central area. There has been determined opposition to the introduction in the main axis of office or quasi-retail activities, such as banks, estate agents, building societies and employment agencies, which were seen to create uninteresting 'dead-spots' in the shopping frontage. Under existing legislation, planning permission is required for a change from retailing (Use Class 1) to office activity (Use Class 11) and this has been withheld wherever possible. For two reasons, this has not been wholly effective. First, certain seemingly office activities, such as travel agents, are actually classified as retailing and therefore would not normally require permission. Secondly, refusal of permission on application may well be followed by a successful appeal (Samuels, 1979). Nevertheless, there have been very few incursions into Above Bar of quasi-retail activities, and this accounts for the dense concentration of offices at both ends of the main axis in London Road and High Street. Other measures were taken to improve access for the increasingly-important motorist shopper. In addition to road improvements, off-street car parking was made available by the local authority and permission was granted for the construction of multi-storey parks. By the early 1970s, approximately 5000 off-street spaces had been provided, and a charging structure adopted by the local authority to encourage short-stay shopping visits. As early as 1963, attention was given to improving the shopping environment with pedestrianisation. A tentative start was made in Manchester Street in 1965, with a substantial part of Above Bar being closed to traffic in 1971 and subsequently landscaped.

In contrast to the situation in many urban areas, however, a policy of retail expansion in the central area was not vigorously pursued in the 1960s, although total retail floorspace in the city as a whole did grow steadily (Table 5.2). This may well have been because the additional retail floorspace incorporated in the rebuilding plan had not been saturated, but also because vacant land and sites suitable for redevelopment close to the retail core were extremely scarce. Nevertheless, towards the end of the decade, two projects were instigated which the local authority considered would enhance the status of the central-area facilities. The initiative for the first came from Capital and Counties Property Company, one of the largest property development organisations. Their proposal for a shopping centre at the eastern end of East Street was approved in principle by the Council in 1969, and in 1973 the East Street Centre was opened. It incorporated the typical design features of contemporary shopping developments. The

Table 5.2

Changes in total retail floorspace in Southampton, 1964-79.

Year	Floorspace ('000m^2)	% change
1964	325.2	
1967	324.9	+5.4
1968	345.1	+0.6
1969	349.6	+1.3
1970	351.1	+0.4
1971	349.8	-0.4
1974	359.8 (406.9)	+2.9
1977	379.4 (424.9)	+5.4 (+4.4)
1978	391.2 (435.4)	+3.1 (+2.5)
1979	399.1 (442.5)	+2.0 (+1.6)

Notes: Figures include the floorspace of catering establishments and office-type businesses in shopping areas, but before 1974 exclude shops with accommodation. Subsequent totals including this category are shown in parentheses.

Source: Floorspace statistics.

23 shops with 8000m^2 of floorspace were arranged along two levels in an enclosed precinct. Although there was no magnet store within the centre, it was strategically situated adjacent to Debenhams (formerly Edwin Jones) and incorporated a substantial car park. The second proposal originated with the local authority and concerned development of a much larger site covering 20 ha at the northern end of the main shopping axis, west of Above bar. Considering the future of this Western Esplanade site, the Council decided in 1970 that it should be developed as a major focus for retail activity, although not until 1980 was a more detailed plan approved. The developers, Heron Corporation, with finance from a pension fund, envisage 30,000m^2 of gross retail floorspace in the new centre, together with industrial and social uses. The plan has aroused considerable opposition from citizens, who question the wisdom of approving a single developer for the whole site, one of the largest available in any European city, and criticise the inadequate provision for residential and recreational uses. Nevertheless, it seems likely that construction will go ahead, adding approximately 20 per cent to the total retail floorspace in the city centre.

It is interesting to observe that these two major new developments are located at each end of the main shopping axis, clearly reflecting the spatial constraints on development elsewhere. Moreover, although when the East Street Centre first opened there were more applicants than shops available, this demand for space was not sustained. Two years later, only four shops were let, and in 1980 more than a quarter of the total floorspace remained vacant. This may be because retail demand cannot support the rents demanded. Evidence for this came from the Chamber of Commerce which claimed that retail spending in the city centre had fallen from 15 per cent above the national average in 1974 to 8 per cent below in 1976 (Southern Evening Echo, 1977). It has also been suggested that, despite the general air of malaise in retail markets, there is little evidence of a reduction in rental values (Lear and Cave, 1980). Alternatively, the East Street Centre may be poorly located to attract shoppers. Not only is it on the periphery of the shopping district, but it is furthest from shoppers arriving from the north, and who probably constitute a majority of central-area customers. If this is the case, then the Western Esplanade scheme, which will undoubtedly increase shopper movements in the northern part of the shopping axis, will exacerbate the problems of this development.

In view of the changes that have taken place in retailing, notably with respect to locational considerations, it is perhaps surprising that there has been no formal declaration by the city authorities of policy for shopping development since the 1950s. Only with the appearance of the South Hampshire Structure Plan could official reaction to more recent developments be gauged. Moreover, although the consultation draft was issued in 1972, a significant amendment in relation to shopping was made by the Secretary of State for the Environment before the Plan was finally approved in 1977. A more detailed plan for Southampton is now in preparation.

The Structure Plan provided substantive proposals for the region based on a number of underlying policies. In general, these statements constitute formal articulation of the general principles outlined above. It is argued that to make the best use of public investment, new shopping developments should not undermine the viability of existing centres. The need to provide adequate and suitably-located facilities for the population was recognised, and proposals were based on a three-tier hierarchy of sub-regional, district and local centres. Enhancement and expansion of the existing sub-regional and district centres, together with the creation of new centres associated with additional housing, were seen as appropriate priorities for the future. In contrast, it was anticipated that the proportion of spending attracted to local centres would decline, and that expansion at this level would, therefore, be more modest. Considerable attention was given to the appropriate location and scale of subsequent developments, taking into account anticipated population changes, increases in consumer spending and the potential of individual centres to accommodate growth. On the basis of these assessments, estimates were made of the additional retail floorspace likely to be required at individual centres in the period to 1991.

For Southampton, the Plan foresaw that, as the main suburban centres continued to expand, the city centre would establish a more specialised role. However, with the likely increase in turnover, an additional 7400m^2 of retail floorspace was likely to be needed in addition to outstanding commitments (including the Western Esplanade development). Shirley was considered well-placed to consolidate its status as the main focus at district level in western Southampton, and an increase in floorspace of 8300m^2 was projected. In the east, this role would continue to be fulfilled by Bitterne, but a new local centre at Miller's Pond would also be established. Together these centres would

116

accommodate a further 9300m^2 of floorspace. In contrast, retail demand in Portswood district centre was not expected to grow substantially and no provision for expansion was made. Similarly, it was recommended that in Woolston expansion should only be allowed to cater for growth in local requirements.

The spatial allocation of additional floorspace has been undertaken by the conventional method adopted for retail planning in structure plans. It provides for co-ordinated development based on quantitative assessment of likely need, whilst allowing detailed planning to be undertaken at a local level. The approach has, however, been criticised because of the unreliable nature of such forecasts at a time of rapidly-changing shopping patterns, particularly with respect to increasing demand for decentralised shopping facilities. The planning authority recognised this danger, but believed that the physical opportunities and build-up in trading potential for large car-based stores outside established centres would not materialise before the 1980s. The submitted Plan, therefore, stated categorically that the local authorities would not be prepared to entertain proposals for such stores, and consequently this element of uncertainty in the forecasts was reduced considerably. The situation has, however, been complicated by the intervention of central government. Before the Plan was approved the Secretary of State for the Environment had in fact given consent for the construction of the Carrefour hypermarket and modified the policy statement to convey a much more lenient attitude to similar applications(3). Moreover, the position of the authorities has been further weakened by the results of impact studies, including one of the Carrefour development, which suggested that the effects of hypermarkets on individual local shops and centres could be relatively small (Department of the Environment, 1976, 1978).

The apparent conflict of views between central and local government has been confirmed by subsequent events. In December 1978, Hampshire County Council approved a reappraisal of its shopping policies, particularly in the light of the trend towards car-based shopping (Hampshire County Council, 1978). The document largely affirmed existing policy, with some revision of floorspace estimates, but recognised that there was a need for further provision for car-borne shoppers. It was maintained, however, that this should be provided within existing district centres and that there was no further need for any freestanding superstores or hypermarkets. In January 1979, the Secretary of State granted permission on appeal for another hypermarket in South Hampshire, and this was followed by a similar response to the application from Tesco for a free-standing superstore on the eastern outskirts of Southampton. There has, therefore, been considerable difficulty in implementing this aspect of the preferred policy, and it may be necessary to make further adjustments to floorspace guidelines in the future to take into account the demand satisfied by these out-of-centre developments.

CONCLUSION

Since 1960 there have been important structural and spatial readjustments in the pattern of retailing in the Southampton area. In many ways, these developments have reflected evolving national trends that have impinged on all facets of retail activity. Consumer behaviour has been affected by changed social and economic environments. Retail organisations have been faced with new economic considerations, and retail planners have had to respond to a dynamic situation in which they have been confronted with new questions. In other respects, Southampton has been shown to be unusual, and consideration of local circumstances has been necessary to account for the pattern of development.

The emergent patterns may be seen as partial reconciliation of the new requirements of retailers and consumers within the constraints imposed by local planners. Within this process, the role of the large multiple firms has been crucial. Through their expansionist approach and with the ability to respond to new market conditions, these firms have strengthened their position to the extent that they now exert a powerful influence on the rate and direction of change quite out of proportion to their number of outlets. The small independent trader, faced with a variety of problems, has found it difficult to respond to their challenge and many have struggled to survive. For consumers, these developments have been a mixed blessing. Shopping opportunities have become more restricted by the reduction in the number of outlets, but widened by the additional floorspace provided. The demands of certain groups have been satisfied by the car-based stores, extended shopping hours, opportunities for one-stop shopping and other innovations. But for others, including the less mobile and households with low incomes, the disappearance of local shops has created new problems. The changes have also placed the local planning authority in an equivocal position. It is not their function to restrict change or to protect established business interests; indeed, the inevitability of certain trends has been recognised. Yet their concern has been aroused by the potentially-detrimental effects of the decline in shop numbers, the establishment of out-of-centre stores and over-provision of shops. Their response, therefore, may be seen as an attempt to accommodate change gradually and in an ordered fashion, with the intention of minimising the disadvantageous consequences. Recognition of the decreasing importance of local shopping and attempts to cater for the car-borne shopper within the system of recognised shopping centres are indicative of this particular approach. Frequently, the requirements of retailer, consumer and planner have been reconciled in this way. However, on the one issue where a major conflict has developed, namely with respect to the establishment of freestanding superstores, it has proved extremely difficult to resist development because of the attitude of central government. The effect of this intervention on the longer-term plans for retail development remains to be seen.

NOTES

(1) Except where stated otherwise, multiples are firms with at least ten branches which are not co-operatives.
(2) The Environmental Health Department is obliged under the Food and Drugs Act (1955) to inspect premises selling food. The figure stated represents the number of discontinued records and includes confectioners but not catering establishments. It is a minimum value because the records may be incomplete.
(3) The attitude of the Department of the Environment to large new

stores is reflected in advice to local authorities provided by two
Development Control Policy Notes:
No.13 (1972) Out-of-town Shops and Shopping Centres.
No.13 (1977) Large New Stores.

REFERENCES

ATKINSON, A G, TULLOCH, A M and ROBINSON, O (1974), Manpower and pay
        research in distribution, in THORPE, D (ed.), Research into
        Retailing and Distribution (Farnborough, Saxon House), 97-123.

BECHHOFER, F, ELLIOTT, B and RUSHFORTH, M (1971), The market situation
        of small shopkeepers, Scottish Journal of Political Economy
        18, 2, 161-180.

BERGER, L (1964), Architecture, in MONKHOUSE, F J (ed.), A Survey of
        Southampton and its Region (Southampton, British Association),
        309-312.

BERRY, R K (1977), Small-unit Retailing in Urban Britain - a Review of
        Present Trends and the Policies affecting the Small Shop
        (Lampeter, St David's College).

BRADLEY, M and FENWICK, D (1975), Shopping Habits and Attitudes to Shop
        Hours in Great Britain (London, HMSO).

DAWS, L F and BRUCE, A J (1971), Shopping in Watford (Garston, Building
        Research Station).

DEPARTMENT OF THE ENVIRONMENT (1976), The Eastleigh Carrefour: a
        hypermarket and its effects, Department of the Environment
        Research Report (London, HMSO), 16.

DEPARTMENTS OF THE ENVIRONMENT AND TRANSPORT (1978), The Eastleigh
        Carrefour after three years, Department of the Environment
        Research Report (London, HMSO), 27.

ECONOMIST INTELLIGENCE UNIT (1973), The future of pedestrianised
        shopping precincts, Retail Business, 190, 20-27.

FERNIE, J and CARRICK, R J (1981), Quasi-retail activity in Britain.
        Paper presented to the annual conference of the Institute of
        British Geographers, Leicester.

GUY, C M (1980), Retail Location and Retail Planning in Britain
        (Farnborough, Gower).

HALL, B D (1969), Analysis of the results of a survey of shoppers in
        South Hampshire, South Hampshire Plan Technical Unit Working
        Paper (Winchester, Hampshire County Council), 8.

HAMPSHIRE COUNTY COUNCIL (1978), Shopping policies in South Hampshire,
        Strategic Planning Paper (Winchester, Hampshire County
        Council), 5.

JONES, P M (1978), Trading Features of Hypermarkets and Superstores
(Reading, Unit for Retail Planning Information).

LEAR, J R and CAVE, C (1981), Shops, in VAIL, L S, Annual Report of the
Property Market in Hampshire 1980 (Southampton).

NORTHEN, R I and HASKOLL, M (1977), Shopping Centres: a Developer's
Guide to Planning and Design (Reading, Centre for Advanced
Land Use Studies).

PICKERING, J P (1974), The retail trades without RPM, in THORPE, D
(ed.), Research into Retailing and Distribution (Farnborough,
Saxon House), 23-41.

ROBINSON, G W S (1964), The central district, in MONKHOUSE, F J (ed.),
A Survey of Southampton and its Region (Southampton, British
Association), 240-246.

SAMUELS, A (1979), Building society 'offices' in shopping areas,
Journal of Planning and Environment Law, December, 819-822.

SOUTHERN EVENING ECHO (1955), 27 October.

SOUTHERN EVENING ECHO (1977), 19 July.

WADE, B (1976), Hypermarkets and superstores: their characteristics and
effects, in Unit for Retail Planning Information (ed.),
Hypermarkets and Superstores: Report of a House of Commons
Seminar (Reading, URPI), 1-4.

Acknowledgements   The author is grateful to Mr Peter Yeates of the
Southampton Environmental Health Department, as well as Mrs Claire
Wratten, Mrs Christina Stringer and other staff at the City Planning
Office, for help in the preparation of this paper.

6 Urban Growth and Social Change

S P PINCH

Few beliefs can have been more widely held in recent years than that in
the decline of the British city. Indeed, the recent Preliminary Report
from the 1981 Census seems to confirm the continuing massive decrease
in the populations of the major British cities (OPCS, 1981). Upon
closer inspection, however, the 'decline of the city' is perhaps better
envisaged as a radical transformation of form. Since the Second World
War considerable numbers of people have moved out from the high-
density, continuously built-up inner areas of British cities and into
surrounding smaller low-density settlements and dispersed suburbs
located beyond the green belt. This process has been given numerous
interpretations ranging from a consumption-intensive life-style foisted
upon individuals in the interests of overcoming problems of under-
consumption in capitalist economies (Harvey 1977, 1981) to a spontaneous
reflection of free-market preferences for 'rural' or 'anti urban' life
styles. Those engaged in this out-migration have commonly perceived
this as a 'flight from the city' and in administrative terms this is
the case. Nevertheless, while there are undeniably enormous
differences in the quality of the environment between the older areas
of cities and newer commuter hinterlands, in functional terms the out-
migrants remain within a 'city region' or 'daily urban system'. Thus,
many commute back into city centres to work, while those who work
outside remain essentially 'urban' in occupation and life style.

Research has indicated that the extent and character of this
decentralisation process vary enormously between different areas of
Britain (Department of the Environment, 1976; Drewitt et al, 1976a,
1976b). The purpose of this essay is to examine the social
consequences of this decentralisation process within the rapidly-

growing Southampton city region. Such a task immediately involves the complex task of defining two elements, first the most appropriate spatial units to encompass decentralisation, and second, the relevant criteria by which social change is to be gauged.

The arguments relating to geographical boundaries have been discussed extensively elsewhere and need not be repeated here (London School of Economics, 1974a). Conventional administrative boundaries are, of course, inadequate since they fail to record the impact of urban growth in suburbs beyond the older city boundaries. This essay, therefore, utilises the well-tried Standard Metropolitan Labour Area (SMLA) framework adopted by Hall and colleagues from the North American SMSA concept (Hall et al, 1973) and later extended at the London School of Economics. The SMLAs are functional urban areas made up of high-density urban cores with surrounding commuter hinterlands termed rings (see Department of Environment, 1976 for a discussion of definitions). In the Southampton case, for example, the core is made up of the older County Borough, to which Eastleigh, Romsey and Winchester municipal boroughs and New Forest, Romsey and Stockbridge and Winchester rural districts are added in the rings (Chapter 1).

Any such framework involves a balance of positive and negative aspects depending upon the task in hand. The main disadvantage of the SMLA concept in the present context is that, since the cores are built up from pre-1974 local authority boundaries, they do not closely correspond with the worst inner-city areas characterised by multiple-deprivation and by the largest rates of population loss in recent years. However, this deficiency is outweighed by the many advantages of the SMLA approach. Most important is the extensive range of studies already undertaken using the SMLA framework which permit a comparison of any local area with trends throughout the whole of Great Britain. Furthermore, recent studies (Berthoud, 1976; Holtermann, 1975) have highlighted the enormous difficulties involved in defining 'inner core' areas of multiple-deprivation. Indeed, the decline of the city would now seem to have 'rippled-out' from many inner areas to affect all areas within cores. In this context, the SMLA divide between the core and the ring is increasingly the crucial division between decline and growth and is the most appropriate framework within which to isolate the consequences of the decentralisation process.

The enormous amount of attention devoted to the choice of spatial units has arguably diverted some interest from the more important problem of defining the appropriate criteria to measure social change. Those wishing to undertake a comprehensive statistical analysis are, of course, heavily constrained by the availability of data. Furthermore, the economic, social and geographical processes at work within regional systems are highly inter-related in complex causal sequences. This gives a unity and underlying logic to the study of regions, but in Haggett's (1965) words makes "cutting into the system" extremely difficult. Nevertheless, there can be little doubt that the driving 'motor' of social change is the basic industrial and commercial change described previously in Chapters 3 and 4. These changes have an impact upon the occupational structure, which in turn affects the cluster of attributes related to income, housing, educational attainment, attitudes and life styles embodied within the notion of social class.

These occupational changes have been promoted by two inter-related, but conceptually-distinct processes. The first process is techno-logical innovation leading to changes in the skills required within particular industries. This process is sometimes termed an 'occupation effect'. Thus within industries there has been a considerable growth of non-manual occupations of a managerial, technical and clerical character and a decline in manual work both of a skilled and unskilled character (Gudgin, Crum and Bailey, 1979). This process has been in operation in Britain throughout most of the twentieth century (Routh, 1965), but much more recent in origin is a second process, namely changes in the relative sizes of industries. This is sometimes termed an 'industry effect' and involves the growth of the post-industrial society with the relative decline of manufacturing employment and the growth of the service sector. Between 1931 and 1961 the service sector remained remarkably stable as a proportion of the British economy, but in the 1960s it began to expand rapidly (Department of Employment, 1975). This expansion of services has led to a considerable growth in professional, managerial and other intermediate forms of non-manual employment which, with the exception of the increase in unskilled forms of manual service employment, has served to reinforce the occupational effects within industries. The net outcome of these 'occupation' and 'industry' effects has been an increase in the volume of upward social mobility.

These processes of occupational change and upward social mobility have been at the heart of the decentralisation process in city regions. The resulting increased standards of living, combined with growing preferences for low-density suburban environments and rigid planning restrictions on the development of green belts surrounding older city boundaries, have led to a greater separation of home and workplace. Consequently, new forms of employment have been attracted into the commuter belts, following the outward movement of population. Hence the changing character of employment has affected the location of the workforce, but the changing location of employees has in turn affected the location of employment. Much of this new employment growth has been of a skilled and technological character, while many of the traditional heavy industries have been in decline in city cores. This has led to the 'selective labour hypothesis', the idea that it is mostly the affluent groups who have moved out into the rings, thereby leaving a growing proportion of the unskilled and unemployed in city centres.

A second major dimension of social change in British cities since the Second World War has been in the realm of ethnic status. During the 1950s there was in Britain, as in other European nations, a considerable demand for labour which was filled by immigrants. In the case of Britain these immigrants were predominantly from the West Indies and the Indian sub-continent. Research has suggested a 'replacement hypothesis' whereby these immigrants have occupied low-paid, semi- and unskilled manual occupations vacated by the British-born population as it moved upwards in social class and outwards from inner-city areas. These patterns vary between different cities and between different ethnic groups, but in general terms these immigrants and their offspring have not subsequently decentralised at the same rate as the British-born population. Rather, they have tended to concentrate (although not necessarily segregate) in the core areas of

123

British cities.

A third major form of social change in British cities lies in the realm of demographic profiles. As an older industrialised nation, Britain's age structure is becoming increasingly top-heavy with the elderly population growing at a faster rate than younger age groups. These changes are again related to basic economic factors which have led to declining birth and death rates. Improved methods of contraception, preferences for smaller families and (until recently at least) increased employment opportunities for women have combined to produce fewer births and smaller numbers in the younger age groups. At the same time, increased living standards and developments in medical technology have eliminated many of the communicable and infectious diseases from early and middle adulthood, with the result that increasing numbers are surviving to retirement age.

These demographic changes are again linked with the decentralisation process. Within small sub-regions it is net migration rather than natural change which is the most important component of overall population change, whilst mobility is closely related to age. It is the 15-29 years age group who are frequently the most mobile and often attracted into cities. Those in the child-rearing age groups are, in contrast, typically attracted by the familial life styles prevalent in suburban commuter belts. Retirement often leads to a move to new surroundings, but many elderly persons lack the income to move out of inner-city areas and are 'trapped' like many other low-income groups.

This essay examines the relationships between these three major dimensions of social change - social class, ethnic status and age - and the decentralisation process within the Southampton SMLA. Emphasis is placed upon the rate of change in Southampton compared with the nation as a whole, and the effects of decentralisation upon the social composition of the core and ring. The bulk of the detailed statistical analysis relates to the period between 1961 and 1971 (the period for which most information is available), but inferences are later made concerning more recent developments.

SOUTHAMPTON IN CONTEXT

As stressed elsewhere in this volume, the dominating feature of the Southampton SMLA since the Second World War has been its considerable growth. Between 1951 and 1961 the SMLA ranked tenth in terms of its population growth, with an increase of over 45,000, whilst during the 1961-71 period it rose to fifth position amongst SMLAs, with an increase of almost 60,000. It is not yet possible to derive population figures for the SMLA directly from the 1981 Census, but the Southampton, Eastleigh, Winchester, Test Valley and New Forest local authority areas (collectively somewhat more extensive than the SMLA) recorded a net increase of some 30,000 between 1971 and 1981. Although less than in previous years and smaller than that originally envisaged in the South Hampshire Structure Plan, this is still a considerable rate of growth. A similar pattern has been revealed by employment statistics. Between 1951 and 1961 the Southampton SMLA ranked seventh in terms of employment growth, with an increase of over 23,000 jobs, but during the period between 1961 and 1971 the Southampton SMLA rose to second position, with an employment increase of over 30,000 jobs.

This growth has occurred in both the core and ring of the Southampton SMLA, but has been larger both in relative and absolute terms in the ring. This means that Southampton belongs to a small group of SMLAs, predominantly in the South of England (including the cities of Exeter, Oxford, Reading, Bath and Bournemouth), which experienced relative decentralisation throughout the period between 1951 and 1971 (London School of Economics, 1974b). There was a net loss of population from the core through out-migration during this period, but this was exceeded by a high rate of natural increase resulting in a net gain of population. In the Southampton ring there was also a relatively high rate of natural increase in population, but this was exceeded by net in-migration; inevitably there was much more rapid growth here than in the core.

DECENTRALISATION AND SOCIAL CLASS

The analysis of changes in class structure is derived from an amalgamation of the 17 socio-economic groups recognised by the Registrar General into four broad divisions. These are termed 'professional and managerial', 'intermediate non-manual', 'skilled manual' and 'semi- and unskilled manual'. The advantages and limit-ations of these divisions have been discussed previously (London School of Economics, 1976a; Pinch and Williams, 1981). In brief, although such broad divisions inevitably obscure similarities between non-manual clerical workers and skilled manual workers, they avoid lumping together both of these intermediate groups into a 'new middle class'. Evidence suggests that there are still substantial differences in material rewards, status and life styles between manual and non-manual workers but the categorisation used here avoids using the manual or non-manual categories in blanket terms.

A potentially more serious problem is the fact that these data are based upon the numbers of economically-active males, thereby ignoring two factors. The first of these is the differing national rates of unemployment in 1961 and 1971 which are likely to have affected the four groups to different degrees and which will obscure rates of change. On the assumption that the unskilled manual jobs will decline most rapidly during an economic downturn, this is likely to exaggerate the decline in manual occupations, although the precise impact of this cannot be known. A second factor to be ignored is the considerable increase in female participation in the workforce in recent years. At the national level between 1961 and 1971 female participation in the workforce increased by 14.3 per cent, while during the same period male employment declined by 6.3 per cent. In the Southampton SMLA the increase in female employment has also been considerable (Table 6.1). While just over 50 per cent of the total increase in employment in the Southampton SMLA consisted of females in the 1950s, this figure rose to almost two-thirds in the 1960s. In the 1950s males were increasing at a faster rate in the core than in the ring, but this pattern was reversed in the 1960s. In the case of females, however, there was a similar high rate of increase in both the core and ring in the 1950s, but a larger percentage increase in the ring in the 1960s. In both time periods and in both zones the percentage increase in female

125

Table 6.1

Employment change in the core and ring of the Southampton SMLA, 1951-71.

| | 1951-61 | | 1961-71 | |
	Absolute change	% change	Absolute change	% change
TOTAL EMPLOYMENT				
Urban core	14,930	17.6	12,590	12.6
Metropolitan ring	8,527	12.3	19,430	25.0
SMLA	23,457	15.2	32,020	18.0
MALE EMPLOYMENT				
Urban core	7,644	12.2	3,260	4.6
Metropolitan ring	3,266	6.1	8,890	15.7
SMLA	10,910	9.4	12,150	9.6
FEMALE EMPLOYMENT				
Urban core	7,286	33.6	9,330	31.5
Metropolitan ring	5,261	33.5	10,540	50.3
SMLA	12,547	33.0	19,870	39.3

participation in the workforce was far in excess of that for males. Much of this employment has been in the service sector (Chapter 4) and the data presented here will, therefore, under-represent the expansion of intermediate non-manual forms of employment in the 1960s. Nevertheless, a reasonable assumption is that the occupation of males is the best indicator of the income and status of a household, although given the growth of dual-career and one-parent families this assumption may need to be questioned in the future.

Some of the enormous recent changes in the British occupational structure are shown in Table 6.2. Overall there has been an upward shift in the class structure, with the greatest changes at the extremes of the occupational hierarchy. Between 1961 and 1971 the largest absolute and percentage increases were in the high-status managerial and professional groups, while the largest absolute and percentage decreases occurred in the low-status semi- and unskilled manual occupations. Smaller absolute and percentage increases were recorded in the intermediate non-manual occupations and smaller absolute and percentage decreases in the skilled manual occupations.

The figures for the Southampton SMLA are also shown in Table 6.2. Given the considerable employment growth in Southampton in recent years, much of it being of a skilled and technological character, together with the high standard of amenities provided in the region, it is not altogether surprising to find the national upward shift in the occupational structure reflected in an exaggerated form. The rate of increase in professional and managerial socio-economic groups, at 41.9 per cent, was over twice the national average, while the percentage increase of intermediate non-manual groups in Southampton, at 20.8 per cent, was over four times the national figure. Even the skilled manual

Table 6.2

Socio-economic change in Great Britain and the Southampton SMLA, 1961-71.

	Great Britain		Southampton SMLA	
	Absolute change	% change	Absolute change	% change
Professional and managerial	469,000	20.5	7,170	41.9
Intermediate non-manual	124,000	4.7	4,460	20.8
Skilled manual	-217,000	-3.3	3,780	7.8
Semi- and unskilled manual	-649,000	15.9	-2,710	-7.9
Armed forces and inadequately described	-41,000	-7.1	-130	-2.6
Total	-314,000	-1.9	12,570	9.9

socio-economic groups increased by 7.8 per cent against the -3.3 per cent decrease throughout Great Britain as a whole. Finally, the decrease in the semi- and unskilled manual groups, at -7.9 per cent, was almost half the national rate of decrease for this socio-economic group. Overall, there was a 9.9 per cent increase in all the socio-economic groups compared with the national decline of -1.9 per cent.

Somewhat different patterns are revealed if these occupational changes are disaggregated into the cores and rings (Table 6.3), but again they have a symmetrical character. At the national level the professional and managerial groups increased in both cores and rings, but with by far the larger increase in the latter. In contrast, the semi- and unskilled manual groups declined in both cores and rings, with the larger decreases in the former. Both of these groups at the extremes of the occupational hierarchy were, therefore, decentralising in relative terms. Both the intermediate non-manual and skilled manual groups decreased in the cores and increased in the rings, thus exhibiting a simpler pattern of absolute decentralisation. In the Southampton SMLA the pattern of absolute change was broadly similar for the professional and managerial and semi- and unskilled manual groups. However, the behaviour of the two intermediate groups was different from the national pattern, with absolute increases in the core as well as in the ring.

The relative magnitude of these changes is clarified by the percentage changes shown in Table 6.3. In Great Britain as a whole the professional and managerial groups increased at the fastest rate in the metropolitan rings, the figure of 38.1 per cent being for above the national percentage increase for this group. However, this figure is

Table 6.3

Socio-economic change in the cores and rings of Great Britain
and the Southampton SMLA, 1961-71.

| | Great Britain | | Southampton SMLA | |
	Cores	Rings	Core	Ring
Professional and managerial	89,000 (8.7%)	305,000 (38.1%)	1,100 (14.6%)	6,070 (63.2%)
Intermediate non-manual	-99,000 (-6.6%)	161,000 (20.8%)	230 (2.0%)	4,230 (43.2%)
Skilled manual	-457,000 (-13.2%)	152,000 (9.0%)	700 (2.7%)	3,080 (13.6%)
Semi- and unskilled manual	-353,000 (-15.2%)	-125,000 (-11.6%)	-1,730 (9.6%)	-980 (-6.1%)
Armed forces and inadequately described	14,000 (6.4%)	-14,000 (-8.6%)	-220 (-13.8%)	90 (2.7%)
Total	-806,000 (-9.51)	479,000 (10.6%)	80 (0.1%)	12,490 (20.3%)

exceeded by the phenomenal 63.2 per cent increase in professional and
managerial groups of the Southampton SMLA ring. This is more than three
times the national rate of increase in this group and is exceeded by the
rings of only 22 of the 126 other SMLAs, these being predominantly in
new and expanding towns in the Outer South East (London School of
Economics, 1976a). The intermediate non-manual group recorded a small
percentage increase in the core of the Southampton SMLA, but showed a
43.2 per cent increase in this group in the ring; this being almost ten
times the national percentage rate of increase in this group and over
twice the national rate of increase in all cores. The percentage
increase in the skilled-manual group was little above the national rate
of increase in the rings, but significantly there was a small percentage
increase in this group in the Southampton core compared with the
substantial percentage decrease for all cores. Finally, the percentage
declines in the semi- and unskilled manual group were less in the core
and ring of Southampton than the national rates of decline for this
group in all cores and rings.

Interpretation of these changes between cores and rings is further
clarified if the influence of national change is extracted from the
data. A positive shift indicates that a socio-economic group in a zone
has either increased more than the national average increase for the
socio-economic group or else has decreased less than the national
average decrease for the particular socio-economic group. Conversely, a
negative shift indicates that the decrease in a zone is greater than the
overall national decrease for the particular socio-economic group or
else that the increase is less than the overall national increase for
the group. In the following analysis these shifts are presented in

percentage terms (formed by dividing the absolute shift of a socio-economic group by the size of the group in 1961) so that the relative changes in the groups can be easily seen.

Table 6.4

Percentage shifts in socio-economic groups in the cores and rings of Great Britain and the Southampton SMLA, 1961-71.

| | Great Britain | | Southampton SMLA | |
	Cores	Rings	Core	Ring
Professional and managerial	-12.9	16.6	-5.9	42.7
Intermediate non-manual	-11.4	16.1	-2.7	38.6
Skilled manual	-9.4	12.7	6.0	16.9
Semi- and unskilled manual	-0.5	3.5	5.5	9.1
Total shift	-7.2	11.3	2.1	22.2

The pattern of shifts for Great Britain reveal that all the occupational groups were decentralising with negative shifts in the cores and positive shifts in the rings (Table 6.4). The rapidly-growing professional and managerial groups had the largest negative percentage shift in the cores and the largest positive percentage shift in the rings. Conversely, the rapidly-declining semi- and unskilled manual groups had the smallest negative percentage shift in the cores and the smallest percentage shift in the rings. Taken together these results suggest a positive relationship between the overall growth rate of a socio-economic group and the extent of decentralisation on relative relocation between core and ring. It is the higher-status professional groups that have relocated into the rings of the SMLAs at the fastest rate. However, the relationship is not one that changes gradually with moves down the occupational hierarchy, for the intermediate non-manual and skilled manual groups reveal a pattern of shifts similar to the professional and managerial groups. In relative terms the most static group is the semi- and unskilled category made up of those who may be assumed to lack the income and or the status required to gain access to the pattern of owner-occupation and to pay for the increased journey-to-work distances prevalent in the rings.

The shifts in the Southampton SMLA once again reveal the national pattern modified by the growth within the region. Thus, compared with Great Britain, all the occupational groupings had larger positive percentage shifts in the ring and either positive shifts or smaller negative shifts in the core. Most striking was the considerable positive percentage shift in the professional and managerial group in the ring, a shift which was over twice the national average. However, a similar pattern was revealed by the intermediate non-manual group. The behaviour of the two manual groups in the core of Southampton was

also contrary to the national pattern. The continuing attractiveness of
the Southampton core for employment in the 1960s is evidenced by the
fact that both manual groups recorded positive shifts in the core. In
the Southampton case, therefore, it was both the manual groups which
appeared relatively static compared with the rapidly-decentralising non-
manual groups.

Such decentralisation trends have led some commentators to argue that
British cities are becoming increasingly polarised with larger
proportions of the higher-income groups in the rings and larger
proportions of the low-income groups in the city cores. Polarisation
has been criticised for creating concentrations of deprivation, reducing
the potential for social interaction and limiting opportunities for
social mobility. As Harris (1973) points out, many of these arguments
appear suspect, but the growing concentration of low-paid persons in
poor environmental conditions is increasingly seen as one symptom of
'inner-city' problems. Constrained by housing and employment
opportunities, it is argued that semi- and unskilled workers are trapped
in the inner-city. However, measuring polarisation in statistical
terms is not a simple matter, for many definitions of polarisation may
be employed. Thus, polarisation may be measured in terms of the
distribution of socio-economic groups at one point in time or by the
rates of change in these groups over a period of years.

Table 6.5

Proportion of socio-economic groups in the cores and rings of
Great Britain and the Southampton SMLA in 1961 and 1971.
(percent of total population)

| | Great Britain | | | | Southampton SMLA | | | |
| | Cores | | Rings | | Core | | Ring | |
	1961	1971	1961	1971	1961	1971	1961	1971
Professional and managerial	12.1	14.7	17.5	22.2	11.7	13.3	15.6	21.2
Intermediate non-manual	17.8	18.3	17.0	18.8	18.1	18.4	15.9	18.9
Skilled manual	41.3	39.3	37.0	36.9	39.9	41.3	36.8	34.7
Semi- and unskilled manual	26.9	24.9	23.6	19.1	27.9	25.2	26.3	20.3

Table 6.5 compares the proportions of the four main socio-economic
groups in cores and rings in Great Britain and Southampton in the years
1961 and 1971. These are comparatively large areal units and as such
none of the zones can be regarded as polarised in the sense of being
dominated by one particular group, although the skilled manual workers
are undoubtedly the largest category. It is, therefore, more
instructive to focus upon the rates of change in the proportions.
Throughout Great Britain the two non-manual socio-economic groups
increased as a proportion of both the cores and rings, while the two
manual groups decreased as a proportion of these zones. Again the

changes in the percentages were greatest at the two extremes, with the professional and managerial groups displaying the largest increases and the semi- and unskilled groups recording the largest decreases. Overall the changes emphasise the importance of the general upward shift in occupational status in the 1960s compared with the effects of decentralisation per se. Thus, the cores became increasingly diverse rather than polarised with larger proportions of non-manual occupations. It was the rings which changed most dramatically in status, however, with their increases in both the non-manual groups, static proportions of skilled workers and declining proportions of unskilled workers. This supports the hypothesis that the low-status occupational groups are excluded by various processes from the growth in the rings.

A broadly similar pattern emerges from the Southampton SMLA, but there are a number of features worthy of comment. First, the rapid rate of growth of professional and managerial groups in the ring started from a comparatively small base and in 1971 the proportion was still below the national average. The largest proportions of persons in this grouping are of course employed in the major conurbations. Second, in contrast to national trends there was an increase in the proportion of skilled manual workers in the core of the Southampton SMLA. This reflects the diverse manufacturing growth manifest in Southampton in the 1960s (Chapter 3).

DECENTRALISATION AND BIRTHPLACE GROUPS

The birthplace group data used in this essay were selected to represent the broad sub-continents which have been the main sources of immigration into Britain in recent years. This criterion, together with the need for maximum compatibility of definitions between 1961 and 1971 produced six categories (Table 6.6). The limitations of these data have been discussed extensively elsewhere (London School of Economics, 1976b and 1976c), but two important caveats should be borne in mind. First, the Census data refer to country of birth and not to nationality or race. When coupled with the fact that such data take no account of children born in this country to immigrants of a previous generation, this means that such birthplace data cannot be strictly equated with colour. Second, it is considered that such data are prone to under-estimation in certain areas of a degree which may be considerable (Peach, 1966). Furthermore, it is known that in 1961 many enumerators made mistakes in their categorisation of birthplace groups. Nevertheless, the Census concludes that these birthplace data "... are considered to give a reliable general indication of the fortunes in the labour market of certain groups born overseas".

The patterns of change in birthplace groups in Great Britain and the Southampton SMLA are shown in Table 6.7. Throughout Britain all the birthplace groups grew at a faster rate in the 1960s than the British-born population, with percentage increases particularly large in the case of the Indian, African and West Indian groups. However, the largest and longest-established immigrant group, from Ireland, increased at a rate similar to that of the British-born population. Some of the percentage increases are exaggerated by the small size of the immigrant groups in 1961, but when the absolute increases of all birthplace groups are added, they total over 932,000, representing over

Table 6.6

Definitions of birthplace groups from the 1961 and 1971 Censuses.

---

1) IRISH - This group includes persons born in Northern Ireland as well as in the Irish Republic, since it was not possible to separate these from the data available for 1961.

2) INDIAN - India, Pakistan and Ceylon.

3) AFRICAN - Ghana, Kenya, Malawi, Nigeria, Rhodesia, Sierra Leone, Tanzania, Uganda, Zambia and other New Commonwealth countries in Africa.

4) WEST INDIAN - Barbados, Guyana, Jamaica, Trinidad and Tobago and other New Commonwealth countries in the Americas.

5) OTHER COMMONWEALTH - Australia, Canada, New Zealand, Gibraltar, Malta and Gozo, Hong Kong, Malaysia, Singapore, and other New Commonwealth countries in Asia and Oceania.

6) OTHER IMMIGRANTS - Other non-Commonwealth immigrants (excluding Eire) and birthplace not stated.

7) BRITISH-BORN - Those born in Great Britain.

Table 6.7

Change in birthplace groups in Great Britain
and the Southampton SMLA, 1961-71.

	Great Britain		Southampton SMLA	
	Absolute change	% change	Absolute change	% change
Irish	35,000	3.8	1,584	26.1
Indian	260,000	125.3	1,404	71.2
African	116,000	296.4	652	248.9
West Indian	123,000	71.3	458	97.5
Other Commonwealth	58,000	21.3	589	17.8
Other Immigrants	340,000	42.3	4,313	82.5
British-born	1,759,000	3.6	50,300	13.1
Total	2,691,000	5.3	59,300	14.8

one-third of the total increase in population. The rates of change within the rapidly-growing Southampton SMLA reveal a number of deviations from the national pattern. The Irish, West Indian and Other Immigrants categories all increased at rates above the national average, while the Indian, African and Other Commonwealth groups increased at rates below the national average. In Southampton moreover, only 10 per cent of the total population increase were immigrants, the

132

Table 6.8

Change in birthplace groups in the cores and rings of Great Britain
and the Southampton SMLA, 1961-71.

| | Great Britain | | Southampton SMLA | |
	Cores	Rings	Core	Ring
Irish	-9,000 (-1.4%)	34,000 (18.4%)	831 (22.9%)	753 (30.8%)
Indian	224,000 (160.6%)	27,000 (60.6%)	1,332 (135.1%)	72 (7.3%)
African	89,000 (344.7%)	20,000 (242.7%)	359 (355.5%)	293 (182.0%)
West Indian	111,000 (70.1%)	10,000 (96.3%)	378 (118.5%)	80 (53.0%)
Other Commonwealth	26,000 (16.0%)	21,000 (30.5%)	-78 (-4.3%)	667 (44.4%)
Other Immigrants	175,000 (37.7%)	122,000 (58.6%)	1,684 (67.9%)	2,629 (95.8%)
British-born	-1,335,000 (-5.3%)	2,269,000 (16.5%)	5,589 (2.9%)	44,711 (23.7%)
Total	-719,000 (-2.7%)	2,503,000 (17.5%)	10,095 (4.9%)	49,205 (25.0%)

vast majority being British-born.

The 'replacement' hypothesis suggests that immigrants have taken up
the poorly-paid, low status jobs at the bottom of the occupational
hierarchy that have been vacated by the upwardly socially-mobile
British-born population as they have moved out into the commuter belts.
A perspective upon this hypothesis is provided in Table 6.8 which shows
the absolute rates of population change for the birthplace groups
disaggregated into cores and rings. Throughout Great Britain the
British-born population displayed considerable population loss from the
cores and an even larger absolute increase in the rings. In contrast,
with the exception of the Irish, all the immigrant groups increased at
a faster rate in the cores than in the rings. The increases were
disproportionately large in the cores compared with the rings in the
case of the Indian, African and West Indian groups. A broadly similar
pattern was revealed by the immigrant groups in Southampton, but again
there were a number of local deviations from the national pattern.
Given the substantial growth of the core, it is not altogether
surprising to find that, contrary to the national pattern of decline,
the British-born population increased in the core of Southampton
(although clearly at a much smaller rate than in the ring). The Irish
and Other Immigrants categories also displayed a similar increase in the
core in contradiction of the national pattern, while the Other

Commonwealth group actually decreased in the core (albeit by a small number) and increased in the ring. In the Hampshire context, the Other Commonwealth growth in the ring probably reflects white persons born in the Commonwealth who have moved to Britain. Nevertheless, the overall trend is one of increasing growth of Indian, African and West Indian groups in the core in comparison with the ring.

The relative rates of growth shown by the birthplace groups are clarified by the percentage changes shown in Table 6.8. Of greatest interest is the fact that the difference between the rates of increase in the core and ring is greater for the Indian, African and West Indian groups in Southampton than in the cores of the nation taken together. Once again this is likely to reflect job opportunities in an expanding local economy compared with the declines experienced in the major conurbations.

Table 6.9

Percentage shifts in birthplace groups in the cores and rings of Great Britain and the Southampton SMLA, 1961-71.

| | Great Britain | | Southampton SMLA | |
	Cores	Rings	Core	Ring
Irish	-5.2	14.6	19.1	27.0
Indian	32.3	-67.7	9.8	-118.0
African	42.7	-59.3	159.0	-114.0
West Indian	-1.3	24.9	47.2	-18.0
Other Commonwealth	-5.5	9.1	-25.6	23.1
Other Immigrants	-4.4	16.5	25.6	53.5
British-born	-8.9	12.9	-0.7	20.0
Total	-8.4	12.7	-0.3	19.8

The patterns are further illuminated by the percentage shifts in Table 6.9. These reveal that throughout Great Britain all the birth-place groups were decentralising in relative terms, apart from the Indian and African groups. In Southampton, however, with the exception of the Irish, Other Commonwealth and Other Immigrants categories, there were larger positive percentage shifts in the cores and larger negative shifts in the rings compared with the nation as a whole.

These patterns would suggest a growing tendency for polarisation of immigrant groups in the core of Southampton at a faster rate than the British average. Table 6.10 shows a comparison of the proportions of the various immigrant groups in the cores and rings of Great Britain and the Southampton SMLA in 1961 and 1971. In Great Britain, the British-born population declined as a proportion of the total population of both cores and rings but at a faster rate in the cores. Conversely, the other birthplace groups increased as a proportion of the total

Table 6.10

Proportion of birthplace groups in the cores and rings
of Great Britain and the Southampton SMLA in 1961 and 1971.
(per cent of total population)

	Great Britain				Southampton SMLA			
	Cores		Rings		Core		Ring	
	1961	1971	1961	1971	1961	1971	1961	1971
Irish	2.4	2.5	1.3	1.3	1.8	2.1	1.2	1.3
Indian	0.5	1.4	0.3	0.4	0.5	1.1	0.5	0.4
African	0.1	0.4	0.1	0.2	0.0	0.2	0.1	0.2
West Indian	0.6	1.0	0.1	0.1	0.2	0.3	0.1	0.1
Other Commonwealth	0.6	0.7	0.5	0.5	0.9	0.8	0.8	0.9
Other Immigrants	1.8	2.6	1.4	2.0	1.1	1.9	1.4	2.2
British-born	94.0	91.4	96.3	95.5	95.5	93.6	95.9	94.9

population in all zones but at a faster rate in the cores. A similar
pattern is revealed in the Southampton context, but the changes in the
proportions being generally smaller. Thus, there was a smaller decline
in the proportion of British-born in the core and smaller increases in
the sizes of the other birthplace groups. This reflects a smaller rate
of net outmigration by British-born inhabitants and a shorter history
of immigrant-group settlement than other major British conurbations.
Hence the rapid rates of increase observed earlier have been upon a
generally smaller base population of non-British born persons than in
the cores and rings of the nation as a whole. The distribution of
immigrant groups is likely to display such variations throughout the
country because of variations in local circumstances. Not only is the
distribution of immigrant groups the most dynamic aspect of urban
change, it is also in one sense the least predictable, being largely an
'injection' of persons into the system rather than merely the outcome
of the rearrangement of the system's internal structure.

DECENTRALISATION AND AGE GROUPS

For the analysis of age structures it is necessary to define groups
which are relatively homogenous in terms of the characteristics
associated with changes in an individual's life cycle (London School of
Economics, 1976d and 1976e). Four age groups are used 0 to 14, 15 to
29, 30 to pensionable age and above pensionable age (65 for males and 60
for females). The first group crudely approximates with those below
school-leaving age and for this category mobility is largely dependent
upon the life style of parents. The 15 to 29 age group contains the
stage of the life cycle when the majority of individuals leave home and
establish their own families, so that mobility rates are usually high.
The 30 to pensionable-age group contains those who are geographically
more stable while their children are growing up. Mobility often
increases again in the final group, however, when the end of employment
leads to a move to a 'retirement area' or to a location closer to

135

offspring or other relatives.

To simplify the analysis these groups are necessarily large and obviously conceal enormous differences. Such large and irregularly-sized groups also limit the analysis because changes in an area in a given ten-year period are not only the result of net migration and natural change but also are a product of the composition of the age structure in the base year. To analyse such cohort changes requires regularly-sized groups. In the present analysis, therefore, it is possible that large changes within age groups may not be reflected in changes between the age groups. Thus, when interpreting changes in age structure between 1961 and 1971, direct inference cannot be made from the age structure as it existed in 1961.

Table 6.11

Age-group changes in Great Britain and the Southampton SMLA, 1961-71.

| | Great Britain | | Southampton SMLA | |
	Absolute change	% change	Absolute change	% change
0-14 years	1,006,000	8.4	12,974	13.3
15-29 years	1,376,000	13.8	23,741	30.4
30 years to pensionable age	-959,000	-4.4	8,969	5.3
Pensionable age	1,689,000	16.8	13,616	23.8
Total	2,689,000	5.2	59,300	14.8

The national pattern of age structure change is shown in Table 6.11. The 1960s produced an increase in the size of three of the age groups, but not in the 30 years to pensionable-age group. The largest absolute increase was in the 15 to 29 age group (reflecting the post-war 'baby boom'), while the largest percentage increase was in the above pensionable-age group. Southampton's status as a growth area is underlined by the fact that throughout the 1960s all the age groups (and especially the 15 to 29 category) increased at rates considerably above the national average. This of course largely reflects the considerable net in-migration to the region of all age groups, but also an above-average rate of natural increase.

Once again if these aggregate results are split between the cores and rings a somewhat different picture emerges (Table 6.12). Nationally the 0 to 14 and 30 to pensionable-age groups decreased in the cores and increased in the rings, while the 15 to 29 and above pensionable-age groups increased in both zones but in greater magnitude in the rings. The direction of absolute changes in Southampton was broadly similar to the national pattern, although there was a small increase in the 0 to 14 age group. The main inference which may be drawn from this pattern

Table 6.12

Age-group changes in the cores and rings of Great Britain
and the Southampton SMLA, 1961-71.

| | Great Britain | | Southampton SMLA | |
	Cores	Rings	Core	Ring
0-14 years	-4,000 (0.1%)	761,000 (22.4%)	52 (0.1%)	12,922 (27.1%)
15-29 years	313,000 (5.9%)	739,000 (27.2%)	9,864 (24.2%)	13,877 (37.1%)
30 years to pensionable age	-1,410,000 (-12.5%)	485,000 (7.8%)	-4,481 (-5.2%)	13,450 (16.2%)
Pensionable age	365,000 (10.4%)	532,000 (26.2%)	4,660 (16.3%)	8,956 (31.3%)
Total	736,000 (-2.7%)	2,517,000 (17.5%)	10,095 (4.9%)	49,205 (25.0%)

is that it was the child-rearing groups aged between 30 years to
pensionable age who (together with their offspring) have been leaving
the inner-city areas for commuter suburbs. In contrast, the 15 to 29
age group has, as usual, been attracted to city centres by employment,
educational and social opportunities. The increase of the older age
group in city cores may be attributed to their unwillingness to move
and/or their inability to relocate through limited incomes.
Nevertheless there is a larger magnitude of growth of the 15 to 29 and
above pensionable-age groups in the rings, so that they are both still
decentralising in relative terms.

The percentage changes in Table 6.12 show that in the Southampton
SMLA all the age groups either increased at an above-average rate or
decreased at a below-average rate in comparison with Great Britain as a
whole. Of particular note is the 15 to 29 group which increased in the
core of the Southampton SMLA at a rate almost four times the national
average. The major exception to the general pattern was the 0 to 14
age group whose increase in the Southampton core was little above the
national decline in this zone.

The relative magnitude of the changes between the cores and rings are
finally illuminated by the percentage shifts shown in Table 6.13. At
the national level there was a remarkably consistent pattern with all
age groups displaying negative shifts of roughly similar magnitude in
the cores and again positive shifts of similar magnitude in the rings.
All these groups, therefore, displayed an underlying trend of
decentralisation, although this was less marked in the case of the
above pensionable-age group. In the Southampton SMLA there were, as
might be expected, much larger positive percentage shifts for all the
age groups in the ring and smaller negative shifts in the core, with a
large positive shift for the 15 to 29 age group in the core.

Table 6.13

Percentage shifts in age groups in the cores and rings of Great Britain
and the Southampton SMLA, 1961-71.

| | Great Britain | | Southampton SMLA | |
	Cores	Rings	Core	Ring
0-14 years	-8.7	13.8	-8.3	18.7
15-29 years	-8.0	13.3	10.8	23.3
30 years to pensionable age	-8.0	12.3	-0.8	20.6
Pensionable age	-6.7	9.1	-0.5	14.5
Total	-8.4	12.7	-0.3	19.8

Table 6.14

Proportion of age groups in the cores and rings of Great Britain
and the Southampton SMLA in 1961 and 1971.
(per cent of total population)

| | Great Britain | | | | Southampton SMLA | | | |
| | Cores | | Rings | | Core | | Ring | |
	1961	1971	1961	1971	1961	1971	1961	1971
0-14 years	22.9	23.5	23.8	24.8	24.5	23.3	24.2	24.6
15-29 years	20.0	21.7	19.0	20.6	19.9	23.5	19.0	20.8
30 years to pensionable age	42.8	38.6	43.3	39.7	41.7	37.7	42.3	39.3
Pensionable age	14.3	16.2	13.9	14.9	14.0	15.0	14.5	15.3

These patterns of demographic change have led to the hypothesis that
our inner cities are becoming polarised in terms of their age
structures, with a tendency for concentration of the child-rearing
groups in the rings and growing proportions of the elderly left behind
in inner-city environments. Some limited support for this hypothesis
may be derived from Table 6.14 which shows the proportions of the four
main age groups in the cores and rings of Great Britain and the
Southampton SMLA in 1961 and 1971. In the cores of Great Britain there
was an increase in the proportions of all age groups, apart from the 30
years to pensionable-age category, but the largest increase was in the
proportion in the above pensionable-age group. However, a similar
pattern was also revealed in the rings, and while the increase in the
proportion of the population above pensionable age is not so large in

this context, there was also a considerable decline in the proportion in the 30 years to pensionable-age group. This would indicate that, at this scale of analysis, it is the overall national patterns of change which have had the most significant impact upon the age structures of the cores and rings rather than the decentralisation processes.

The age profiles for the Southampton SMLA reveal a number of deviations from the national pattern (Table 6.14). In contrast to the national pattern of increase in the core, there was a decrease in the proportion in the 0-14 age group in the Southampton core, but a substantial increase in the 15 to 29 age group. The 30 years to pensionable-age group again decreased as a proportion in the Southampton core, but the increase in the proportion in the above pensionable-age group was considerably less than the national average. The pattern of change in the Southampton ring again followed the national pattern with declines in the 30 years to pensionable-age group. Overall, there was a smaller degree of difference between the age profile for the core and ring of the Southampton SMLA than the aggregate profiles for cores and rings in all British SMLAs. Hence the Southampton core has a rather more youthful profile than the national average for all cores, with a larger proportion of the 15 to 29 age group and a smaller proportion of the elderly. Conversely, the Southampton ring has a more 'elderly' profile than the national average for all rings, with a larger proportion of the population in the above pensionable-age category. This would seem to reflect the fact that, as a growing SMLA in the 1960s, Southampton's core did not reveal old-age characteristics of some larger northern cores with considerable population declines and ageing demographic profiles. While the Southampton ring grew at an even faster rate, its location in the South and in attractive Hampshire settlements (particularly around the New Forest) have encouraged the in-migration of elderly persons looking for a retirement home.

RECENT DEVELOPMENTS

The Southampton SMLA clearly displays a number of significant differences from the national pattern of change in the period between 1961 and 1971. The results are even more remarkable when compared with the patterns of decline observed previously in the major conurbations and especially those in the North (Cameron, 1980; Goddard and Hodgson, 1977). Most striking in Southampton is the relationship between economic growth and the rate of decentralisation. Thus, it is the more affluent and most rapidly-growing professional and managerial workers who have decentralised at the fastest rate in Southampton, but a similar pattern is also displayed by the growing intermediate non-manual groups. In contrast, the relatively poorer and declining semi- and unskilled manual groups displayed the smallest rate of net decentralisation. Immigrant growth in Southampton has in some cases been faster than the national average but upon a smaller base number in 1961. As a result, the overall pattern has been one of greater relative concentration than in the major conurbations with a longer history of immigrant settlement. All the age groups have increased at rates faster than the national average as befits a growth area.

These results relate to the period from 1961 to 1971 and it is not yet possible to reconstruct in detail comparable patterns of change over the period 1971 to 1981. What is clear, however, is that the 1970s were in many respects different from the years of growth in the 1960s. Continuity was maintained by the decline of Britain's manufacturing base but this was accelerated by the recession which followed the first major increase in oil prices by OPEC. The resulting increased energy costs and hence reduced mobility, the declining investment in construction and the general rundown of regional assistance and new town policy, all dictated a less dynamic spatial structure than in the 1960s.

These trends were reflected in a reduced national increase in population. Between 1971 and 1981 the population of England and Wales increased by only 1.5 per cent, compared with almost 6 per cent between 1961 and 1971. There was also a reduced rate of growth for the Southampton SMLA, but significantly this reflects a growing difference between the relative fortunes of the core and ring. The commuter hinterlands embodied within the Winchester, Eastleigh, Test Valley and New Forest districts grew at rates comparable with and, in some cases, in excess of those in the 1960s. In contrast, the enumerated population of the Southampton SMLA core declined by some 11,000 between 1971 and 1981. Indeed, estimates derived from the 1979 Hampshire Enhanced Electoral Registration Survey (Hampshire County Council, 1980) indicate that, while in the 1960s only the inner-city wards of Southampton were losing population, by the 1970s a majority of the wards in the city were experiencing net population loss. In these cases a reduced rate of natural increase has no longer compensated for the net out-migration of population. This means that the Southampton SMLA has moved one step forward in the postulated 'life-cycle' of SMLAs (Department of Environment, 1976) from a situation of relative decentralisation between 1951 and 1971 to a position of absolute decentralisation (i.e. with a declining core and growing rings) during the period between 1971 and 1981.

Table 6.15

Age-group changes in districts of the Southampton area, 1971-79.

	Southampton	New Forest	Test Valley	Winchester	Eastleigh
0-14 years	-9,500 (-19.2%)	-3,300 (-11.2%)	-200 (-1.0%)	-1,400 (-7.3%)	300 (1.5%)
15-34 years	3,000 (5.2%)	6,000 (20.1%)	4,300 (16.9%)	2,700 (13.4%)	6,700 (31.9%)
35-64 years	-4,100 (-5.6%)	4,200 (9.1%)	700 (2.7%)	2,100 (7.1%)	3,500 (12.6%)
65+ years	5,800 (22.0%)	6,600 (30.4%)	3,000 (35.7%)	2,200 (19.8%)	2,400 (27.3%)

Source: Hampshire Enhanced Electoral Registration Survey, 1979.

The effects of these changes upon the age structure of the South-ampton district may also be derived from the Hampshire Enhanced Electoral Registration Survey (Table 6.15). Neither the age groups, the district boundaries or the method of data collection are strictly compatible with the Census-based SMLA data presented previously but, despite these and other limitations, the data are the best available guide to the general pattern of recent changes. The major interest is the difference between developments in the Southampton core and those in the surrounding commuter hinterlands.

Now that the Southampton district has started to decline, its pattern of age-structure change more closely follows that of the national pattern observed previously for the period 1961 to 1971. The falling birth rate combined with high net out-migration has led to a substantial decline in the numbers of the population aged under 15 (Table 6.15). There was also a continuing decrease in the child-rearing and middle-age groups between 34 and 65 years, a smaller increase in those aged between 15 to 34, but a continued large increase in the population aged above 65. The districts surrounding Southampton all experienced either larger increases or smaller decreases in all the age groups. However, the extent of the fall in the birth rate is again emphasised by the fact that (with the exception of Eastleigh which recorded a small increase) all the districts had declines in the population aged under 15 years. All the other age groups increased in size in the districts, the major contrast with Southampton being the increase in the 34 to 65 age group.

The relative growth rates of the four age groups in the districts are also shown in Table 6.15. In the case of Southampton they reveal an exaggerated form of the 1960s pattern, with changes greatest at the extremes of the age structure. There was a substantial -19.2 per cent decline in the 0 to 14 age group, matched by a 22.0 per cent increase in the above 65 age group. The percentage increase in the 'young adult' group was substantially less than in the period between 1961 and 1971, but the rate of decline of the child-rearing and middle-aged groups in Southampton between 1971 and 1979 was broadly comparable with the earlier period. The percentage changes also emphasise the contrasting fortunes of the core and surrounding ring. The remaining districts had smaller percentage declines in the 0 to 14 age group but larger percentage increases in the young adult group. With the exception of Winchester (which had a small amount of population increase upon an already above-average proportion of the elderly), there were also larger percentage increases in the 65 plus age group in the districts surrounding Southampton. This, of course, reflects continued high rates of retirement migration, especially to the New Forest area. The percentage increases for the 34 to 65 age group emphasise the diversity of the ring and the concentrated nature of certain types of growth. Thus Test Valley recorded a small percentage increase in this instance, this contrasting markedly with the growth of Eastleigh.

The effects of the changes upon the overall age structures are shown in Table 6.16. In Southampton there was an accelerated decrease in the proportion of the population aged under 15 years and a corresponding increase in the above 65 age group. The intermediate age groups changed by much smaller proportions. The patterns of change in the surrounding districts were generally less extreme. There were overall smaller

Table 6.16

Proportions of age groups in districts of the Southampton area in 1971 and 1979.
(per cent of total population)

	Southampton 1971	Southampton 1979	New Forest 1971	New Forest 1979	Test Valley 1971	Test Valley 1979	Winchester 1971	Winchester 1979	Eastleigh 1971	Eastleigh 1979
0-14 years	24.0	19.9	23.0	18.6	26.7	23.0	24.1	20.9	25.5	22.2
15-34 years	28.0	30.1	23.5	25.6	28.2	28.9	25.2	26.7	27.2	30.8
35-64 years	35.4	34.3	36.4	35.8	34.2	35.1	24.6	25.8	36.0	34.8
65+ years	12.6	15.8	16.1	20.2	10.9	13.0	13.8	15.5	11.3	12.4

Source: Hampshire Enhanced Electoral Registration Survey, 1979.

declines in the proportions in the 0 to 14 age group and (with the exception of the New Forest) smaller increases in the proportions in the old age group. The two intermediate age groups reveal a more complex pattern which once again serves to emphasise the diversity of the ring areas. As in Southampton, there were increases in the proportion of the population aged 15 to 34, but the increases were smaller in the Test Valley and Winchester, equal in the New Forest and larger in Eastleigh. The patterns of change are even more complex in the 34 to 65 age group, for the Test Valley and Winchester districts increased their proportions while the other districts all decreased but by amounts which did not vary significantly. All told, these estimates derived from the Hampshire survey suggest that, while powerful net-migration trends are at work within the decentralising SMLA, national patterns of population decline have had a profound effect upon the structure of all the districts. However, they also indicate a growing difference between the age structure of the core, which like the major cities is becoming more elderly, and the surrounding ring areas (apart from those with large amounts of retirement migration).

However, it would seem unlikely that this accelerated decentralisation and reduced growth have radically altered the patterns of change observed for socio-economic groups and birthplace groups in the Southampton SMLA. Thus the increase of non-manual socio-economic groups in the ring, the decrease of semi- and unskilled manual socio-economic groups in the core, and the increase of Indian, West Indian and African immigrant groups in the core are likely to have continued in the 1970s, albeit at perhaps reduced rates in some instances. In this respect, the performance of the Southampton SMLA may be contrasted with that of the large conurbations where the bulk of population loss exists (Department of Environment, 1976; OPCS, 1981). In the latter the continued decline of Britain's traditional manufacturing industries has led to and accelerated the decrease in skilled manual forms of employment. In contrast to the 1960s, this decrease has not been compensated by the growth of services. Indeed, the decline of traditional forms of blue-collar service employment is now seen as playing an important part in causing increased unemployment in inner-city areas (Townsend, 1977).

It remains to be seen, therefore, whether developments in the 1980s will produce a fundamental shift from the pattern of economic growth and population increase which has been sustained in the Southampton SMLA since the Second World War towards a more 'conurbation-like' pattern of decentralisation within decline. The Southampton ring is certain to continue to grow, for unlike the major conurbations it possesses many features, including a desirable residential environment and skilled workforce, which are conducive to economic growth. However, it is possible that the Southampton core may fare less well in the future. As indicated in Chapter 3, a large proportion of the city's employment is concentrated in a small number of large firms, many of which are multi-nationals. It may be, therefore, that the industrial base of Southampton is vulnerable to the transference of future investment to plants in other countries with lower production costs. AC Delco recently announced some 800 redundancies in Southampton; this represents the largest single contribution to unemployment in the city in recent years and this might be the forerunner of developments elsewhere. However, even if growth is sustained, both Southampton and the wider city region will face considerable problems in the future. Unemployment has risen in recent years and, although less than the national average, there are considerable difficulties in providing employment for school-leavers and those made redundant in middle age (Hampshire County Council, 1980b). The problems of finding suitable jobs for school-leavers are likely to be particularly acute in the next few years, because of the demographic bulge of those aged between 15 to 29 caused by the increased birth rate in the 1960s. There are also considerable social strains imposed by a rapidly-growing elderly population. In Hampshire these strains are intensified by a high rate of in-migration amongst retired persons combined with a County Council which is not prepared to spend as much on social services as authorities elsewhere in the country. Furthermore, the experience of the last twenty years has shown that above-average economic growth does not eradicate basic inequalities in living conditions between declining cores and rapidly-growing commuter hinterlands. In this context, it is of perhaps some significance that Southampton has not escaped entirely from the pattern of rioting and looting which has affected certain major British cities in the middle of 1981.

REFERENCES

BERTHOUD, R (1976), Where are London's Poor? Greater London Council Quarterly Bulletin, 36.

CAMERON, G C (ed.)(1980), The Future of the British Conurbations (London, Longman).

DEPARTMENT OF EMPLOYMENT (1975), The Changing Structure of the Labour Force (London, HMSO).

DEPARTMENT OF ENVIRONMENT (1976), British cities: urban population and employment trends 1951-1971, Research Report 10 (London, HMSO).

DREWETT, J R, GODDARD, J B and SPENCE, N A (1976a), What's happening in British cities? Town and Country Planning, 44, 14-24.

DREWETT, J R, GODDARD, J B and SPENCE, N A (1976b), Urban Britain: beyond containment, in BERRY, B J L (ed.), Urbanisation and Counter-urbanisation (London, Sage).

GODDARD, J B and HODGSON, J (1977), Urban change in the Northern Region, in FULLERTON, B (ed.), North Eastern Studies, 1977 (University of Newcastle, Department of Geography).

GUDGIN, S, CRUM, R and BAILEY, S (1979), White collar employment in UK manufacturing industry, in DANIELS, P W (ed.), Spatial Patterns of Office Growth and Location (Chichester, Wiley).

HAGGETT, P (1965), Locational Analysis in Human Geography (London, Arnold).

HALL, P, THOMAS, R, GRACEY, H and DREWETT, R (1973), The Containment of Urban England (London, Allen and Unwin), 2 vols.

HAMPSHIRE COUNTY COUNCIL (1980a), Enhanced Electoral Registration Survey 1979 (Winchester, County Planning Department).

HAMPSHIRE COUNTY COUNCIL (1980b), Hampshire Strategic Monitoring Report 1980 (Winchester, County Planning Department).

HARRIS, M (1973), Some aspects of social polarisation, in DONNISON, D and EVERSLEY, D (eds), London: Urban Patterns, Problems and Policies (London, Heinemann).

HARVEY, D (1977), Government policies, financial institutions and neighborhood change in United States cities, in HARLOE, M (ed.), Captive Cities: Studies in the Political Economy of Cities and Regions (London, Wiley).

HARVEY, D (1981), The urban process under capitalism: a framework for analysis, in DEAR, M and SCOTT, A J (eds), Urbanisation and Urban Planning in Capitalist Society (London, Methuen).

HOLTERMANN, S (1975), Areas of urban deprivation in Great Britain: an analysis of 1971 Census data, Social Trends, 6, 33-47.

LONDON SCHOOL OF ECONOMICS (1974a), The definition of Standard Metropolitan Labour areas and Metropolitan Economic Labour areas, Part 1 - Commentary, Urban Change in Britain Working Report (London School of Economics, Department of Geography), 1.

LONDON SCHOOL OF ECONOMICS (1974b), Synopsis of inter-urban and intra-urban population change: net migration, natural change and population density, Urban Change in Britain Working Report (London School of Economics, Department of Geography), 12.

LONDON SCHOOL OF ECONOMICS (1976a), Socio-economic change in the British urban system, 1961-1971, Urban Change in Britain Working Report (London School of Economics, Department of Geography), 21.

LONDON SCHOOL OF ECONOMICS (1976b), Inter-urban changes in the birth-place structure of the British urban system, 1961-1971, Urban Change in Britain Working Report (London School of Economics, Department of Geography), 31.

LONDON SCHOOL OF ECONOMICS (1976c), Intra-urban changes in the birth-place structure of the British urban system, 1961-1971, Urban Change in Britain Working Report (London School of Economics, Department of Geography), 32.

LONDON SCHOOL OF ECONOMICS (1976d), Inter-urban changes in the age structure of the British urban system, 1961-1971, Urban Change in Britain Working Report (London School of Economics, Department of Geography), 25.

LONDON SCHOOL OF ECONOMICS (1976e), Intra-urban change in the age structure of the British urban system, 1961-1971, Urban Change in Britain Working Report (London School of Economics, Department of Geography), 26.

OFFICE OF POPULATION CENSUSES AND SURVEYS (1981), Census 1981: Preliminary Report for England and Wales (London, HMSO).

PEACH, C (1968), West Indian Migration to Britain: a Social Geography (London, Oxford University Press).

PINCH, S P and WILLIAMS, A (1981), Social-class changes in British cities, in GODDARD, J B (ed.), The Urban and Regional Transformation of Britain (London, Methuen).

ROUTH, G (1965), Occupation and Pay in Great Britain (Cambridge, Cambridge University Press).

TOWNSEND, A R (1977), The relationship of inner-city problems to regional policy, Regional Studies, 11, 225-252.

7 Area-Based Housing Improvement

S P PINCH

It has been suggested that one of the most remarkable features of the English local government system is the large degree of conformity displayed by the numerous local authorities to national shifts in policy (Dunleavy, 1980). In the field of housing, for example, there has been a dramatic and universal swing away from slum-clearance and comprehensive redevelopment programmes towards the renovation of older housing. The City of Southampton has not been a major exception to this trend. Throughout much of the post-war period, there was a considerable local authority building programme in the city designed to overcome the long waiting lists and to replace slum housing. By 1970, however, the worst dwellings had been replaced, and in the last decade the emphasis has been upon the renovation of the existing housing stock. Indeed, Southampton declared one of the first General Improvement Areas in the country in 1970. The magnitude of the shift in emphasis is demonstrated by the fact that, while some 23,000 new dwellings have been constructed in the city since the Second World War, in 1979 the total of new dwellings completed totalled only 279.

What is also becoming clear from research, however, is that this apparent conformity of cities such as Southampton takes place within broad limits. The nature, extent and impact of national changes in policy vary enormously in different localities, and nowhere is this demonstrated better than in the field of renovation policies. The effectiveness of housing improvement policies has differed greatly, both between local authorities (Kirby, 1979; Sigsworth and Wilkinson, 1973), and also between areas within local authority boundaries (Bassett and Short, 1978; Duncan, 1974). Furthermore, the reasons for these variations in policy are now seen to be the result of a complex interaction between many processes operating at different scales - national, local and individual. To some extent, these variations are a function not only of differing problems in the areas concerned (the terms 'inner-city' and 'multiple deprivation' now being seen as gross over-simplifications), but also the result of variations in the response of the numerous agencies and institutions involved in formulating housing policies. Some of these factors may be envisaged as general or 'structural', affecting all authorities, whereas others are evident in particular areas, reflecting the complex interaction of local factors. Sorting out the relative importance of these various influences has proved to be one of the most difficult tasks facing researchers seeking to understand resource allocations in cities. It is against this background that this essay attempts to document the experience of housing improvement in Southampton in the 1970s. It is not the intention to provide a detailed account of the evolution of improvement policies in various parts of the city. Indeed, it would be impossible in the space available to do full justice to the spate of conflicting reports, newsletters, information sheets and local correspondence which have accompanied improvement policies in Southampton in the last decade. Instead, an attempt is made to select a limited number of issues of general interest.

THE BACKGROUND TO RENOVATION POLICIES

The background to housing policy in the 1970s has by now been well documented (e.g. Duncan, 1971; Monck and Lomas, 1980; McKay and Cox, 1979; Paris and Blackaby, 1979; Pepper, 1971; Roberts, 1978) and requires only the briefest outline in this context. The shift away from large-scale slum clearance and comprehensive redevelopment towards smaller-scale renovation (or rehabilitation) of the existing housing stock can now be seen to have been the result of numerous pressures. Amongst the most important of these pressures were undoubtedly the escalating economic costs of redevelopment and the growing public hostility to the social disruption caused by such housing schemes, especially when associated with the construction of high-rise blocks of flats. There was also a shift in the perception of the housing problem by planners and academics towards the end of the 1960s. The traditional division between 'fit' and 'unfit' housing was seen as inadequate when increasingly the problem was one, not of slums requiring demolition, but of essentially sound houses lacking modern amenities and being in need of improvement. The principal tool of policy to encourage such improvement was the improvement grant and the most notable innovation of the 1969 Housing Act was the General Improvement Area (GIA). Local authorities were empowered to designate areas of cities consisting of some 300 to 500 households within which it was hoped the uptake of improvement grants could be concentrated. Comprehensive improvements were sought by the widespread adoption of high-standard discretionary grants intended to guarantee the future life of the areas for at least thirty years.

The policy was thus one of a set of area-based policies introduced at this time. The rationale for the approach was the belief that a principal barrier to the improvement of housing was the so-called 'neighbourhood effect'. This implied that there was little incentive for an individual to improve his dwelling if similar action was not taken by neighbours, since the surrounding environmental deterioration would negate the effects of improvements and diminish any capital gain. It was also hoped that the policy would renew confidence in areas which had suffered from low investment through years of blight over planning uncertainty. General environmental improvements, such as the removal of 'un-neighbourly' activities, landscaping, the creation of off-street parking and play areas, were seen as a way of stimulating confidence in the future of an area and encouraging grant uptake.

Although initially little guidance was given to local authorities over the designation of GIAs, it was soon realised that this policy would be inappropriate in areas where poor physical conditions were compounded by a range of social problems. These include low incomes, unemployment, overcrowding, multiple occupation, crime, large proportions of one-parent families, concentrations of ethnic minorities, much rented accommodation and associated problems of eviction and harassment. To cope with housing problems in such areas, local authorities were empowered to declare Housing Action Areas (HAAs). Within such areas, high rates of improvement grant are payable to enable owners to improve their properties. Although as in the GIAs, the emphasis is upon voluntary improvement by persuasion and cooperation, local authorities have enhanced powers to force landlords to improve their properties or else purchase properties on a compulsory basis if no improvements are made. The primary emphasis in such areas is upon household rather than environmental improvements, and it is intended that declaration of a HAA should lead to a rapid improvement in the quality of dwellings within five years. 'Priority neighbourhoods' can be declared in districts adjacent to HAAs to prevent the 'rippling out' of problems from the HAA. Such areas are to receive more intensive treatment when further resources are available to declare other HAAs. Although substantially different in detail, both GIAs and HAAs may be seen as part of a general thrust towards improvement in the 1970s and are treated together in this essay under the general term of 'improvement areas'.

Over the years, both forms of area-based improvement have been subject to a barrage of criticism. In essence, these criticisms have been twofold. It has been claimed first that the areas have been relatively unsuccessful in so far as their rate of grant uptake has frequently been limited, and second that the areas have been too small to have had a significant impact upon the overall housing problems of British cities. After a brief outline of Southampton's housing problems and improvement strategies, each of these major issues is considered in turn.

SOUTHAMPTON'S HOUSING PROBLEMS IN CONTEXT

As a free-standing medium-sized city in the south of England, Southampton's housing problems are less serious than those in many other parts of the country. This assertion is easily demonstrated with a few statistics selected from the 1971 Census (roughly the beginning of the period of interest to this study)(Table 7.1). Southampton is broadly similar in overall population size to nearby Portsmouth, the other major urban centre within Hampshire. Both cities have similar

Table 7.1

A comparison of indices of housing disadvantage in selected cities.

| | HOUSEHOLDS | | | | | |
	With shared use of hot-water supply	With shared use of fixed bath or shower	Without hot-water supply	Without fixed bath or shower	With exclusive use of outside flush toilet	Without exclusive use of all amenities
	No. (%)	No. (%)	No. (%)	No. (%)	No. (%)	No. (%)
Southampton	1,995 (2.8)	3,610 (5.0)	5,390 (7.5)	3,805 (5.3)	5,600 (7.8)	12,315 (17.1)
Portsmouth	2,145 (3.1)	3,975 (5.8)	6,175 (9.1)	5,390 (7.9)	10,555 (15.5)	17,420 (25.6)
Birmingham	11,230 (3.4)	15,415 (4.6)	26,125 (7.8)	27,640 (8.3)	49,925 (14.9)	73,145 (21.9)
Liverpool	6,180 (3.2)	9,080 (4.7)	23,135 (11.9)	33,095 (17.0)	43,055 (22.1)	57,075 (29.3)
England and Wales	336,940 (2.0)	561,460 (3.4)	1,055,015 (6.4)	1,442,810 (8.7)	1,691,580 (10.2)	2,956,130 (17.9)

Source: 1971 Census.

numbers and proportions of households sharing standard amenities, but
Portsmouth has larger numbers and proportions of households with more
serious indices of housing deficiency. Thus, more households in
Portsmouth have no hot-water supply, no fixed bath or shower or have to
use an outside toilet. Overall, therefore, Southampton has a smaller
proportion of households without exclusive use of all amenities.
However, Table 7.1 shows that the housing problems of both Southampton
and Portsmouth are significantly less, both in relative and absolute
terms, than the major cities of Birmingham and Liverpool. Indeed, with
a few minor exceptions, Southampton's housing conditions are in
relative terms remarkably close to the national average.

The character of Southampton's housing problem is also arguably
different from that of northern industrial areas. There is not the
same degree of physical deterioration of the housing stock or the same
extent of blight from industrial dereliction. Although there is a wide
range of social and economic problems, there is not the same history of
chronic unemployment and urban deprivation that characterises other
parts of the country. Nevertheless, housing problems inevitably exist
and, as in most English cities, the bulk of these problems lie in the
older inner-city areas built largely before 1914. These dwellings
extend in a broad band around the medieval core of the city and along
the lower-lying areas of the rivers Itchen and Test. The worst
dwellings built in the nineteenth century were removed after the Second
World War in a vigorous slum-clearance programme, in which some 4500
dwellings were cleared and over 23,000 new dwellings constructed.
However, the reduction of the local authority waiting lists and the
removal of the worst housing served to emphasise the disparity between
the newly-constructed, low-density peripheral housing estates with
their modern amenities and the high-density inner areas with their poor
conditions.

These inner-city dwellings are typically of a two-storey construction,
with an outside toilet on the ground floor. The houses are often of
sound construction but, due to a combination of age and lack of
maintenance, they frequently reveal a wide range of defects. Amongst
the most common deficiencies are slate roofs in poor condition,
structural movement of certain walls, rising damp, inadequate
plasterwork, decayed window frames and inadequate electrical
installations (Southampton City Council, 1980a). These problems are
often compounded by a range of environmental deficiencies, such as
heavy traffic, inadequate parking facilities, a lack of open space and
local amenities, and the infiltration of un-neighbourly business and
commercial activities. Certain areas have suffered from years of
planning blight, especially that associated with uncertainty over the
construction of major roadworks through the city. Had the policy of
clearance and redevelopment continued at the level of the 1960s, then
many of these areas would have fallen to the local authority bulldozer,
and lack of maintenance of many houses has undoubtedly stemmed
from an expectation of slum clearance.

Roberts (1978) points out that one of the most remarkable features of
GIA policy is the enormous discretion it gives to local authorities over
the choice of areas and the means of implementing the policy. In the
absence of conventional guidelines from central government, local
authorities have varied considerably in their approach. Some have

declared a large number of improvement areas, while others seem to be reluctant to use the policy. Some authorities have pushed improvement policies with considerable vigour, making a wide range of environmental improvements, while others appear to have relied upon the mere act of declaration as the basis for the policy.

In Southampton the approach can be described as having been restricted and cautious, for only four improvement areas have been declared in ten years (Fig.7.1). The first GIA was declared in Freemantle in May 1970 and terminated in 1980. This was one of the first GIAs in the country and regarded locally as a pilot scheme in which experience could be gained to aid the implementation of the policy in other parts of the city. It was a relatively large GIA consisting, at the time of declaration, of 517 dwellings. Of 473 dwellings initially inspected, more than three-quarters lacked one or more of the standard amenities or were in need of repair (Southampton City Council, 1967). Nevertheless, the majority of houses were in a structurally-sound condition and were regarded as having considerable potential for improvement. The second GIA was declared in the St Denys area in 1974 and is assumed to finish in 1982. This area lies nearly 3km north of the city centre, on the west bank of the river Itchen. Once again, with over 500 dwellings, this is a relatively large GIA and in many respects is similar to Freemantle.

The first HAA was declared in the Derby Road area of the city in 1976 (Fig.7.1). The normal five-year life of this HAA has been extended with Department of the Environment (DoE) approval, and it is hoped that area status can be terminated between 1981 and 1983. In contrast to the stable working-class areas of Freemantle and St Denys, Derby Road displays many 'classic' symptoms of areas usually termed 'transition zones'. Compared with Southampton as a whole, there is an above-average proportion of privately-rented accommodation and thus an above-average proportion of single-person households with a high population turnover. There is also an above-average rate of unemployment in the area. In 1974 a total of 6.6 per cent of the Derby Road area were referred to the social services and the area accounted for 17 per cent of all the problems dealt with by the Southampton Housing Aid Centre. The area has also gained considerable notoriety in recent years, being the location of a highly-visible prostitution zone. This activity has caused conflict with many local residents who see this as exerting a stigma on the area, lowering house values and putting the district in an unfavourable position with building societies.

Local authorities are given firmer guidance by central government over which areas would be suitable for HAA status than was initially the case with GIAs. Nevertheless, there is again room for local discretion, and the work of Monck and Lomas (1980) has indicated that a wide range of types of area have been declared as HAAs. This serves to emphasise the dangers of conceptualising areas, such as Derby Road, in a stereotyped manner. Derby Road emerges from the Monck and Lomas analysis amongst a cluster of HAAs characterised by an above-average proportion of both immigrants and large families, but a low incidence of overcrowding. Most areas of this type are in the large conurbations such as London and Birmingham; indeed, Derby Road is the only HAA in this cluster not in a metropolitan district. Compared with HAAs in other clusters of the Monck and Lomas analysis, such areas have a

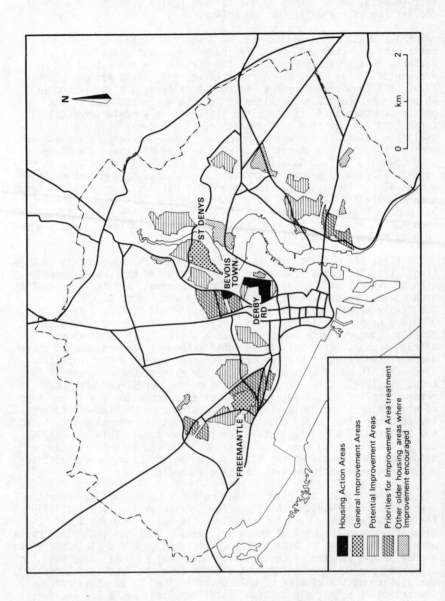

Figure 7.1 Housing improvement areas in Southampton.

152

below-average proportion of privately-rented accommodation and an above-average proportion of owner-occupied properties. They are also typified by below-average proportions of single-person households, one-parent families and multiple occupancy.

Finally, the Bevois Town HAA was declared in May, 1978 (Fig.7.1). This area lies approximately 2km north of the city centre and consisted of 173 dwellings at the time of declaration. Compared with Derby Road, this is an extremely small HAA and, as will be shown below, in many respects it more closely resembles the two GIAs. Nevertheless, it was given HAA status to help cope with the poor condition of many of the dwellings in the area. Indeed, in January, 1977 a report was submitted to the city council which recommended clearance of the area, but this policy was later altered (Southampton City Council, 1978).

AREA-BASED IMPROVEMENT AND GRANT TAKE-UP

Debates about the aims of area-based improvement policies have seldom been explicit. A range of vague and possibly conflicting social objectives are often mentioned, but the most obvious immediate goal is the physical improvement of the housing stock. A crucial test for an improvement area, therefore, is the extent to which owners come forward and take up grants to make improvements of sufficient standard to ensure a future dwelling life of thirty years in a GIA and of at least fifteen years in a HAA. The most frequent criticism of area-based improvement policies is that physical improvement has been limited because of a low rate of grant uptake.

The Southampton record is extremely varied. Freemantle, the first GIA, has in many respects been successful. By 20th October 1980, when GIA status was terminated, the number of dwellings constructed prior to declaration now in a good state of repair totalled 448 out of the original total of 513 (Southampton City Council, 1980b). This reflects some 129 dwellings improved with grant aid since 1970. To put these results in perspective, however, it should be recognised that this reflects ten years' effort, working out at an average of only one improvement grant per month. Furthermore, over 70 dwellings had already been improved with grant aid in the area prior to declaration and, given the general increase in improvement grant activity in the early 1970s, one might wonder if the designation of GIA status has had any major impact in this context. Indeed, a large amount of the overall improvement in the area has resulted from owners making improvements with their own financial resources and without recourse to local authority assistance. In effect, it took a number of years before sufficient confidence could be created in the area for significant numbers of owners to come forward and take up grants (Southampton City Council, 1980b). The initial moves were made by small local builders, who improved properties for sale on a speculative basis. Nevertheless, such 'lumpiness' in grant applications seems to be a feature common to many improvement areas (Monck and Lomas, 1980), and the rate of grant take-up in Freemantle compares favourably with that recorded in other GIAs. Roberts (1978), for example, recorded an average rate of only one improvement grant every four to five months in his sample of GIAs. Furthermore, there now appears to be a high level of confidence expressed in the area by planners, local residents and building societies.

In St Denys, the second GIA, there were at the time of declaration in July 1974 375 dwellings (roughly 70 per cent of the initial total of 524) lacking one or more of the basic amenities or in need of substantial repair. This figure has now been reduced to 30 per cent, but this represents only 48 improvement grants completed in the private sector by July 1980 (with approval given for another 17)(Southampton City Council, 1980c). Over a six-year period, this rate of grant uptake compares somewhat unfavourably with Freemantle. Indeed, it is improvements made by owners themselves, without grant aid, which have formed the lion's share of developments, as represented by an estimated 163 dwellings. Although the overall rate of improvement in St Denys is not as poor as that in some unsuccessful GIAs in other parts of the country, there appears in some quarters to be a general feeling of disappointment with the progress made in the area. Furthermore, since Freemantle was a pilot scheme designed to gain experience, it might have been thought that from the lessons learnt the rate of improvement would be greater in this second GIA.

According to DoE Circular 14/75, HAAs are supposed "to secure a significant improvement in the living conditions in the area and to do so within about five years". Preferential rates of house-renovation grants, together with strengthened coercive powers, are intended to compensate for the additional social and housing stresses experienced in such areas. In this respect progress in the Derby Road HAA in Southampton has hardly been dramatic, but it has attained moderate success avoiding the near disastrous performance of some HAAs in inner-city environments. At the time of declaration in February 1976 there were no less than 510 dwellings out of a total of 765 in the area either lacking standard amenities and or in need of repair (Southampton City Council, 1980b). At the end of five years, only 50 full improvement grants had been completed in the private sector, but approval had been given for a further 57. To this must be added the 77 properties acquired and improved by the city council, together with 81 other types of intermediate, repair and frontage grant. Once again, however, it is the number of dwellings improved or partly improved without grant-aid which, at an estimated 185 dwellings, provides the largest overall contribution to improvement.

It is as yet too early to make firm conclusions about the success of the second Bevois Town HAA. Although consisting of only 173 dwellings, progress in the first year was officially described as "disappointing", with only 12 applications approved and work completed on only three dwellings (Southampton City Council, 1979). However, slow progress in the period immediately after declaration has been a feature of all the improvement areas in Southampton. Furthermore, after two years, there are signs of an increase in the rate of grant uptake, with 22 applications made and work completed on nine dwellings. The city council has purchased 32 properties in the area and completed renovation work on 17, with work planned for a further nine (Southampton City Council, 1980c). While in overall terms this is limited compared with other areas and given the poor condition of the housing, what is remarkable and requires explanation is the fact that so many residents have sufficient confidence to make the substantial investment needed to undertake renovation.

Judged by the rate of grant take-up, area-based improvement policies in Southampton have had varying degrees of success. Thus the relatively good progress made in the Freemantle GIA contrasts with the smaller amount of improvement made in St Denys GIA. The moderate rate of progress made in the Derby Road HAA contrasts with the so far limited rate of grant take-up in the Bevois Town HAA. A multitude of factors have been suggested to account for such variations in the success of area-based improvement policies. In essence, these factors point to the inadequacy of the legislative framework in relation to the three sets of agents who are responsible for such schemes. First, there are the local residents, who are supposed to volunteer for grants for improvement; then there are the local authorities, who are supposed to instil confidence in the areas, and finally, there are the various private-sector agencies (building societies, banks, builders, etc.), who are responsible for ensuring a buoyant private market in housing. As will be shown later, the behaviour of these three sets of agencies is closely related.

AREA-BASED IMPROVEMENT AND LOCAL RESIDENTS

The most basic criticism of area-based improvement policies is that the approach is beyond the limited incomes of the majority of inhabitants of such areas. Even with contributions of grant of up to 60 per cent in GIAs and 90 per cent in HAAs, it is argued that the low income of many inner-city inhabitants prevents them from incurring the substantial costs of improvement (Kirwan and Martin, 1972). As might be expected, given their housing conditions, GIAs and HAAs tend to have above-average proportions of persons in low-paid, semi-skilled and unskilled manual occupations and below-average proportions of higher-paid professional and managerial groups. Table 7.2 confirms that this is certainly the case in Southampton (the figures for occupational groupings are derived from those enumeration districts in the 1971 Census which are most closely aligned with the improvement areas). However, there is little difference in the social-class structure of the two GIAs (and by inference their income levels) which would suggest why the areas should have differing rates of grant uptake. Freemantle has a higher proportion of professional and managerial workers, but smaller numbers of the intermediate occupations and a higher proportion of semi- and unskilled category. The statistics for the two HAAs reveal a more diverse social structure than the GIAs, with higher proportions of professional and managerial occupations. Again however, there is insufficient difference in the occupational structure of the two areas which might account for the greater success rate of Derby Road. Indeed, Bevois Town has higher proportions of the intermediate occupational category who might have been expected to take advantage of improvement grants.

However, these data do not mean that income can be discounted in explaining variations in grant take-up in the areas concerned. One of the most notable features of both GIA and HAA policy has been the way in which the rapid inflation of building costs in the late 1970s and the time lag between this and increases in the ceilings payable on improvement grants have served to reduce the improvement grants proportion of total costs and served to increase the owner's contribution to improvement. This time-lag effect has been observed in national

Table 7.2

Occupational structure of improvement areas in Southampton.
(% of total occupied)

	Professional and managerial	Intermediate non-manual	Skilled manual	Semi- and un-skilled manual
Freemantle GIA	5.0	8.4	37.8	48.7
St Denys GIA	0.8 (9.7)	13.7 (19.7)	55.0 (35.7)	30.5 (31.9)
Derby Road HAA	9.0	8.5	36.5	46.0
Bevois Town HAA	9.6	15.4	48.1	32.7
Southampton	18.2	18.8	40.0	23.5
Great Britain	17.3	17.5	38.3	23.0

Source: 1971 Census. Figures in parentheses refer to later local
          authority surveys prior to declaration.

data, the rapid general increase in the uptake of improvement grants
after the 1969 Act being followed by a general decline after 1974. In
the case of St Denys, the GIA declaration corresponded with the
national fall in improvement grants and this must have had the initial
effect of inhibiting improvement. The value of grants in HAAs has also
been affected by inflated building costs. Indeed, progress reports for
the Derby Road HAA refer to considerable fluctuations in the uptake of
grants depending upon the eligible expense limits (Southampton City
Council, 1980d).

The influence of income is also suggested by the fact that, while the
rate of grant take-up varies considerably between the improvement
areas, there is in all areas, with the exception of the recent Bevois
Town HAA, a large proportion of improvement made by owners without
recourse to local authority funds. This would support the assertion
that the full 10 point standard of renovation embodied in the
improvement grants is beyond the means of many residents. Interviews
with residents indicate in some cases a preference for improvement in a
series of smaller incremental steps, while some owners claim to be
deterred from taking up improvement grants by restrictions upon the
sale of property within five years (Witt, 1981).

Another characteristic of improvement areas, which is closely related
to low income and which has also been suggested to account for the low
rate of grant uptake, is the age of the residents. The argument
states that elderly persons in improvement areas lack either the
financial resources or the personal incentive to embark upon the
considerable upheaval involved in modernisation. For example, the
cost of redecoration is not covered by grants and the elderly in
particular are less likely to be able to do their own redecoration
after improvement (Monck and Lomas, 1980). Roberts (1978) has argued

Table 7.3

Age-structure of improvement areas in Southampton.
(% of total population)

	AGE RANGES (Years)							
	0-9	10-19	20-29	30-39	40-49	50-59	60-69	70+
Freemantle GIA	13.0	12.3	15.4	10.0	12.8	12.1	12.1	12.5
St Denys GIA	14.6	13.6	14.5	10.2	10.5	14.7	13.4	8.3
Derby Road HAA	22.9	17.3	14.4	12.3	11.1	9.4	7.9	4.9
Bevois Town HAA	14.8	12.8	9.9	10.8	9.1	13.0	15.9	9.7

Source: 1971 Census.

that it is the middle-age groups, without the financial burdens of
child-rearing or the short-term commitment to the area of some younger
age groups, who are most likely to take up grants, but who are
frequently under-represented in GIAs.

However, the age structure of the four improvement areas in
Southampton shown in Table 7.3 reveals little difference between the two
GIAs. Indeed, the rather more successful Freemantle had a larger
proportion of the very old age groups than St Denys in 1971.
Nevertheless, progress reports for both GIAs leave little doubt that
amongst those households that have not made improvements, the elderly
constitute a significant proportion. The Derby Road HAA deviates from
the classic inner-city picture by having a relatively small proportion
of its overall population in the older age groups. By far the largest
proportions are to be found in the younger age groups, reflecting to a
large degree the immigrant presence in the area. The Bevois Town HAA,
in contrast, has an age structure which accords closely with the two
GIAs. There are particularly large proportions in the 50-59 and 60-69
age groups in 1971, many of whom would have been elderly at the time of
HAA declaration. Bevois Town is clearly an 'old age' HAA and this is
likely to have initially inhibited the rate of improvement in contrast
with Derby Road. The local authority has thus undertaken an active
campaign to rehouse those elderly persons in Bevois Town who wanted to
move out of the area and not participate in the development of the HAA.

A third factor suggested to explain variations in grant take-up in
improvement areas relates to the tenure of the dwellings. The
properties most in need of renovation are frequently in the privately-
rented sector, but improvement policies have often failed to induce
landlords to upgrade their properties. Despite the financial incentives
embodied within the legislation, many landlords have neither the
personal capital nor the inclination to improve their properties
(Roberts, 1978). Limited support for the influence of tenure conditions
upon rates of grant take-up in Southampton may be derived from Table

Table 7.4

Tenure characteristics of improvement areas in Southampton.
(% of households)

	Owner-occupied	Council	Rented unfurnished	Rented furnished	Total privately-rented
Freemantle GIA	60.3	10.9	27.8	3.3	30.1
St Denys GIA	55.7	11.5	25.8	5.6	35.4
Derby Road HAA	53.0	10.9	22.1	18.5	40.6
Bevois Town HAA	37.5 (50)	8.8 (10)	42.9 (37)	8.8 (3)	51.7 (40)
Southampton	45.9	31.7	16.2	6.1	22.3

Source: 1971 Census. Figures in parentheses relate to later local
authority surveys prior to declaration.

7.4. Compared with the Freemantle GIA, St Denys has a larger
proportion of privately-rented accommodation and a smaller proportion of
owner occupation. As might be expected, both the HAAs have larger
proportions of privately-rented accommodation, but the figure is
particularly large in the Bevois Town HAA.

The condition of the dwellings may also have an effect upon grant take-
up in improvement areas. It is argued that the greater the extent of
housing problems, the greater will be the costs of improvement as a
proportion of the total capital cost of the dwelling, and the less will
be the incentive for the owner to improve his property. In this context,
there is a frequent 'valuation gap', whereby the value of the
unimproved house and the cost of improvement (minus the grant-aided
element) exceed the value of the improved property. Evidence for the
effect of housing conditions upon improvement grant performance may be
derived from Table 7.5, which shows selected indices of amenity
deficiency in Southampton. Amongst the GIAs, housing is in a poorer
condition in the less successful St Denys area. Amongst the HAAs, Derby
Road has the greater incidence of overcrowding, but on all the indices
of amenity deficiency the housing is in a worse condition in the Bevois
Town HAA. This has meant that the costs of renovation have been
considerable in Bevois Town, approaching and even exceeding the cost of
new dwellings. However, continued rapid inflation in the housing market
has meant that the market value of improved dwellings is exceeding the
costs of acquisition and renovation by the local authority.

These factors of income, age, tenure and housing quality are
frequently inter-related. For example, the social survey undertaken in
the Bevois Town area indicated that 54 per cent of the dwellings
lacking one or more of the basic amenities were in the privately-rented
sector, and of these two-thirds were tenanted by pensioners, usually
with extremely low incomes (Southampton City Council, 1978). In half of
the remaining owner-occupied dwellings lacking one or more of the basic

Table 7.5

Housing conditions in Southampton's improvement areas.
(% of households)

	Without exclusive use of all amenities	Sharing or lacking hot-water supply	Sharing or lacking a bath	With no inside WC	With over 1.5 persons per room
Freemantle GIA	34.3	20.2	20.9	24.9	1.4
St Denys GIA	42.9	28.0	28.6	31.0	0.9
Derby Road HAA	50.6	31.3	31.3	23.0	7.0
Bevois Town HAA	53.3	31.7	36.4	39.8	1.6

Source: 1971 Census.

amenities, the head of household was over 60 years of age.

AREA-BASED IMPROVEMENTS AND THE LOCAL AUTHORITY

The second set of hypotheses used to account for variations in the success of improvement policies points to the activities of local authorities. The legislative framework surrounding area-based renovation gives considerable discretion to local authorities in the implementation of policy and puts much of the onus upon the local authority to make the policy work. Without sufficient local authority commitment to improvement, neither the confidence of the local residents nor the desired level of voluntary improvement will be attained. Environmental improvements are thus seen as crucial to the success of GIAs in order to remove blight. Paradoxically, therefore, one criticism of area-based improvement policies is that these environmental works have been given too much attention. They are the only major visible features separating GIAs from surrounding tracts of housing, and Roberts (1978) argues that planners, architects and engineers have often been preoccupied by these features rather than the more important task of encouraging grant take-up. The alternative and more frequent criticism is that local authorities have not done enough in the way of environmental improvements. In some cases, it appears authorities have made improvements only after a significant response has been shown by residents, that is in the form of grant applications made following declaration of GIA status.

It would seem difficult to apply the former charge in the Southampton context. Certainly, a wide range of typical environmental improvements has been made. In Freemantle these include the construction of a play area, lock-up garages, a church and flats for the elderly, while in St Denys the environmental improvements include a community centre (with

159

Urban Aid support), a substantial block of new dwellings, landscaping of the riverbank and (unique in GIAs) the renovation of a houseboat site. Nevertheless, neither GIA begins to approach the 'showpiece' character of certain areas in other parts of the country. Indeed, it is difficult in certain parts to perceive that one is actually in a GIA. St Denys in particular has in places an untidy and unkempt appearance, with poor roads and areas of waste land. There would also seem to be a substantial feeling of dissatisfaction among some residents with the amount of progress made in the area by the local authority (St Denys Residents' Association, 1978).

The history of participation and improvement in Southampton is complex, but some general features can be distinguished in both GIAs. First, there were undoubtedly substantial delays between the declaration of area status and the completion of environmental works. To a large extent, these reflect the elaborate participation exercises and a desire to ascertain the wishes of local inhabitants. Nevertheless, these activities cannot justify the many years which elapsed before many of the relatively simple landscaping improvements were undertaken. It cannot, therefore, be mere coincidence that this inertia corresponded with the initially slow response rate to grant take-up in both areas. The crucial lesson is that without fairly rapid and substantial visible evidence of environmental improvement following area declaration, years of suspicion over local authority intentions will not be overcome. In this context, it is encouraging to note that in the latest Bevois Town HAA the local authority has moved swiftly to purchase the worst properties in need of repair in order to eliminate blight and instil confidence in the area. Another lesson to emerge from Southampton in this context is that it is not only the appearance of the GIA itself but also of neighbouring areas which is crucial for public confidence. A clearance site adjacent to the Freemantle GIA had for many years had a deleterious effect upon the scheme, leading many residents to question whether it was actually an improvement area. Coupled with this is the need for adequate maintenance of environmental improvements. Criticism of the local authority's neglect of landscaping schemes has been made in St Denys and clearly environmental improvement is not a 'once-and-for-all' affair.

A second feature to emerge from developments in Southampton is that the improvements most eagerly sought by residents in both GIAs (the removal of local 'non-conforming' businesses and the prevention of heavy through traffic) were the fields in which the local authority was often least able to take effective action. In Freemantle, for example, many un-neighbourly uses have been removed, including a scrap-metal yard and car-repair works, but some larger activities, including a laundry and engineering works, have not been relocated, primarily because of the costs involved and the difficulties of finding land elsewhere in the city. However, it is in the less successful St Denys GIA that the problems of undertaking improvements have been most severe. Indeed, in this context there is evidence of considerable disagreement between the views of the local residents' association and those of local planners, with the views of residents somewhere in between (St Denys Residents' Association, 1978; Witt, 1981). The local residents' association feel that the local authority has 'betrayed' the area by not fulfilling the initial expectations raised by the declaration of the GIA. A limited number of un-neighbourly uses have been removed, but in other cases the local authority has had to resort to cosmetic treatment through frontage grants. There is evidence that the local residents as a whole feel less strongly than the St Denys Residents' Association about these business activities, but both groups seem united in their hostility to what is seen as the failure of the city council to curb the problems of heavy traffic (Witt, 1981). There is also considerable opposition to the untidiness of the area and condemnation of the local authority for failing to resurface roads and improve pavements. The lack of funds to implement garage and rear-access schemes, the poor maintenance of areas of open space and the limited impact of frontage grants are also sources of discontent.

Many owner-occupiers feel that the local authority has made relatively little impact upon the improvement of tenanted properties in the area. Following central government advice, which encouraged the use of housing associations to aid the policy of improvement, Southampton encouraged the Hythe and South Bank Association to help in the city. However, the impact of the Association in St Denys and the other areas has been negligible. The major problem appears to have been the difficulties experienced by the Association in working within the cost constraints imposed by the Housing Corporation.

Taken as a whole, it seems clear that Southampton has not pursued the policy of environmental improvements with the vigour of certain authorities elsewhere. However, it is important to see these developments in the overall context of the constraints of finance imposed upon GIAs. The limited environmental budget makes it impossible to deal comprehensively with problems, such as widespread intrusive industries, which have caused years of blight in an area like St Denys. In this context, it is also important to note that the physical layout of a GIA can place important constraints on the overall success of the policy. Whereas in Southampton, there is a shortage of building land and/or the area is badly blighted by intrusive activities, the difficulties of making significant improvements within cost constraints are greatly magnified. Similarly, compulsory-purchase powers designed to force landlords to improve their properties or to remove non-conforming users are widely regarded as limited and cumbersome. Even relatively simple rear-access schemes can be obstructed by one individual who objects. It is, therefore, difficult to escape the conclusion that when GIAs are blighted by processes operative over many years, environmental improvements are little more than cosmetic.

AREA-BASED IMPROVEMENT AND MARKET INSTITUTIONS

The third set of hypotheses used to explain the success or failure of improvement policies refers to the activities of various private-sector institutions. Despite substantial state intervention, improvement policies are critically dependent upon local builders to undertake the renovation and building societies to provide mortgages for improved dwellings. As part of the 'hidden hand', it has proven much more difficult to investigate the influence of these agencies in the same systematic manner as local authorities.

Working speculatively, local builders in Freemantle were amongst the

161

first to take advantage of the possibilities created by the area. However, there is little evidence to suggest that the availability of building capacity has affected the relative success of improvement areas in Southampton. This is much more likely to be a factor which can explain the differences in the uptake of improvement grants between, rather than within, local authorities. A local survey in Southampton indicated that improvement work was undertaken by many small firms (the local authority having a list of 41 firms approved for this type of work)(St Denys Residents' Association, 1979). This survey suggested that there was a greater demand for improvement work than could be met by the availability of builders, the restraints including shortages of skilled labour, the inherent difficulty of improvement work, problems of meeting standards within cost constraints and difficulties in getting payment for work from the local authority. These difficulties have been replicated nationally, but it is possible that if there had been the scale of improvement in Southampton initially anticipated in improvement legislation, there would have been severe shortages of building capacity to meet the demand.

Building societies have frequently been accused of discriminating against improved properties by their reluctance to grant mortgages for such properties. Accusations of 'redlining', the deliberate with-holding of grants from inner-city areas, are often difficult to substantiate, but in market terms it is clearly prudent to invest in newer properties in suburban areas where there is less risk. Although public statements may differ from actions, research into the attitudes of building-society managers in Southampton reveals a wide range of attitudes concerning the status of inner-city areas (Easterbrook, 1981). In some cases, however, these attitudes amount to suspicion and hostility, especially regarding the intentions of the local authority. Significantly, some managers claim to have no overall policy, but rely upon the advice of their surveyors. Apparently, the main preoccupation of the managers, and the chief criterion by which they will be judged, is not lending policy, but their ability to attract investment. Five societies in the city participate in the Building Societies Support Scheme, but a recent document by the local authority describes the performance of building societies in older areas of the city as "disappointing" (Southampton City Council, 1980a). Certainly, many residents in areas such as Derby Road feel that the building societies discriminate against them. Nevertheless, it is not possible to isolate the building societies per se as being directly responsible for the success of one improvement area over another in Southampton. Rather they are part of the general process of under-investment in housing in certain inner-city areas when compared with rapidly-growing commuter belts.

AREA-BASED IMPROVEMENT AND STRATEGIC HOUSING NEEDS

The second major type of criticism of area-based improvement relates not to the internal functioning of the policy, but to its relationship with the overall housing need. It is argued that improvement areas have been too small to cope with the extent of housing problems found in English cities. This charge is easily translated to the Southampton context. The four improvement areas in Southampton at the time of their declaration represented a total of 1984 dwellings (most, though by no

Table 7.6

Southampton's enumeration districts classified by percentage of households without exclusive use of all standard amenities.

| | NUMBER OF EDs | | | | | | | | | |
	0-9.9%	10-19.9%	20-29.9%	30-39.9%	40-49.9%	50-59.9%	60-69.9%	70-79.9%	80-89.9%	90%+
All EDs	55	33	35	38	26	19	11	4	4	0
GIAs	0	0	4	1	1	1	0	0	0	0
HAAs	0	0	0	0	4	4	1	0	0	0

Source: 1971 Census.

means all, of which were in need of improvement). However, this figure must be set against estimates produced in the early 1970s of some 9250 dwellings in the city lacking at least one of the standard amenities and being in need of some form of improvement (Southampton City Council, 1972). Since the 1969 Housing Act, some 3880 improvement grants have been taken up in the city, but the majority of these are the result of voluntary take-up in areas outside the GIAs and HAAs. This reflects the general promotion of improvement grants in the 1970s and testifies to the rather limited impact which area-based policies have had upon housing problems. In this respect, Southampton's approach compares unfavourably with that of Portsmouth, which has already declared 18 GIAs and has a larger number planned to cover an area of 14,000 dwellings.

The above evidence suggests that improvement areas in Southampton, as in other parts of the country, have been too selective to deal with the extent of substandard housing. A sharply contrasting criticism, however, suggests that these areas have lacked selectivity by avoiding the areas of worst housing conditions (Roberts, 1978). This criticism was initially applied to GIAs declared prior to the 1974 Act. For example, Duncan (1974) observed in Huddersfield that GIAs were not declared in the areas of worst housing stress as defined by the absence of standard amenities and by large proportions of immigrants and rented accommodation, but were in areas of better-quality housing which had already showed indications of a willingness to take up grants. This he argued was a manifestation of the 'inverse-care law' and the tendency for planners to concentrate upon areas in which their objectives were most assured.

A similar pattern may be observed in Southampton. Table 7.6 shows the enumeration districts of the city classified according to the percentage of their households without exclusive use of all amenities in 1971. Taking all 229 districts with recorded data into account, there is a progressive decline in numbers as the percentage of households without exclusive use of all amenities increases. If one examines those enumeration districts which are located wholly or substantially within a GIA, it may be seen that they lie in the 20 to 60 per cent range and not in the worst areas in terms of amenity deficiency. As described previously, both Freemantle and St Denys are relatively stable working-class areas with few of the symptoms of social stress displayed by the HAAs. Furthermore, in the case of the Freemantle pilot scheme some 70 improvement grants were taken up prior to declaration, indicating a willingness amongst the inhabitants to invest in the area (Southampton City Council, 1970). The area also displayed a number of other characteristics which Ministry circulars suggested might point to the area being favourable for GIA status, such as proximity to the city centre, access to amenities and essentially sound housing. However, it would be misleading to assume that the area was chosen simply because of a strong expectation of success. As in many other cities, the reasons for the choice of area seem essentially pragmatic in character. Freemantle was one of a number of inner-city areas in the pipeline for clearance in the late 1960s and the efficacy of improvement in this context was doubted by some planners in the initial years.

Returning to Duncan's criticism concerning the apparent avoidance of the areas of greatest housing stress, one might reflect that planners would no doubt have also been criticised if they had concentrated the policy of GIAs on areas where it was not likely to have been successful! Indeed, many planners would appear to have displayed much good sense in realising that the provisions of the 1969 Act would do relatively little to attack the severe problems of housing stress areas.

As might be expected, the HAAs in Southampton are in areas of poorer conditions, being concentrated in areas with larger percentages without exclusive use of all amenities. However, these are by no means the worst areas defined in terms of amenity deficiency. The latter are considered too poor in quality even for short term renovation, but the present decline in clearance policies makes the position of such marginal areas highly problematic in the overall context of renovation policies. Paradoxically, many of these poorest areas have not even had the benefits of the additional incentives for improvement embodied in the GIAs, let alone those associated with HAAs. Even if a policy of 'gradual renewal' is acknowledged, such a policy inevitably blights many dwellings in these areas.

CONCLUSIONS

There are two dominating and seemingly contradictory impressions which emerge from this review of renovation policies in Southampton in the 1970s. The first impression is one of the enormous complexity of developments in each area. Even with only four improvement areas, there are considerable differences between what might otherwise be labelled superficially as 'twilight areas'. The reasons for variations in the success rate of the policy in each of these areas are also enormously complex, such that they cannot be explained by any uni-causal hypothesis which points simply to age, class, tenure or 'degree of public participation' as an explanation. There is in each area a complex interaction of individuals and organisations which takes place within the overall constraints imposed by the legislative framework. It is, of course, impossible to be conclusive about these processes from the aggregate statistical data presented here, but the evidence does suggest a number of clear conclusions. In St Denys a combination of inflation and delays in raising grant ceilings, the limited impact of environmental improvements, an above-average proportion of tenanted properties, the poor condition of many dwellings, the limited impact of a housing association and the poor communication between a local residents' association and the city council, have produced a relatively limited rate of improvement grant uptake. Freemantle also experienced problems with intrusive activities and limited environmental works, but had fewer disadvantages compared with St Denys, and as a consequence the policy has been more successful. In the Bevois Town HAA a combination of particularly bad housing, a high proportion of tenanted properties and a large number of elderly households have so far produced a limited (but apparently increasing) rate of grant take-up. In contrast, despite its many symptoms of 'social stress', the younger and more dynamic community in Derby Road has produced a relatively high success rate compared with many HAAs elsewhere. The below-average proportions of the elderly, privately-rented accommodation and multiple occupancy would also seem to have helped Derby Road.

The second more important impression, however, is one of the remarkable similarity of developments in Southampton compared with other cities. While different combinations of factors affect the development of improvement policies in different areas, these cannot be envisaged as 'unique' or 'local' to those areas. The limited impact of environmental improvements in certain areas, the problems involved in renovating tenanted properties, the difficulties of promoting improvement grants in dwellings occupied by the elderly and the difficulties imposed by delays in raising the grant ceilings are all features which could be replicated in many other parts of the country. The substantial number of dwellings in the city improved by owners using their own financial resources, but at standards different to those demanded by the local authority, also provides additional support for the common observation made elsewhere that the full discretionary grant standards intended for improvement areas are often either above what is considered necessary by the residents and/or above what their limited incomes will support. Improvement grants are intended to promote a further life of thirty years, but whether some of the private work undertaken so far will support this goal must be open to considerable doubt.

The most important feature of renovation policies in Southampton, but one common to other areas, is the limited impact which area-based improvement policies have had upon the overall magnitude of housing problems. This judgement arises, not so much because of the limited take-up of improvement grants in certain areas, but because of the small number of districts which have been subject to the area-based approach. In 1972 a report by the City Planning Officer delineated fifteen areas of the city which were in need of housing and environmental improvement (Southampton City Council, 1972). These comprised 10,600 dwellings, far in excess of the numbers of dwellings incorporated into GIAs and HAAs. A larger number of improvement areas was planned, but never implemented because of limited finance and staff. Instead, a compromise policy was adopted whereby areas were recognised in which "house improvement policy" would apply. In these areas, owners were actively encouraged to take up grants and the general aim was to "protect the residential environment", but without the added inducements and facilities available in GIAs or HAAs. The intention was to achieve a target of between 800 to 900 improvement grants per annum, but after the peak of 540 grants in 1974 the rate of grant take-up in the city has declined to about 350 grants per annum (City of Southampton, 1980a).

The net result is that today many of Southampton's dwellings are deteriorating rapidly and approaching the point where wholesale rehabilitation or redevelopment is necessary. Estimates from house-condition surveys suggest that about 13,500 houses in the city in the private sector are either unfit, lack amenities, or are in need of improvement. On the assumption that as many houses requiring major repairs are being improved without grant aid as are being improved with grants, it is estimated that it will take about twenty years, at the present rate of progress, to deal with the current disrepair to the private-housing stock (Southampton City Council, 1980a). This of course pays no attention to the fact that many dwellings are deteriorating every year into a state of serious disrepair. At present rates of clearance of unfit dwellings, however, it would take about 350 years to replace the city's pre-1914 housing stock.

166

It would be wrong, however, to view the policy of improvement as one of complete failure. The decline of some areas has been halted, and much has been learnt about public participation and the wishes of local residents. Many hours have been spent by local authority staff in an attempt to grapple with complex management problems, sometimes in situations where there is a lack of social concensus amongst inhabitants about future developments. There is evidence of a good deal of satisfaction with the results of improvement in certain areas (Witt, 1981). Many people are strongly attached to the older parts of Southampton and would have been dissatisfied if they had been bulldozed in widespread clearance policies. It is clear that after a slow start, the end result of a decade of improvement policy in Southampton has been better than that suggested by those researchers who elsewhere have examined progress in improvement areas after only a few years. Also on the credit side, there is the fact that the local authority has devoted resources to those areas which have been declared rather than using the mere act of declaration itself as an instrument of policy.

Nevertheless, the progressively deteriorating housing situation in Southampton testifies to the enormous shifts in housing policy noted at the beginning of this essay. The policy of renovation rather than demolition has in the 1970s commanded a great deal of support (including from both major political parties), but has been associated with an enormous decline in housing investment. Consequently, a massive injection of resources into both the private and public sectors is necessary to make up the lost ground. In Southampton, this would involve rehabilitating or redeveloping at least 1500 properties per year to deal with those properties currently in need, plus those likely to deteriorate in the next ten years (Southampton City Council, 1980a). It would also involve a more rigorous use by the local authority of powers to induce compulsory improvement, a re-instatement of a selective slum-clearance programme and a larger area-based improvement programme. However, by itself a policy of simply declaring more GIAs and HAAs is likely to be ineffective. The experience of the 1970s makes it clear that, without substantial modifications, the area-based approach will be unable to cope with the problems of the poorest properties most in need of improvement. In particular, effective powers are necessary to enforce improvements in the privately-rented sector. It should also be noted that an estimated 47 per cent of the properties in the city in need of improvement are dispersed or in areas where the area-based approach is deemed inapplicable. Finally, at the root of many of the 'housing' problems is the lack of income status and of power commanded by the inhabitants of inner-city areas. Solving these particular problems would involve actions in social and economic spheres usually regarded as being outside the realms of housing.

A recent local policy document notes that in the current economic climate, with a reduced Housing Investment Programme allocation, there are insufficient resources to instigate a comprehensive programme of action to deal with Southampton's housing problems (Southampton·City Council, 1980a). Even trying to contain the problem, so that by 1984 the city council would be dealing with 700 dwellings per year would, at present-day prices, cost £3 million (almost double the current level of expenditure at £1.6 million). With increased pressures from central government for financial stringency in local authorities, with declining living standards, growing unemployment and increasing numbers of elderly households on low incomes, the current prospects for a substantial improvement in housing conditions in Southampton in the 1980s look decidedly bleak.

REFERENCES

BASSETT, K and SHORT, J (1978), Housing improvement in the inner city: a case study of changes before and after the 1974 Housing Act, Urban Studies, 15, 333-342.

EASTERBROOK, R P (1981), Mortgage Lending in the City: a Pilot Study, Unpublished BA Dissertation, Department of Geography, University of Southampton.

DUNCAN, S S (1974), Cosmetic planning or social engineering? Improvement grants and improvement areas in Huddersfield, Area, 6, 259-271.

DUNCAN, T L C (1971), House Improvement Policies in England and Wales (Birmingham, Centre for Urban and Regional Studies).

DUNLEAVY, P (1980), Urban Political Analysis (London, Macmillan).

KIRBY, A (1977), Housing action areas in Great Britain, 1975-77, University of Reading, Department of Geography, Geographical Papers, 60.

KIRWAN, R and MARTIN, D B (1972), The Economics of Urban Residential Renewal (London, Centre for Environmental Studies).

McKAY, D H and COX, A W (1979), The Politics of Urban Change (London, Croom Helm).

MONCK, E and LOMAS, G (1980), Housing Action Areas: Success and Failure (London, Centre for Environmental Studies).

PARIS, C and BLACKABY, B (1979), Not Much Improvement: Urban Renewal Policy in Birmingham (London, Heinemann).

PEPPER, S (1971), House Improvement Goals and Strategy (London, Lund Humphreys).

ROBERTS, J R (1978), General Improvement Areas (Farnborough, Saxon House).

SIGSWORTH, E M and WILKINSON, R K (1973), Constraints on the uptake of improvement grants, Policy and Politics, 1, 131-141.

SOUTHAMPTON CITY COUNCIL (1967), Report on a Scheme for Area Improvement at Freemantle (Southampton, Housing Committee).

SOUTHAMPTON CITY COUNCIL (1970), Proposed Freemantle No.1 General Improvement Area (Southampton, Housing Committee).

SOUTHAMPTON CITY COUNCIL (1972), Area Improvement Policy Report (Southampton, Housing Committee).

SOUTHAMPTON CITY COUNCIL (1978), Bevois Town Housing Action Area Declaration Report (Southampton, Housing Committee).

SOUTHAMPTON CITY COUNCIL (1979), Bevois Town HAA Annual Report (Southampton, Housing Committee).

SOUTHAMPTON CITY COUNCIL (1980a), Housing Renewal (Southampton, Housing Committee).

SOUTHAMPTON CITY COUNCIL (1980b), Freemantle GIA Annual Report (Southampton, Housing Committee).

SOUTHAMPTON CITY COUNCIL (1980c), St Denys GIA Annual Report (Southampton, Housing Committee).

SOUTHAMPTON CITY COUNCIL (1980d), Derby Road HAA Annual Report (Southampton, Housing Committee).

SOUTHAMPTON CITY COUNCIL (1980e), Bevois Town HAA Annual Report (Southampton, Housing Committee).

ST DENYS RESIDENTS' ASSOCIATION (1978), St Denys General Improvement Area Report (mimeo).

ST DENYS RESIDENTS' ASSOCIATION (1979), Builders and House Improvement in Southampton (mimeo).

WITT, S (1981), Perceptions of the St Denys General Improvement Area by residents, planners and residents' association, Wessex Geographer, 16, 19-26.

8 The Impact of Residential Growth on the Rural Hinterland

B J WOODRUFFE

This essay sets out to examine the distribution and temporal pattern of
new residential development in the areas surrounding the urban centres
of the Southampton region over the last two decades. It attempts to
place such changes within a theoretical framework of city-region
development and to relate them to some of the planning policies which
have operated in the region during this time. In so doing, a
perspective is gained of the differential nature of residential growth
and of the factors influencing and controlling it. The pattern of
change is summarised in the form of a descriptive model which would
appear to be applicable to other metropolitan areas.

In recent years there has been no shortage of research on expanding
villages and communities within commuting distances of large cities and
towns; significant amongst this research are the investigations by Pahl
(1965), Connell (1978) and Livingston (1975). Scores of studies have
been made of individual settlements and many of these have concentrated
on the modifications of the socio-economic structure and the differences,
sometimes the divisiveness, between newcomer groups and the so-called
local population (Pacione, 1980; Ambrose, 1974; Radford, 1970; Laux,
1971 and Rodger, 1979). Other authors have been concerned with
physical, aesthetic and commercial changes (Jackson, 1977 and Vulquin,
1971). Furthermore, discussion and illustration of these far-reaching
changes has gradually been introduced into the popular topographic
literature (Brode, 1980; Cave, 1976; Woodruffe, in press).

The addition of new people and housing to villages and settlements in
close proximity to cities is by no means a recent phenomenon, as
careful observation of building styles and housing types will reveal

(Coppock, 1964). But what is different about the post-war period is the scale, extent and continuity of building that has taken place. This process is not simply related to the increase in personal mobility through the private car, but it is a reflection of higher incomes and personal attitudes and aspirations. To live in or near to the countryside is, as was shown by the Hampshire County Council (1966) survey, a desire of many townsfolk. It is also the outcome of planning authorities restricting the outward growth of cities and large urban areas, thus deflecting the demand for developable land to outlying locations. It is fashionable to refer to this influx of new people and the construction of new property in the rural surroundings as 'urbanisation', a blanket term which is notoriously difficult to define. Lewis and Maund (1976) quote Hauser's (1965) statement that urbanisation is "the process of intensification of typically urban behaviour as a result of the diffusion of ideas and behaviour patterns from towns and cities." But not all newcomers to rural areas originate from the city, and it is becoming increasingly apparent that much household migration in rural areas is village-to-village rather than town-to-village. Herington and Evans (1979) in their migration study in Leicestershire write:

> "It is interesting to note that almost 75 per cent of all moves into the rural settlements in Charnwood do not originate in the two major cities of Leicester and Nottingham or other urban areas."

Moreover, it is clear (Woodruffe, 1974) that many new village residents are seeking a way of life different and distinct from their urban or suburban counterparts, and that the design of new property in villages is becoming more specific to the locality (Hampshire County Council, 1976) and less suburban in appearance.

It is not the intention of this essay to debate the perceptual niceties of urbanisation nor to get inveigled by the issues surrounding the allegiancies of newcomers or locals. These are two topics of metropolitan development which have attracted the interest of geographers, but from which little theory has as yet been produced. On the other hand, the spatial evolution of a settlement pattern and the impact of development on particular settlements, topics which are essentially geographical, have permitted some theoretical ideas to develop which have applicability in the planning realm. Whilst planning approaches are necessarily dominated by the land use/ development theme, it is worth noting that several authorities are now aiming for a greater awareness and understanding of the social and cultural life of the communities under their jurisdiction (Avon County Council, 1981). Nevertheless, often because of the complexities of administrative boundaries and local council affiliations, much residential development around major cities has tended to be planned in a piecemeal fashion. Such has partly been the case in South Hampshire where, prior to the 1974 local government reorganisation, eleven authorities were responsible for development control. The problem of unco-ordinated development was fully appreciated as the County Planning Officer stated (Smart, 1969):

171

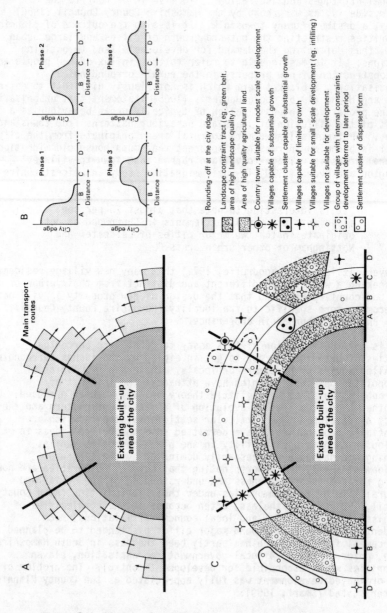

Figure 8.1 Models of residential development in the hinterland
of an urban area.

172

"... settlement policy should evolve from a social
and economic analysis of alternative ways of meeting
city regional housing need in urban areas and
villages, with alternative spatial patterns, taking
into account accessibility, services and physical
constraints."

With the advent of structure plans and the partial erosion of the urban-
rural division of responsibilities after 1974, more coherent approaches
to development issues and schemes were expected and yet the boundaries
between the three Hampshire Structure Plan areas (South, Mid- and South
West Hampshire) certainly do not encourage a city-region approach. This
is not the case in some metropolitan areas where local plans have been
prepared within the context of co-ordinated structure plans (Warwick
District Council, 1976; Torfaen Borough Council, 1979).

A THEORETICAL FRAMEWORK

Whilst residential development in the Southampton region during the
1960s and 1970s has not followed a carefully directed strategy, it is
clear that it has not been a haphazard process. Growth and
modifications to settlement structures have occurred in particular
spatial and temporal directions which are best introduced by reference
to a selection of theoretical models (Fig.8.1).

Assuming that a city or large town is the core area of employment
growth and that the employed population wish to keep home-to-work
distances to a minimum, the pattern of new residential development is
likely to take the form of accretions at the city edge (Fig.8.1A).
Land close to the main transport routes would be built up in the first
stage, the process gradually extending around the city periphery to
meet up with development associated with other transport routes. But
development would spread outwards simultaneously in phases before each
peripheral ring was completed. The result would be the star-shaped form
characteristic of the inter-war period in British and other European
cities.

With the introduction of planning controls on the release of land, but
with continual pressures for housing, the rings of development may be
phased rather differently; one effect might be to produce a series of
'growth waves or ripples' spreading outwards from the city (Fig.8.1B).
Each ring, apart from the inner one, would experience a slow build up of
growth to a peak period of construction, then a tailing off as
commitments are completed. Clearly, since the area of successive rings
increases with distance from the city, the more widely distributed
development would become. A second wave of growth may start at the city
edge before the previous one is complete. A variant of this model can
occur when the inner ring is sterilised by some constraint such as a
green belt policy; in this instance the waves of development would
radiate from the outer boundary of the inner ring and the peaks of
construction would be higher to compensate for the loss of the city-edge
tracts.

Beyond the city edge new residential development is not free to locate
in the space available, since it is normally attached to an existing

173

settlement. Consequently, the location of such settlements and their internal characteristics may well determine the scale, rate and timing of any construction. Factors such as the size of the settlement, the provision of facilities and especially of utilities (water, drainage, electricity, etc.), accessibility availability of land, the quality of agricultural land and landscape come into play and influence the role the settlement might take in any development strategy within the city region. Taking the simple ripple model, the distribution of one wave of growth within one ring can take many forms along a concentration-dispersion continuum. Differences will occur from ring to ring, because the settlement structure will change and because in general the number of settlements available to partake in any growth wave will in theory increase outwards. Figure 8.1C is an attempt to model some of the situations which might arise, and it can be termed a nodal growth model to distinguish it from the ripple model. The two, however, are not mutually exclusive. Exemplification of how planning policies may be derived from such a model is given in the MHLG (1967) document Settlement in the Countryside.

There are, of course, complications with the application of such models. Figure 8.1B assumes constant rates and equal amounts of development within each ring; in reality house building fluctuates from year to year and developers or builders complete at different speeds. Furthermore, the length of each phase of growth is likely to vary from place to place within each ring, and clearly any such rings are not readily identifiable morphologically. Other urban areas and small towns may be situated within the city region and may augment the pressures for development. This is very much the case in South Hampshire where the housing markets of Southampton, Winchester, Eastleigh, Bournemouth and Salisbury overlap with one another. Employment locations may exhibit a diversified distribution rather than a city-based concentration, another point which is valid for this region. At the settlement level, villages respond differently to demands for housing development. Some are suited to substantial growth, and it has been argued by planners that villages, which have been expanded rapidly, should be permitted subsequently a period of quiescence for the new community to stabilise. Given this argument, it would be possible in theory to devise a strategy of rotating development among a number of settlements such that when the growth of one village is nearing completion, that of another is gaining momentum.

These theoretical possibilities present planning authorities with different means to the same end - that of directing, programming and controlling the development of land. In practice, such possibilities now normally appear in the form of alternative strategies, an approach used in the preparation of the South Hampshire Structure Plan (Hampshire County Council, 1972c) and the Winchester and District Plan (Hampshire County Council, 1974). The detailed diversity of such approaches is considerable, not only at a sub-regional level but also at local level (see, for example, Bedfordshire County Council, 1976; Dorset County Council, 1980; Parry Lewis, 1974 and West Wiltshire District Council, 1980).

174

RESIDENTIAL DEVELOPMENT IN SOUTHAMPTON'S HINTERLAND, 1963-80(1)

For reasons already outlined, the rural area surrounding Southampton does not lend itself to a simple slicing up into a ring form. But since some division of the region is essential for analytical purposes, the seventy parishes comprising the hinterland have been grouped into the following three basic categories(2):

- a) Urban edge parishes, adjacent to a built-up part of the city,
- b) Rurban fringe parishes, located within a short distance of the city edge or the built-up parts of Eastleigh, Winchester or Bournemouth,
- c) Parishes in the rural surroundings beyond. Since this group is large in number, it has been sub-divided into:
  - i) Rural centres and planned growth villages/parishes,
  - ii) Medium-sized nucleated villages/parishes,
  - iii) Small nucleated villages/parishes,
  - iv) Parishes with a nebulous or dispersed cluster pattern of settlement.

Table 8.1

New housing in the regional divisions.

	No. of parishes	No. of new houses built 1963-80	Average no. per parish	% increase on 1963 housing stock
Urban edge	5	4390	878	79.5
Rurban fringe	16	10015	626	95.7
Rural hinterland:	(50	6591	132	37.2)
i)	7	3841	549	67.8
ii)	9	1283	142	30.6
iii)	16	496	31	17.7
iv)	18	971	54	19.1
Total	71	20996	296	62.1

The overall distribution of new housing by parish is mapped in Figure 8.2. The immediate impression is one of growth concentrating close to Southampton, Eastleigh and Bournemouth, with a nodal pattern developing away from these centres. That the volume of new construction decreases with distance from and, to some extent, ease of accessibility to the urban centres is clear from Table 8.1. This general rule is one that would be expected in principle even if it cannot be substantiated theoretically. Whilst it is possible to interpret in Table 8.1 the falling off of the average growth per parish, from 878 in the urban edge, 626 in the rurban fringe to 132 in the rural hinterland, in terms of a ring pattern it is very evident from the map that there is considerable variation in absolute increases from parish to parish in each category. Furthermore, when the annual increases are taken into account (Table 8.2), the seemingly simple pattern becomes yet more complicated. Perusal of these figures reveals few growth ripples which are traceable across the whole parish spectrum and little coincidence of peaks of building activity between categories.

Urban edge parishes

Between 1963 and 1980 this small group of parishes accommodated almost 21 per cent of the total residential growth, a much lower proportion than the rurban fringe parishes (48 per cent), but a proportion similar to the rural centres and planned villages (18 per cent). Year by year the share has varied from 17 per cent of new housing in 1964 to around 30 per cent in 1969 and 1975. Despite these relative fluctuations, the urban edge parishes have been significant locations for residential growth throughout the whole period, and it is difficult to integrate this general pattern with a growth-ripple concept.

However, the distribution of growth has not been spread equally among the five parishes concerned. By far the greatest amount (49 per cent) has been centred in Hedge End, a village characteristically metropolitan (Masser and Stroud, 1965) which has mushroomed in size by over 145 per cent since 1963. Hedge End is not strictly contiguous with Southampton's built-up edge and the development which has occurred there is not a city edge accretion. Interestingly, the village has grown both outwards, towards Botley and Bursledon, and inwards towards Southampton, and now only a narrow neck of open country, penetrated by the M27 motorway, separates the two. No green belt policy has operated around Southampton (the green belt proposed was never officially approved), hence here is a case of residential development at the nearest feasible location beyond the city edge. The rate of development has slowed in recent years with only 22 per cent of the 2155 new dwellings being built in the period 1976-80 compared to 55 per cent between 1963 and 1969.

Classic urban edge augmentation can be appreciated nearby in West End which adjoins directly the built-up structure of Southampton. Though it still describes itself as a village, it has expanded and consolidated steadily to a size of over 1500 households; over 800 dwellings have been added since 1963, an increase of some 52 per cent. Different again is the parish of Nursling and Rownhams close to the north-west edge of the city. Its overall increase is 73 per cent, though it was still a pleasant fringe village until 1974. Suburban expansion up to the city boundary gradually reduced the intervening open land until in 1974 residential development started apace and has subsequently linked the village of Rownhams with the continuous built-up part of Southampton. The dramatic change in growth rates is illustrated by the fact that only 67 new houses were built in the parish in the 1963-73 decade, since when almost 500 have been added. Once the current phase of estate construction is complete, it seems likely there will be a lull until perhaps some of the remaining agricultural and pasture land adjoining the boundary is released for development. This change in Rownhams might be seen as a ripple, or rather a wave, of growth spreading out but a

176

Table 8.2

Annual additions of new housing in the regional divisions, 1963-80.

	Urban edge	Rurban fringe	Rural centres/ Planned villages	Medium villages	Small villages	Dispersed parishes	Total
1963	102	206	60	29	19	15	431
1964	192	421	253	115	46	83	1110
1965	351	629	259	126	40	86	1491
1966	186	505	218	82	23	55	1069
1967	197	509	180	41	24	56	1007
1968	355	645	277	116	47	68	1508
1969	375	504	216	87	17	43	1242
1970	167	459	229	64	21	74	1014
1971	154	575	163	59	13	57	1021
1972	122	505	294	92	32	48	1093
1973	180	454	168	92	18	58	970
1974	127	370	97	61	51	43	749
1975	307	462	131	67	13	37	1017
1976	367	686	280	46	41	80	1500
1977	279	824	279	50	30	74	1536
1978	369	834	187	51	17	42	1500
1979	197	582	212	44	22	24	1081
1980	363	843	338	61	22	28	1655
Totals	4390	10015	3841	1283	496	971	20996
Average per year	244	556	213	71	28	54	1166

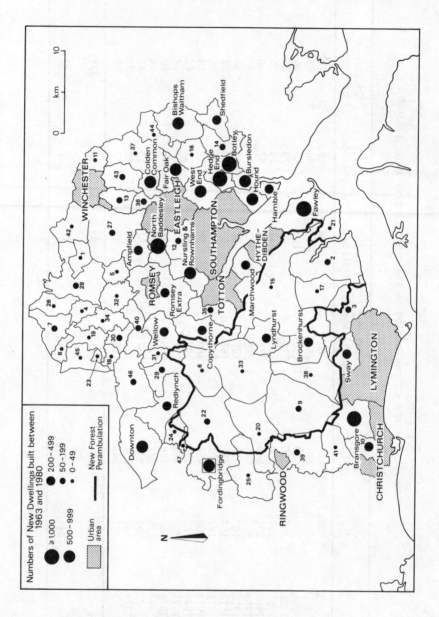

Figure 8.2 Distribution of new housing in Southampton's
hinterland, 1963 – 80.

Key to Figure 8.2

1   Ashley
2   Beaulieu
3   Boldre
4   Bossington
5   Braishfield
6   Bramshaw
7   Broughton
8   Buckholt
9   Burley
10 Burton
11 Chilcomb
12 Chilworth
13 Compton
14 Curdridge
15 Denny Lodge
16 Durley
17 East Boldre
18 East Dean
19 East Tytherley
20 Ellingham
21 Exbury and Lepe
22 Fordingbridge (outer parts)
23 Frenchmoor
24 Hale
25 Harbridge and Ibsley
26 Houghton
27 Hursley
28 Kings Somborne
29 Landford
30 Lockerley
31 Melchet Park and Plaitford
32 Michelmersh
33 Minstead
34 Mottisfont
35 Netley Marsh
36 Otterbourne
37 Owslebury
38 Rhinefield
39 Ringwood (outer parts)
40 Sherfield English
41 Sopley
42 Sparsholt
43 Twyford
44 Upham
45 West Tytherley
46 Whiteparish
47 Woodgreen

short distance beyond the city before dissipating its impetus. The sudden but limited phase of construction would fit a 'short-sharp growth' model for a village with the ensuing stability phase about to begin. Development on such a scale has changed the image and identity of Rownhams beyond recall; a study carried out when the estate construction was well under way (Ferguson, 1977) asked residents to classify the village. Almost half regarded it as an 'urbanised village' but the majority of these respondents were newcomer households of less than 20 years' residence. Few expressed it to be either 'a suburban area' or 'an attractive village'; the long-term residents of 20 years or more regarded it as 'a place without identity', clearly a reflection of the impact of recent change.

Of the other parishes in this group Hound, which includes the large settlement of Netley, is comparable to Hedge End's pattern, but with development tending to accelerate in recent years rather than decrease. Chilworth, on the northern edge of the city, has increased only by about 18 per cent (62 new dwellings). It is a parish of low-density, high-status property set within an attractively wooded environment. Opportunities for additional housing have come about largely through subdivision of large garden plots.

Rurban fringe parishes

This group of parishes forms an almost continuous arc of settlements around the estuary from Fawley to Romsey, Winchester and around the eastern periphery of Eastleigh to Hamble. Two parishes, Bransgore and Sopley, on the north-east margins of Bournemouth are also included. As noted above, it is within these parishes that the largest share of residential growth has taken place since 1963 and very few parishes have escaped a substantial increase. Scales of increase are higher than in the urban edge parishes (Table 8.1); in all the number of dwellings in the rurban fringe settlements has almost doubled (a 95.7 per cent increase), whereas the urban edge settlements grew overall by almost 80 per cent. Annual increments (Table 8.2) display a remarkable consistency, more so than the urban edge or rural hinterland groups, but to some extent this comes about through a levelling out effect between the various settlements. Growth rates have tended to rise throughout the period; between 1966 and 1970 annual additions averaged about 525 dwellings, but between 1976 and 1980 these had risen to a figure of 750 dwellings.

Several settlements are now considerably larger and consequently much altered in structure and appearance. Botley, close to Hedge End, has experienced an addition of 1330 new dwellings, an increase of 282 per cent. Substantial increases were also experienced by North Baddesley (1530 dwellings; 217 per cent increase), Fair Oak (950; 161 per cent), Bransgore (1150; 160 per cent) and Fawley (2200; 96 per cent). Only four of the sixteen parishes grew by less than 25 per cent. These were Netley Marsh, where a fragmented pattern of settlement exists, Compton and Twyford, on the southern edge of Winchester, where the road network and sewerage capacities have limited new building, and Sopley, a small village in the Avon Valley where several constraints prevail, not least of which are those of land and landscape quality.

In one or two parishes the pattern of inward growth towards the urban

area can be noted again. Fair Oak village has linked up with
Bishopstoke, a suburban part of Eastleigh. Botley, Bursledon and
Bransgore have all expanded and thereby reduced the relatively narrow
tracts of countryside separating them from neighbouring communities.
Much of the new building in Romsey Extra parish relates to peripheral
extensions to Romsey and some of the increase in Ampfield comprises
expansion on the western edge of Chandler's Ford, part of Eastleigh
Borough. Though Fawley parish contained the largest number of new
dwellings, these are split among three separate settlement clusters -
Hardley-Holbury, Blackfield-Langley and Fawley village. Elsewhere, new
housing has tended to round off and infill villages, but such processes
may comprise very sizeable additions in the shape of estates and linked
closes.

In the majority of parishes, this residential growth was permitted and
has been completed without the benefit of a local or village plan. This
may account for the widespread and continuous pattern of growth, which
does not fit in with the ordered pattern suggested by the theoretical
models. However, development in Botley and Bursledon, together with
nearby Hedge End, West End and Hound parishes, was controlled by a Town
Map (the Southern Parishes of Winchester Rural District) which was part
of the County Development Plan. This map provided for development into
the early 1970s, until such time as the Structure Plan came into
operation. Pressure for development was intense while the Structure
Plan was in preparation and interim plans were implemented to programme
a continual release of land and to guide public investment in services
and utilities (Hampshire County Council, 1969a and 1971a). Many of the
areas of land identified in these plans were in or close to rurban
fringe settlements. Simultaneously, and also subsequently, local plans
were prepared to determine the detailed limits and phasing, as well as
examining the restraining characteristics and issues within individual
settlements. In the rurban fringe, plans were prepared for Colden
Common, Blackfield-Langley, Hardley-Holbury and Marchwood (Hampshire
County Council, 1973 and 1972a; New Forest District Council, 1975a and
1975b). Where no local plan existed, development of particular sites
has been guided by 'development briefs', such as those employed at North
Baddesley (Test Valley Borough Council, 1977).

Where such plans are now operative, the nature of any development is
able to be controlled more specifically. At Colden Common, for
instance, where housing has been added at a steady rate since 1963, a
plan has permitted the coordination of new growth with the provision of
facilities, in particular a new primary school. It has also directed
the evolution of the form and structure of the settlement and has
allowed for open space and the retention of some of the landscape
features. Though there was a recognisable settlement in the area prior
to the plan, the later programmed growth has helped to create here an
essentially 'new village', along the lines suggested by Thorburn (1965).
A similar situation applied at Bransgore (Hampshire County Council,
1970).

Marchwood illustrates pertinently two of the points touched upon in
the discussion on the theoretical framework for development. From 1963
to 1978 only small amounts of new building occurred in the parish, due
partly to inadequate road access and partly to insufficient capacity in
the sewer and drainage system. Only about 140 dwellings had been

completed by 1978, but in 1979-80 over 200 were built on land scheduled in the local plan which contains provision for an additional 600. The lack of substantial building in Marchwood prior to 1979 appears to conflict with the growth-ripple concept, but only if it is assumed that the development wave should affect all settlements within each ring equally and simultaneously. Conversely, it is possible to argue that, for various reasons, initial waves may be deflected from certain areas which can, however, succumb to later ones. Secondly, it is evident that Marchwood is entering upon a phase of rapid growth after a dormant or slumbering period. By contrast, development in nearby Fawley parish is nearing the end of a growth phase. The concept of rotating, or perhaps in this case, alternating growth between neighbouring settlements is clearly applicable here.

One feature apparent in respect of the rurban fringe parishes of the Southampton region is that there is little evidence of a diminishing role for them. There appears to be considerable spare capacity within many of the settlements, a situation which is not the case in the urban-edge parishes.

The rural hinterland

Beyond the rurban fringe, the remainder of the region is made up of a mosaic of some 50 rural parishes, most containing main or nucleated settlements of varying sizes, though there are several parishes consisting solely of nebulous strings or small dispersed clusters of habitation. The topographic setting, the aesthetic character, the location and availability of facilities and amenities, and the accessibility of all these parishes are quite diverse and account for much of the internal variation in the siting and nature of new building. Taken as a whole, these rural hinterland parishes absorbed 31 per cent of the region's residential growth and this addition of around 6600 dwellings increased the housing stock by almost 37 per cent.

The greatest share of the housing growth was concentrated (Table 8.1) in two types of settlement - the acknowledged rural centres, like Lyndhurst and Downton, and the planned growth villages of West Wellow and Sway. With the exceptions of the New Forest parishes of Brockenhurst and Lyndhurst, all these places grew substantially over the period, some on a scale comparable with rurban fringe parishes; Downton increased by 110 per cent, Fordingbridge by 99 per cent, Wellow by 93 per cent, Bishops Waltham by 89 per cent and Sway by almost 50 per cent. Though their proportionate increases were lower, Brockenhurst and Lyndhurst augmented their respective housing stocks by 330 and 240 dwellings, which have filled in tracts of grazing land within the built-up framework of each village, largely in accordance with the planning policies eventually adopted for them (Hampshire County Council 1971b and 1972b). In both, growth has been steady rather than spasmodic or in waves.

By contrast, the growth of Downton and Fordingbridge in the Avon Valley, west of the New Forest, has been characterised by periodic influxes. Both benefit from a wide range of shopping facilities, A-class road links to Salisbury and Bournemouth, a good provision of social and educational amenities and there is some local employment, especially at Downton. One wave of new building occurred in

Fordingbridge between 1968 and 1971, and another began in 1976 culminating with the completion of 175 dwellings in 1980. This later phase coincided with the construction of a by-pass, which took through traffic away from the confined centre and eased problems of access to land on the settlement edge. Downton witnessed an unprecedented phase of building between 1965 and 1970, when over 450 dwellings were added. Since then increases have been of the order of 7 dwellings per year, a remarkable reduction in rate of construction. The lack of a by-pass, landscape considerations and village centre congestion have militated against anything other than small-scale infilling. On the eastern border of the region, Bishops Waltham is a centre of small-town proportions whose clear potential for residential development has been realised by consistent growth throughout the last two decades.

At Wellow, and to a lesser extent at Sway, the recent expansion has been programmed in conjunction with formal village plans (Hampshire County Council 1969b and 1969c). These two villages abut the perambulation of the New Forest and prior to the modern development taking place, both were unconsolidated settlements straggling along lanes and around a patchwork pattern of smallholdings and pasture land. Both were classed as suitable for further growth because of the opportunities their structure afforded for substantial infilling and because of their good accessibility. Wellow adjoins the A36 Southampton-Salisbury road four km from the M27 junction whilst Sway, like Brockenhurst, has a station on the Southampton-Bournemouth railway line. Two waves of housing construction occurred at Sway, one in the late 1960s before the adoption of the village plan, the other between 1976 and 1980. In all, over 400 dwellings have been built here. With an average increase of 10 dwellings per year before 1972, Wellow grew slowly but, following the implementation of an improved mains drainage scheme, development has since averaged over 50 dwellings a year. The growth has now exceeded the provision in the village plan and small estate groups of houses and bungalows have been constructed on land which was to remain as open space. Like Sway, Wellow was intended to act as a local service centre and, though its commercial activities are limited (six shops, two garages and two public houses), three of the shops are new, purpose-built enterprises. In addition, social and health facilities have been improved with the completion in 1980 of a community hall. If the small amount of pre-20th century building is ignored, both Sway and Wellow are essentially new villages designed largely with the commuter in mind, though not planned in detail from initiation to a target population. Both reflect the continued pressure since the 1920s for housing in a country setting from essentially middle-class families. The problem from now on will be how to curtail the growth, since both have been successful expansions from a planning point of view and many of the social problems recognised in other Hampshire villages by Margaret Livingston (1975) do not appear to have arisen here.

Parishes containing distinct nucleations of settlement grade from places with sizeable housing stocks, like Shedfield (700 dwellings) and Redlynch (775 dwellings), to small clusters such as are found in Michelmersh (220 dwellings) and Mottisfont (125 dwellings). A minimum of 300 dwellings categorises the 'medium-sized villages', the remainder being termed 'small villages'. At such levels the general rule would seem to be that the scale of new development diminishes with decreasing size of settlement. There are, however, some exceptions, and the two largest parishes mentioned above approached scales of growth more typical of rural centres and some rurban fringe parishes. Redlynch, a parish which lies on the north-west edge of the New Forest and within the employment catchment of Salisbury, grew by over 55 per cent; Shedfield, located east of Southampton but also well placed for Fareham, Portsmouth and Winchester, increased by almost 37 per cent. Both are composite parishes with several differentiated settlements and new building has been distributed amongst these separate parts, not always in a manner according to initial size but more to where land was available.

More characteristic of the medium-sized villages are Kings Somborne (123 new dwellings; 29 per cent growth), Broughton (96 new dwellings; 29 per cent growth) and Whiteparish (118 new dwellings; 35 per cent growth). This last village is within easy access of Salisbury, Romsey, Totton and Southampton and has a good basic range of services and amenities. New development rates here have been very steady averaging 7-8 dwellings a year, with no peak construction periods apart from 1973-4 when a group of 28 local authority bungalows was added. Development has been divided between small closes of similar dwelling types and infilling of sites within the recognised structure of the village with more varied properties. Bungalows were dominant in the 1960s, but latterly almost all developments have been houses. The completion of a mains drainage scheme here in 1971 was followed by an application to build over 300 dwelling units in estate format; this proposal exceeded the capacity of the scheme very substantially and subsequently was refused after a public enquiry. Only three of the medium-sized parishes have not shared the overall proportions of growth for this group. These are Beaulieu, East Boldre and Burley, all three located within the New Forest, where conservation policies for landscape and village character are pre-eminent, though not to the point of exclusion, for Burley, a spacious village, has grown slowly at a rate of over 4 dwellings per year.

Given the low levels of development, it is difficult to fit either the medium-sized or small villages concisely into the general models of development. Since many are located 13 and more kilometres from the main urban areas, pressure from any growth wave has dissipated considerably at such distances and spread itself among a greater range of settlements. As illustrated at Whiteparish, the only evidence of any peaks of growth tends to be in association with the construction of one estate or a small number of residential closes, the development phase rarely lasting more than two years. In the smaller villages, more often than not such bursts of building activity are council developments, as at Kings Somborne (50 dwellings in 1964-66), East Boldre (20 dwellings in 1968) and Lockerley (40 dwellings in 1973). In Kings Somborne and Lockerley such additions were clearly out of character with the structure of the villages, but are perhaps unlikely to occur again within the foreseeable future because of a tightening up of planning policies. Apart from this aberration, Lockerley has witnessed changes conforming with its attractive layout around three separated village greens. Selective infilling at low densities, some redevelopment and plot division and a certain amount of cottage improvement and extension have all taken place. The exceptional estate occupies a backland site which does not greatly impinge on the established structure, though it has clearly created a new element in the form of the village.

In general, few of the small villages have been affected markedly by modern development and some have remained almost untouched by new construction. Such absences of building must be attributed only partly to size; agricultural character, the pattern of land ownership, and landscape and village conservation policies are perhaps more significant in denoting such localities as 'unsuitable for development'. Such reasons can account for the fact that several parishes close to Southampton's rurban fringe have experienced low levels of growth, whereas in theory development levels should have been quite substantial. Upham and Durley are two such examples (Fig.8.2). Overall, the medium-sized villages have accommodated around 6 per cent of the growth in the urban hinterland and the small villages only some 2.3 per cent. It is clear from Table 8.2 that in the 1970s rates of growth decelerated, and in view of the revised policies in the current structure plans, few villages are likely to see the extent of development they experienced in the 1960s.

Finally, there is the group of 18 parishes with a nebulous or dispersed pattern of settlement filling in the rural mosaic between nucleated parishes and villages. Some contain small clusters and strings of settlement where, given the trend in the small villages, one would not anticipate any notable growth. Such a tendency holds true only for half of these parishes; in the remainder increases in excess of 10 per cent, and as high as 54 per cent, are found, and it is in these parishes that the bulk of the 970 dwellings built since 1963 are located. In all, the housing stock in these dispersed settlements increased by over 19 per cent, a quite remarkable scale considering the planning policies operative at the time.

Apart from several small parishes in the Test Valley, most of these areas of fragmented settlement lie within or close to the New Forest. As already appreciated above, the scale of new residential development in the New Forest tends to be one of relatively low proportions; growth has been deflected to the fringes in what may be described as a 'polo-mint' pattern. The presence of such a major landscape-restraint tract close to the urban agglomeration severely complicates any growth ripples that radiate outwards. Moreover, because of its pleasant environment, the New Forest attracts residential development which otherwise might have been distributed more widely. Whilst planning policies have attempted to temper demands for building within the Forest settlements, they have not tried to curtail unduly the desires of people to live close to the area. Hence the growth ring around the Forest fringe.

In the five parishes with a dispersed settlement distribution lying within or partly within the New Forest (Denny Lodge, Ellingham, Harbridge and Ibsley, Minstead and Rhinefield), less than 70 new dwellings were completed in the period under review. The majority of these were in Minstead, where new building has been inserted selectively yet loosely into the incipient but diffuse clusters of Newtown and Minstead itself. In rather stark contrast, over 750 dwellings were built in the fragmented settlements in five fringe parishes. Adjacent to, indeed almost part of, the rurban fringe is Copythorne, where residential growth has been taking place more or less continuously since the early part of this century. In 1963 it was already a large parish with over 850 dwellings, but it has subsequently increased by some 200 or 23 per cent. A wave of growth occurred between 1969 and 1971, since when additions have been relatively steady. At Landford, five kilometres beyond Copythorne, a lower total of 150 dwellings was added, but this represented an increase of some 54 per cent. Peaks of growth occurred in 1965-66, 1971-73 and 1976-77, but the height of these waves was relatively low, the latter two reflecting the start and completion of an out-of-character estate of private houses. This estate apart, Landford comprises four strings of settlement which have been compacted without producing anything resembling a village format. Over 100 dwellings have been added in the outer parts of both Fordingbridge and Ringwood parishes on the western boundary of the New Forest. In Ringwood some of this development comprises an extension to the town, but in Fordingbridge additions have been made in many of the discontinuous clusters of settlement that characterise the Forest fringe hereabouts. Development here tailed off in the 1970s, evidence of a tightening up of planning controls with a consequent deflection of new building into Fordingbridge itself.

Typical of these nebulously-settled parishes is Sherfield English which is located north of the New Forest. Here the settlement pattern consists of six open groupings, only one of which approaches the appearance of a small village. All have shared in the growth which has affected the parish (90 new buildings, an increase of 22 per cent) since 1963, despite the County Planning Department's description that such clusters were "too dispersed for new development to be satisfactorily integrated" (Hampshire County Council, 1969d). Most of these clusters have been extended outwards as well as infilled at low densities, and ribbons of housing winding along lanes have been the result. Whilst this modest and continuous expansion can be criticised in the light of national policies against building in the open countryside, it does reflect the unusual nature of the pre-existing settlement distribution in this part of Hampshire. Moreover, it has provided some new residents with the opportunity to purchase homes with space and an immediate country setting, rather different from the situation in many villages where infilling of gaps is now the rule. Of those parishes in this group where new building has been very limited, it should be recorded that the development which has occasionally occurred has largely been in association with farms or landed estates and hence appropriate to its location.

THE OVERALL PATTERN OF DEVELOPMENT IN SOUTHAMPTON'S HINTERLAND

Discussion in the previous sections has attempted to discern those features of the region's residential development which tie in with the theoretical models outlined initially, and also to note where and why discrepancies within the general trends have occurred. It is clear that, though a number of directions and trends are very evident in the pattern and timing of growth, the temporal sequence and spatial locating of new housing construction are more complicated than the development models would lead one to believe. Such a complex situation arises from the vagaries of the housing market, the programmes, hunches and whims of developers and builders large and small, and of course the pattern and nature of land ownership and land availability. Planning control is simply the modest decision-making layer of icing of a 'demand-and-supply' housing cake baked with a multitude of ingredients. In spite of such complications, there is evidence of waves of growth in many

186

Table 8.3

Summary model of residential development.

I Urban edge parishes:	a) Outward expansion of the city beyond its administrative boundary to incorporate proximate villages; b) Steady expansion and consolidation of settlements close to the city built-up area; c) Expansion, often rapid, of metropolitan villages within the immediate countryside, reducing the open land between themselves and the city. Complementary overlap of development phases may occur between villages.
II Rurban fringe parishes:	a) Substantial growth of settlements with a sound range of public and private services and amenities; b) Large-scale rounding-off and infilling of villages with an unconsolidated form or structure, thus creating a later generation of metropolitan villages; c) Development in conjunction with a local plan of simulative new villages; d) Settlements not participating in the growth trends of the region but held in reserve or until certain constraints are removed.
III Rural hinter- land parishes:	
i)Rural centres and planned villages	a) Substantial development of rural centres in nodal locations where considerations of landscape and other restraining factors are not highly significant; b) Comparatively large-scale consolidation of settlements with an open structure in accessible locations. Growth programmed by means of a village plan.
ii)Medium- sized and iii)Small villages	c) Selective expansion of medium-sized nucleated villages with development occurring steadily over a long period; d) Small villages growing slowly by the process of infilling, but with spasmodic bursts of growth largely related to local authority developments; e) Villages, either in landscape-restraint areas or with limiting factors, growing at below-average rates or remaining essentially unaffected by new building, despite relative proximity to urban areas.
iv)Parishes with nebulous or dispersed patterns of settlement	f) Modest but notable additions to clusters where demand for housing is high. Growth waves may be evident though rarely pronounced; g) In less accessible localities, occasional new dwellings largely in association with agricultural or other local employment.

settlements, though the form of the wave varies in amplitude and height. There is also evidence of growth deflection from one area to another, and of nodal concentrations, especially with increasing distance from the city. In essence, most of the characteristics of the theoretical models are present, but not in the same ordered format. The ring pattern shown in the models and identified around other cities is, however, not particularly clear around Southampton. To simplify the variable nature of recent residential development in the city's hinterland and to demonstrate the similarities with the theoretical framework, a summary model has been constructed (Table 8.3).

This model identifies the characteristics of housing growth at parish and village level within the broad regional divisions employed for analysis. It does not incorporate the detail relating to the format of new housing within individual settlements, interesting and varied as this certainly is, but clearly beyond the scope of this essay. In tabular form the summary model does not express the particular spatial patterns of development in the region, but it augments the data displayed in Figure 8.2. Furthermore, it is clear that the model is a variant of that shown in Figure 8.1C, but one peculiar to the intrinsic characteristics of the Southampton area. Nevertheless, some of the settlement types and changes will be applicable to other city hinterlands. For example, the 'selected villages' in Nottingham's rural ring, where 'bursts of residential building' have taken place, seem to equate with the rural centres and planned villages (Type IIIa) around Southampton (Griggs, 1970). On the other hand, the village types studied by Connell (1978) in the Surrey green belt are not readily found in South Hampshire, although there are similarities in parts of the New Forest. This may be because the villages themselves were traditionally different or because a green belt policy has never been effectively pursued in South Hampshire. Similarly, industrial villages, like those in West Yorkshire or on the south-eastern fringes of Bristol, are missing. Conversely, the fragmented settlements of the New Forest fringes are rarely found elsewhere in England. Hence, any transference of the summary model to other city hinterlands must be undertaken with some caution.

One further aspect of the overall settlement structure worth outlining is the relative change in size between the six parish and village categories. A simple rank-size distribution is shown in Figure 8.3. If development occurred proportionate to the initial size of each settlement, the ranking would not alter. In fact, only 10 of the 71 parishes have maintained their ranking over the period, but it is also apparent from the way the distribution hugs the axis that there have not been major shifts in relative size. The upper sector shows settlements which have gained rank, and predominant here are the rurban fringe parishes. In the lower sector, denoting loss of rank, there is a more mixed pattern though seven of the nine medium-sized villages are to be found here and half of the parishes with a dispersed settlement form, especially the larger ones. The diagram adds substance to some of the earlier findings and particularly to the fact that residential development has become increasingly concentrated in the parishes of the urban edge and rurban fringe.

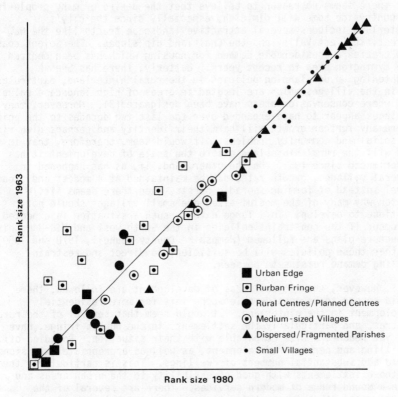

Figure 8.3   Rank - size distributions, 1963 and 1980.

Legend:
- ■ Urban Edge
- ▣ Rurban Fringe
- ● Rural Centres / Planned Centres
- ◉ Medium - sized Villages
- ▲ Dispersed / Fragmented Parishes
- • Small Villages

A FUTURE PERSPECTIVE

This trend towards concentration around, rather than within, the urban areas of South Hampshire seems likely to continue in the 1980s. The greater part of the region's future housing development is certain to be associated with the areas identified in the South Hampshire Structure Plan (Chandler's Ford, Totton and the West End-Fair Oak area). But there seems no reason to believe that the desire of many people for a countryside home will diminish, especially since the city's hinterland includes several attractive landscape tracts like the New Forest, the Test Valley and the Chalkland dip slopes. The Solent coast too creates a considerable demand for housing which has been centred in the Lymington area in recent years. Latterly, there has been a tightening up of planning policies in the rural hinterland, particularly in the villages which are located in areas of high landscape value and where conservation areas have been designated(3). Moreover, many villages appear to have expanded over the last two decades to the point where any further growth will harm their identity and perhaps give rise to social and community problems. It would seem, therefore, that in no way will the rural hinterland absorb the scale of development it has experienced since 1963. On the other hand, if, as has happened in several villages, growth rates can be maintained at a modest and steady level instead of forming sporadic bursts, then there seems little reason why many of the medium-sized and small villages should not continue to develop. To a large extent, such a situation is expected to occur if the constraint policies in the South West and Mid-Hampshire structure plans are followed (Hampshire County Council, 1978 and 1980). Whether these policies will be sufficient to direct and restrain housing demand remains to be seen.

If, however, theoretical ideas of development are followed, there would appear to be considerable scope left for more residential development in the hinterland. It would seem that several of the rural centres, and particularly the settlements in the rurban fringe, have not yet reached a size comparable with their situation. Rounding-off, infilling and perhaps redevelopment, as well as appropriate extensions, could add substantial numbers of dwellings. This is particularly true of those settlements with good accessibility to the urban areas and with a sound range of modern services. There are several of the settlements with a fragmented pattern which could, like Wellow and Sway, be programmed for growth and new villages created. Finally, it could be argued that many small villages, attractive though they may be, are hardly viable socially and that a modest influx of population would be to their advantage. To appreciate fully, however, the impact of residential growth on these individual settlements, further investigation is required to examine the ways in which they have developed in recent decades. Only then could a comprehensive strategy for housing development in the whole of the Southampton metropolitan region be conceived and accomplished.

NOTES

(1) Data on residential development were obtained from the Valuation Lists and Direction Sheets. The latter list new properties as they are valued for rating purposes on completion of construction.

(2) The parishes comprising each category are
    a) Urban edge: Hound, Hedge End, West End, Chilworth,
                        Nursling and Rownhams.
    b) Rurban fringe: Fawley, Marchwood, Netley Marsh, Romsey Extra,
                        North Baddesley, Ampfield, Compton, Twyford,
                        Otterbourne, Colden Common, Fair Oak, Botley,
                        Bursledon, Hamble, Bransgore, Sopley.
    c) Rural hinterland:
        i) Rural centres/planned growth villages: Lyndhurst,
                        Brockenhurst, Sway, Downton, Fordingbridge,
                        Wellow, Bishops Waltham.
       ii) Medium-sized villages/parishes: Redlynch, Whiteparish,
                        Broughton, Kings Somborne, Curdridge,
                        Shedfield, East Boldre, Burley, Beaulieu.
      iii) Small nucleated villages/parishes: Upham, Owslebury,
                        Hursley, Houghton, West Tytherley, East
                        Tytherley, Lockerley, Mottisfont, Michelmersh,
                        Brais field, Bramshaw, Hale, Woodgreen,
                        Exbury and Lepe, Ashley, Sparsholt.
       iv) Parishes with a nebulous or dispersed pattern of
                        settlement: Sherfield English, Landford, Melchet Park and
                        Plaitford, Durley, Copythorne, Minstead,
                        Rhinefield, Denny Lodge, Ellingham, Ringwood
                        (outer parts), Fordingbridge (outer parts),
                        Harbridge and Ibsley, Boldre, Bossington,
                        Chilcomb, Frenchmoor, Buckholt, East Dean.
(3) Conservation areas have been designated in Hamble, Bishops Waltham,
    Hursley, Botley, Broughton, Kings Somborne, Beaulieu,
    Fordingbridge, Lyndhurst, Sopley, Downton and Whiteparish.

REFERENCES

AMBROSE, P (1974), The Quiet Revolution: Social Change in a Sussex
        Village 1871-1971 (London, Chatto and Windus, and University
        of Sussex Press).

AVON COUNTY COUNCIL (1981), Village Life in Avon (Bristol, Planning
        Department).

BEDFORDSHIRE COUNTY COUNCIL (1976), County Structure Plan - Alternative
        Strategies (Bedford, County Planning Department).

BRODE, A (1980), The Hampshire Village Book (Newbury, Countryside
        Books).

CAVE, L F (1976), Warwickshire Villages (London, Hale).

CONNELL, J (1978), The End of Tradition - Country Life in Central
        Surrey (London, Routledge and Kegan Paul).

COPPOCK, J T (1964), Dormitory settlements around London, in COPPOCK, J
        T and PRINCE, H C (eds), Greater London (London, Faber and
        Faber).

DORSET COUNTY COUNCIL (1980), Dorset Structure Plan - DSP8: Settlement Policy Choices (Dorchester, Planning Department).

FERGUSON, C F (1977), Environmental Changes in an Urban Fringe Settlement - a Case Study of Rownhams Village (Unpublished dissertation for the Certificate in Environmental Science, University of Southampton).

GIGGS, J A (1970), Fringe expansion and suburbanization around Nottingham: a metropolitan area approach, in OSBORNE, R H et al. (ed.), Geographical Essays in Honour of K C Edwards (Nottingham University, Department of Geography).

HAMPSHIRE COUNTY COUNCIL (1966), Village Life in Hampshire (Winchester, Planning Department).

HAMPSHIRE COUNTY COUNCIL (1969a), The Waterside Parishes Interim Policy Plan (Winchester, Planning Department).

HAMPSHIRE COUNTY COUNCIL (1969b), West Wellow Area Village Plan (Winchester, Planning Department).

HAMPSHIRE COUNTY COUNCIL (1969c), Sway Village Plan (Winchester, Planning Department).

HAMPSHIRE COUNTY COUNCIL (1969d), The Policy for Villages in Romsey and Stockbridge Rural District (Winchester, Planning Department).

HAMPSHIRE COUNTY COUNCIL (1970), Bransgore Village Plan (Winchester, Planning Department).

HAMPSHIRE COUNTY COUNCIL (1971a), South Hampshire Interim Policy Plan (Stage Two)(Winchester, Planning Department).

HAMPSHIRE COUNTY COUNCIL (1971b), Brockenhurst Village Plan (Winchester, Planning Department).

HAMPSHIRE COUNTY COUNCIL (1972a), Blackfield and Langley Local Plan (Winchester, Planning Department).

HAMPSHIRE COUNTY COUNCIL (1972b), Lyndhurst Planning Policy (Winchester, Planning Department).

HAMPSHIRE COUNTY COUNCIL (1972c), South Hampshire Structure Plan - Draft Document for Participation and Consultation (Winchester, Planning Department).

HAMPSHIRE COUNTY COUNCIL (1973), Colden Common Local Plan (Winchester, Planning Department).

HAMPSHIRE COUNTY COUNCIL (1974), Winchester and District Study - Stage Two Report (Winchester, Planning Department).

HAMPSHIRE COUNTY COUNCIL (1976), Design in Villages and Small Towns, Design Leaflet, 10 (Winchester, Planning Department).

HAMPSHIRE COUNTY COUNCIL (1978), Mid-Hampshire Structure Plan (Winchester, Planning Department).

HAMPSHIRE COUNTY COUNCIL (1980), South West Hampshire Structure Plan - Consultation Draft (Winchester, Planning Department).

HAUSER, P M (1965), Folk urban ideals, in HAUSER, P M and SCHNORE, L F (eds), The Study of Urbanisation (New York, Wiley).

HERINGTON, J and EVANS, D (1979), The spatial pattern of movement in key and non-key settlements, Working Paper No.3 (Loughborough University, Department of Geography).

JACKSON, A A (ed.)(1977), Ashtead - a Village Transformed (Leatherhead, Leatherhead and District Local History Society).

LAUX, H-D (1971), Der sozial-ökonomische Wandel der Gemeinde Waldesch bei Koblenz seit 1945, Arbeiten zur Rheinischen Landeskund, 32, 91-112.

LEWIS, G J and MAUND, D J (1976), The urbanization of the countryside: a framework for analysis, Geografiska Annaler, 58B, 17-27.

LIVINGSTON, M (1975), Rapidly Expanding Rural Communities - A Case Study of Four Hampshire Villages (Winchester, Hampshire Council of Community Service).

MASSER, F I and STROUD, D C (1965), The metropolitan village, Town Planning Review, 36, 111-24.

MINISTRY OF HOUSING AND LOCAL GOVERNMENT (1967), Settlement in The Countryside: Planning Bulletin No.8 (London, HMSO).

NEW FOREST DISTRICT COUNCIL (1975a), Hardley-Holbury Local Plan (Lyndhurst).

NEW FOREST DISTRICT COUNCIL (1975b), Marchwood Local Plan (Lyndhurst).

PACIONE, M (1980), Differential quality of life in a metropolitan village, Transactions, Institute of British Geographers, New Series 5, 185-206.

PAHL, R E (1965), Urbs in Rure: the Metropolitan Fringe in Hertfordshire (London, London School of Economics).

PARRY LEWIS, J (1974), A Study of the Cambridge Sub-region (London, HMSO).

RADFORD, E (1970), The New Villagers: Urban Pressure on Rural Areas in Worcestershire (London, Cass).

RODGER, I (1979), A subtle genocide, New Society, 49, 512-513.

SMART, A D G (1969), Rural planning in the context of the city region, Report of the Town and Country Planning Summer School, 34-38.

TEST VALLEY BOROUGH COUNCIL (1977), Hoe Lane North Baddesley - Review Development Brief (Romsey).

THORBURN, A (1965), The new village, Report of the Town and Country Planning Summer School, 112-122.

TORFAEN, BOROUGH OF (1979), South East Pontypool Local Plan - Draft Written Statement (Cwmbran, Borough Planning Office).

VULQUIN, A (1971), Guilers: L'urbanisation d'un village proche de Brest, Norois, 18, 25-46.

WARWICK DISTRICT COUNCIL (1976), Lapworth District Plan (Leamington Spa).

WEST WILTSHIRE DISTRICT COUNCIL (1980), Trowbridge District Plan: Report of Survey and Issues (Trowbridge).

WOODRUFFE, B J (1974), A Guideline Document for Future Planning in the Parish of Idmiston (Unpublished report to Idmiston Parish Council).

WOODRUFFE, B J (in press), Wiltshire Villages (London, Hale).

Acknowledgements I would like to thank the following people for granting permission to collect data from valuation lists and direction sheets: Mr Hollingsworth (Southampton Valuation Office), Mr Welch (Test Valley District Council), Miss Jean Hall (Winchester City Council) and Mr Hanslip (Eastleigh Borough Council). The following students assisted with some of the village investigations: Deborah Allen (Lockerley), Philip Walker (Sherfield English), Anne Goodwin and Jonathan Mitchell (Wellow) and Sue Jackson (Minstead and Wellow).

9 The Physical Environment and Urban Growth: Potential and Constraint

M J CLARK

The economic growth and social change experienced by South Hampshire have taken place within the context provided by a varied, but moderate physical environment. Moderation is apparent in the relief, climate, hydrology and soils of the region. Rarely do we find physical attributes so advantageous that they could be said to have rendered economic growth almost inevitable, but at the same time it is equally rare to detect any physical constraint so insurmountable or extensive that it could be regarded as an absolute barrier to development. In this respect, South Hampshire is representative of much of the urbanised, temperate mid-latitudes in that its physical environment tends to be perceived on the two disparate planes of (i) the site-scale technical considerations of the civil engineer or water authority, and (ii) the macro-scale, largely aesthetic, viewpoint of architectural, recreational and conservational interests. It appears, therefore, to be academically and professionally unfashionable to regard environment as a fundamental component of the growth system itself, triggering change through the potential offered by physical resources, yet constraining development through limitations which operate both as cost disincentives and perception inhibitors. The following consideration of land-, water- and bio-systems will certainly not claim that environment is the key to development, nor that it exerts an inflexible negative or positive control on growth rates and directions. It may, however, give grounds for suggesting that the link between development and environment is closer and stronger than is envisaged by any exclusively socio-economic model of growth. The discussion will indicate that there is a growing professional acceptance of the practical advantages to be gained from incorporating environmental attributes as standard planning and management criteria.

Whilst increasing emphasis has been given to the academic importance of recognising the connectivity between components of the environmental system, the boundaries of planning responsibility are drawn along more traditional lines and offer a clear basis for subdividing the theme. Thus, for this purpose, hydrology and the ecosystem can conveniently be considered as separate topics, generating their own research programmes and falling within the remit of largely separate institutional structures. The fact that an increasingly important focus for research even in South Hampshire encompasses the present and past links between vegetation, hydrology and geomorphology is just one of many indications that environmental research has tended to restructure more rapidly than environmental management. It follows that in the present context the remaining environmental elements, grouped loosely under the heading of Land Resources, can also most appropriately be classified on management rather than physical criteria. For South Hampshire, it is suggested that emphasis can justifiably be given to three broad topics: mineral resources (particularly aggregates and hydrocarbons), slope and land stability, and the coastal zone. Such an approach has the added advantage that it provides a framework within which to review the major dimensions of the Man-environment relationship, namely resource, constraint, hazard and impact.

The theoretical antecedants on which studies such as this can be based are restricted, having developed for most practical purposes in the period since the late 1960s. At risk of oversimplification, one might suggest that the impetus has been greatest in North America, where development pressure, coupled with land and finance availability, provided the incentive for increasing activity, further encouraged by the growing and maturing environmental lobby and facilitated by the absence of the inertia of a complex, historically-rooted planning legislation and bureaucracy. In the North American terminology, environmental geology (Flawn, 1970; Knill, 1970) emerged to reflect the growing awareness of practical links between physical land attributes and land-use potential, and within this broad field there developed a specific strand of urban geology (Yelverton, 1971) to cater for the problems of existing or proposed built-up areas. Environmental geomorphology (Coates, 1971), urban geomorphology (Coates, 1976a) and geomorphic engineering (Coates, 1976b) crystallised the topic further in recognition of the need to differentiate between subsurface (geological) and surficial (geomorphological) attributes, though the distinction has not been rigorously defined.

One product of this North American focus has been a literature and theoretical (or model) base which is dominated by elements not entirely appropriate to British environment. Thus, for example, the 1973 Urban Geology Master Plan for California (Alfors et al, 1973), which was produced by the California Division of Mines and Geology early enough to have had a substantial influence on subsequent North American work, incorporated management strategies for an impressive series of urban hazards, including landslides, flooding, earthquakes, expansive soils, tsunamis, seiches, erosion, fault slippage, subsidence and volcanic activity. In comparison with this level of physical dynamism and response, the justification for describing the South Hampshire environment as moderate is immediately clear, but in consequence much of the theory and technique of North American urban geomorphology is rendered only marginally relevant in the British context. Perhaps

196

rather closer in environmental attribute and planning approach is the long history of urban physiography in Eastern Europe (e.g. Różycka, 1964), or the applied geomorphology of some other Western European countries (e.g. Tricart, 1973). Nevertheless, although progress has been made in refining and standardising some techniques, such as geomorphological mapping (Demek, 1972), there is no current European concensus on the role and methodology of urban geomorphology itself. Inevitably, therefore, the following consideration of environmental priorities in South Hampshire tends to be pragmatic and site-specific rather than theory-based and generalised.

MINERAL EXPLOITATION - AGGREGATES AND HYDROCARBONS

Mineral production in Hampshire is varied, though few components are of a scale and nature that render them environmentally significant at more than a local level. Some chalk and clay are exploited, but production is such that it has restricted environmental impact, and the materials themselves do not play a key role in any regional growth-linked process. Control is thus possible through the normal county planning procedure, and no major environmental problems need be envisaged. Deep bores for obtaining geothermal energy from hot water offer an interesting prospect for limited future development in the region. The potential has been proved at Marchwood, and plans are well advanced for production-scale projects (with DoE support) at Eastleigh and to provide heating for the major new Western Esplanade development at Southampton. But again the matter is largely a local concern in the present context, with no substantial environmental impacts or constraints. Indeed, since it can be argued that it is energy rather than water which is being extracted, this does not strictly classify as "mineral" at all and the planning responsibility thus devolves to district rather than county level. The remaining two mineral production categories, aggregates and hydro-carbons, have a quite different order of importance based on economic value, development constraint, environmental impact and the complexity of the planning issues that are raised.

Aggregates

Sand and gravel supplies are an essential requirement for major urban, industrial and route development. Since such materials have high bulk and weight, they attract punitive transport costs if long distances are involved, and it follows that regional supplies are important to regional growth. As a consequence, the aggregate industry acts as a sensitive barometer for regional construction activity, and through its pricing levels it potentially presents a significant development constraint if supply fails to meet demand by any substantial amount. The important alternative source of material provided by road and rail imports of crushed rock from the Mendips and East Midlands is not further considered here, since it has no major local environmental implications.

Total aggregate reserves present no problem whatever, since Hampshire is well endowed with both sand and gravel in the form of land-based valley and terrace deposits and extensive submarine banks (Hampshire County Council, 1969). Exploitable reserves are much smaller, being limited by material quality, market price (which influences the degree

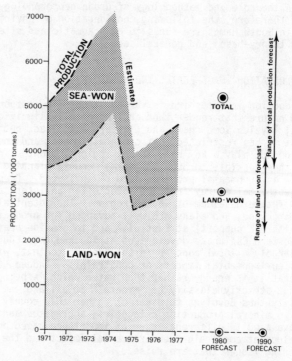

Figure 9.1 Estimates of aggregate production for Hampshire
(excluding the Isle of Wight), 1971–90.

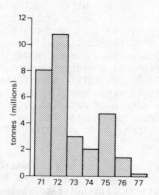

Figure 9.2 Sand and gravel reserves granted planning
permission in Hampshire, 1971–77.

of processing and transport distance that can be accepted economically), available technology (especially for deep marine dredging) and investment levels in the industry (processing plant, wharfage and number of dredging vessels) provide important limitations on future maximum output. Nevertheless, by far the most important potential constraint on supply is the granting of planning permission for exploitation, since permitted (land) or licenced (marine) reserves are only a small fraction of the economically-exploitable total. Data confidentiality, together with major changes in units of measure, material classification and statistical region boundaries, render extensive analysis difficult, but available data of varied quality (Hampshire County Council, 1977; Standing Conference on London and South East Regional Planning, 1980) allow compilation of the tentative production trends shown in Figure 9.1.

The assessment of permitted reserves to compare with these production rates is complicated by the fact that companies periodically review their reserve estimates, both in the light of continued site investigation and on the basis of price changes which alter the economic exploitability of marginal materials. The latest estimates available (Standing Conference on London and South East Regional Planning, 1980) suggest the 1977 permitted reserves for Hampshire (excluding the Isle of Wight) to be 37.2 million tonnes, sufficient for eleven years at 1977 production rates. Since these rates slumped following the regional construction peak (particularly of motorway building) in the mid-1970s (Fig.9.1), the pressure of new applications for planning permission also dropped dramatically (Fig.9.2). But there is no reason to believe that this threatens any future absolute restriction on supplies. Rather, the environmental planning implications are twofold, namely the environmental impact of exploitation, and the balance between land-based and sea-won aggregate.

It is unfortunate that much of the county's reserve lies in either important amenity areas or zones of environmental sensitivity. About 30 per cent of county production comes from the New Forest Production Area and almost 50 per cent from the Southampton/Portsmouth Production Area; between them they include many aesthetically- and economically-valuable sites. Given the importance of aggregate supply, it is unrealistic to expect that conservation issues would be allowed to disrupt urban growth to any great extent, but a decade of increasingly effective environmentalism has certainly produced a great increase in the number of conditions attached to planning permissions. This can, of course, lead indirectly to an upward price drift, which in its turn might have detrimental development consequences falling short of outright constraint. Nevertheless, there is little sign of overall change in the sentiment expressed in the South Hampshire Structure Plan, whereby aggregate priorities are to be safeguarded by avoiding the 'sterilisation' of important reserves by other forms of development. County policy has also long included guidelines on the reinstatement of worked land, though in this respect the late 1970s gave some concern in that the rate of land uptake outran the rate of reclamation, prompting initiation of a more vigorous enforcement policy for planning permit conditions.

Perhaps the most important outcome of the environmental and economic pressures on land-based production has been the substantial increase in

offshore aggregate winning, a change which has important policy
implications. In 1950 the offshore operation in the Wessex Region had
still not recovered to its pre-war level of 200,000 cubic yards (about
235,000 tonnes) a year, yet even so the prospect of expansion was
viewed with suspicion:

> "... careful consideration of the problems involved
> has led us to the unanimous conclusion that we should
> be advocating the taking of unwarrantable risks if we
> were to recommend the diversion to off-shore
> production of any major proportion of the demand for
> sand and gravel now met from more normal land
> working" (Ministry of Town and Country Planning,
> 1950, 10).

The reasons for this caution included the fear that extensive offshore
extraction might increase the risk of coast erosion by reducing onshore
sediment feed and increasing shorewards transport of wave energy
(Jolliffe, 1974), the suggestion of deleterious impact on market trends
within the industry, and the economic and environmental problems of re-
handling marine aggregate at the entry ports. To this list there has
since been added a substantial inventory of the ecological impacts of
dredging, particularly on fish-spawning grounds (Thompson, 1973).
Nevertheless, the 1970s saw a production increase to five or ten times
the pre-war levels, so that marine sources were supplying over 30 per
cent of the county's total (almost three times the national average
percentage). As the long-term county and national importance of these
supplies became recognised, the environmental caution began to be
replaced by a lobby in favour of exploitation (Standing Conference on
London and South East Regional Planning, 1971). By the middle of the
decade the policy transformation was almost complete, and national
policy-makers were being urged by the Verney Committee to take a more
aggressive line:

> "We recommend ... the existing studies of the
> Hydraulics Research Station should be expanded with
> a view to establishing ... whether the large areas
> sterilised for coast protection reasons ... may now
> be dredged without the risk of unacceptable damage
> to the coast. To this end all existing refusals on
> coast protection grounds should be reviewed and
> classified as (a) proven and (b) not proven. Each
> area designated not proven should then be
> reconsidered and experiments carried out to prove ...
> whether the fears are justified..."

> "The extent to which dredging for sand and gravel
> has long term adverse effects on fisheries must be
> established beyond doubt by experiment before it
> is accepted as axiomatic that permanent
> sterilisation of valuable aggregate deposits is
> justified on these grounds" (Department of the
> Environment et al, 1975, 40, 41).

The reasoned tone of these statements thinly disguises a massive shift
towards the viewpoint of the aggregate industry. Again the emotive

200

word 'sterilisation' is used to suggest that environmental protection is somehow negative. Whilst much of Europe and North America moves towards the 'environmental impact statement' philosophy that the exploiter/ developer carries the responsibility of demonstrating that his proposals are environmentally acceptable, the aggregate planning system is being encouraged to adopt the policy that it is up to 'environmental interests' to establish why the exploitation should not be allowed a free hand. Important though the aggregate industry undoubtedly is, this is a philosophy that should be approached with the utmost caution. Hampshire County Council did not accept the Verney Committee recommendations unequivocally, and the downturn in demand in the late 1970s reduced the immediate pressure on supply. Nonetheless, the underlying issues remain to be resolved.

Hydrocarbons

Most planners would regard the formulation of policies to handle hydrocarbon exploration and production as a far more pressing matter, though it is somewhat doubtful whether the potential environmental impact is really much greater than is already the case with aggregates. The national importance of oil and gas, together with the rather negative way in which oil companies are perceived by the public, combine to make oil exploration an emotive issue, despite the fact that the exploration phase at any one site rarely lasts more than two months and there is only a 2 per cent chance of any well yielding a commercial discovery (Lawrence, 1980). If all possible precautions are taken, there is no reason why exploratory drilling should cause more than temporary disruption in most areas, and complete site restoration should be possible. The conflict of interest becomes severe only when a proposed drilling site is either very close to residential development or lies in an area of exceptional environmental value or sensitivity. Rigorous use of planning powers can ameliorate these difficulties by insisting on a more expensive deviated borehole which drills obliquely from a more acceptable site, but there remains a residue of cases where a direct choice has to be made between environmental sanctity and national energy need. The alternative more jaundiced view that the choice is actually between environment and profit can only be partially true, since (as will be discussed below) the final decision rests firmly with the county planners and the national Departments of Environment and of Energy.

Onshore oil exploration and production in Britain started seriously in 1917, but it took the accelerated effort of the Second World War to lift production to 2300 barrels a day, and this figure was not substantially exceeded until supply pressures related to the Korean War and the Suez Crisis raised output to 2500 barrels a day by 1964 (Gilmour and Deacon, 1980). The 2000 barrel level was not breached again until the impact of the 1973 Arab-Israeli War prompted a traumatic increase in oil prices. Within this context, regional production first became significant with the BP discovery of a small commercial field at Kimmeridge (Dorset) in 1959, to be overshadowed after 1973 by the nearby Wytch Farm field (Dean, 1981) which was producing 4000 barrels a day by 1980. Hampshire itself is now virtually covered by exploration and production licences (Fig.9.3), and in April 1980 the Carless Consortium announced recoverable reserves of 16-40 million barrels of low-sulphur, light crude oil at their Humbly

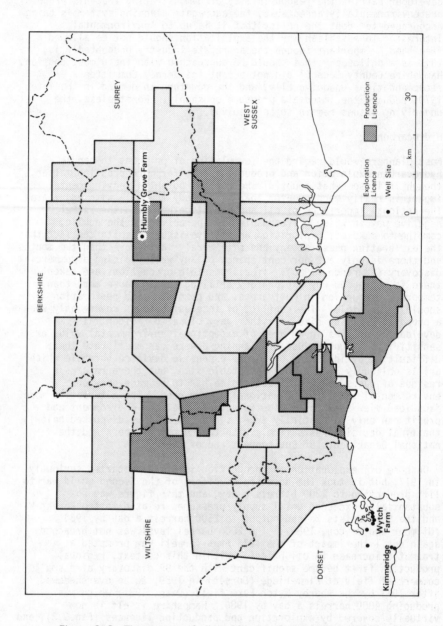

Figure 9.3 The context of oil exploitation in Hampshire, 1981.

Grove exploration site near Basingstoke. This is the first commercial
find in the county, though it is still not on the scale of Wytch Farm.

The main source of oil in Hampshire and Dorset is currently Jurassic
rocks folded and faulted into suitable traps in the Cretaceous. This
is the case at Humbly Grove, though in the Wytch Farm field down-
faulting of Jurassic source rocks has also produced a lower reservoir
in Permo-Triassic rocks (West, 1980). Most Hampshire traps are a few
miles long and trend approximately east-west. Although there is no
suggestion of major international-scale finds, the prospects for a
continued increase in commercial discoveries are good. Since the
Department of Energy allows drilling only after planning consent has
been given by the county, there is scope for local control of both
exploration and production, but the exciting economic prospect is
tempered somewhat by some remaining disparity between the interests of
the producer and the broader remit of the planning department or of the
community at large. In as far as has been possible, the county has
taken a positive line towards constructive compromise based both on
public information (Hampshire County Council, 1980) and policy
designation (Hampshire County Council, 1981). The need for compromise
can hardly be denied in view of the stated policy of the Department of
Energy:

> "The Department's general policy with regard to the
> search for petroleum in the onshore areas of Great
> Britain is to give all possible encouragement to
> such activity.... However, in implementing this
> policy the Department is not unmindful of the need
> to ensure that licence operations do not conflict
> with the requirements of planning legislation....
> Thus there can be no question of the award of a
> licence prejudicing in any way the discretion of
> planning authorities to determine planning
> applications in accordance with their
> responsibilities" (Hampshire County Council, 1981,
> 10-11).

This apparently moderate stance is seen in clearer perspective in a
separate written comment from the Minister of State for Energy:

> "If this objective is to be pursued successfully,
> it is essential that all areas which are believed
> to have petroleum-bearing potential should be
> thoroughly explored including, if possible, those
> areas, such as the New Forest, where there are, or
> may be special environmental considerations..."
> (Hampshire County Council, 1981, 10).

It would seem that as long as the county uses its powers to guide or
even constrain hydrocarbon development, then a balance of interests can
be achieved. However, should there be an attempt to curtail exploration altogether on environmental grounds, then moves may be taken to
impose the priority of national need. The authority to implement such
a shift of control away from the county exists in the power of the
Minister for the Environment to interpret or even reject the
recommendation of the inspector appointed to chair any public enquiry

that might be set up to consider opposition to a proposed drilling programme. If the inspector or minister were to find in favour of an oil company application, then the Department of Energy might well feel justified in issuing a Landward Petroleum Exploration Licence, despite previous county misgivings. Just such a test case is about to be fought to decide on proposed drilling at Denny Wood within the environmentally-contentious New Forest. A formidable local and environmental lobby opposed to drilling has built up, but it is not possible to foresee the outcome of this conflict of argument and power.

Ironically, it is possible that offshore oil and gas exploration might in the long term provide much greater economic benefits to the region, as well as posing correspondingly greater environmental threats along the coastal zone and at the point of landing or centre of processing. As yet the process is at too early a stage to permit prediction of the scale or nature of impact, but a Standing Conference on Offshore Exploration to co-ordinate interests already links Hampshire with neighbouring counties, with central government and with the oil industry. There is no reason to doubt the ability of the county and districts to guide and control developments associated with large-scale offshore production, so for the moment the balance of advantage would appear to lie in the region's favour. Nevertheless, as with aggregates, it is easy to underestimate the potential impact of apparently remote submarine activity. To maintain the advantage will, therefore, require the fullest multi-disciplinary and inter-institutional cooperation (Mitchell, 1976; Kwamena, 1980), but the Shetland experience provides a comprehensive and reasonably encouraging foundation for positive expectations (e.g. Nature Conservancy Council, 1976; Ritchie, 1981).

SLOPE AND LAND STABILITY

Topographic slope can be viewed as an architectural and landscape resource or as an engineering handicap. Geomorphological assessment, which incorporates several slope-related forms and processes, is well established in principle as a criterion for the engineering design and location of major development projects (Doornkamp et al, 1979). This is particularly the case in highway engineering (Brunsden et al, 1975), but many of the proven applications concern extreme or hazardous environments. Progress towards including a geomorphological element in the planning of areas such as Hampshire is relatively slow, though it can be demonstrated that there are several extremely important environmental attributes.

Surface slope

Slope has both direct and indirect influence on people, vehicles and buildings. For people it affects choice of route or location, for vehicles it acts through speed and fuel-efficiency, and for buildings it is a control of stability and pre-construction ground preparation costs. Many, but not all, of these influences can be reduced to a cost equivalent. It is not easy to establish the extent to which, and means by which, topographic information is used in individual decision-making (Sheppard and Adams, 1971), and indeed it has been shown that even in the apparently obvious case of choice of dwelling location by elderly people in Southampton, the slope gradient in the vicinity ranks extremely low in the personal perception of residential attributes (Barnard, 1978).

The slope factor is usually evaluated through a series of threshold values of gradient which are taken to be the limits of steepness for specific land uses in specific regions (e.g. Cooke and Doornkamp, 1974). This approach has been adopted in Hampshire, where the slope categories specified in Table 9.1 provided the basis for slope mapping of the major Park Gate North development by the County Planning Department. This classification has since been published (Hampshire County Council, 1981b) as a guideline for developers and for use at district level. In this context, slope gradient is being used as a planning constraint at site scale rather than regional scale, but is nevertheless an important component in a set of designated environmental planning attributes including orientation, drainage, microclimate, soils and vegetation.

Land stability

Land stability depends greatly on rock type, and therefore varies markedly across the county. For example, the Chalk which covers over a third of the county is a relatively strong but varied rock whose structure closely influences stability, particularly through the orientation of lines of weakness with respect to the slope. Coles (1980) suggests that in areas of simple structure with dips of less than 25°, surface slopes are stable up to 65° gradient, whilst complex steeply-dipping structures give unstable surface slopes above 25° gradient. Most natural chalk slopes have gradients below 32° (Clark, 1965), which is close to the residual shear strength angle of internal friction. Thus slope stability becomes a significant consideration only in oversteepened areas such as coasts or artificial cuttings. It has been noted (Coles, 1980) that the main danger on chalk railway cuttings in Hampshire comes from periodic spalling and small-scale rock falls, whilst major collapse has been rare, despite the gradients of $75-80^{o}$ used by early engineers. For chalk road cuttings, the standard approach adopted by Hampshire County Council uses a 1:1½ (34°) slope, which may be a very conservative design for short (geological) time scales. Extensive field and laboratory analysis employed in the design of the 47m deep M40 cutting across the Chiltern Hills in Oxfordshire in 1972 concluded with a two-stage profile having an upper 40° slope and lower 65° slope. Again, no substantial problems have arisen, and it thus appears that chalk presents few development constraints apart from the absence of surface water and the occasional steepness of slopes.

Other rock types in Hampshire have proved considerably less stable. Major landslides in the 1970s affected the M27 Chilworth Link just north of Southampton, the A3(M) Horndean-Bedhampton motorway north-east of Havant, and the M27 at Funtley, north of Fareham (Elliott, 1978). In each case artificial slopes were involved, and it appears that the inherent instability of these unconsolidated materials is sometimes underestimated by design engineers. Nevertheless, it should not automatically be assumed that the adoption of more conservative lower-angle design slopes would be preferable, since this alternative requires use of considerably more land and involves greater construction costs. Minor landslips are a regular occurrence on the Tertiary sands, clays and gravels that cover almost two-thirds of the county. Eight garages demolished after subsidence on the Walkford Park estate (New Forest

205

Table 9.1

Design implications of slope analysis specified as site guidelines by Hampshire County Council.

SLOPES STEEPER THAN	1:5 (=c.11°)	- identifies slopes potentially dangerous for public access. <u>No development.</u>
SLOPES STEEPER THAN	1:10 (=c.6°)	- usually the accepted maximum limit (1:10) for house building without special construction details/methods/layouts. No industrial development: <u>residential development with severe limitations.</u>
SLOPES STEEPER THAN	1:20 (=c.3°)	- gradients noticed by pedestrians (e.g. maximum ramp gradient recommended 1:15 or 1:12 for short stretches). <u>Not really suitable for industrial development.</u> <u>Residential development with some limitations</u> (contour footpaths).
SLOPES STEEPER THAN	1:30 (=c.2°)	- limit of sloping land capable of being modified for playing fields. Ideal slope for playing fields is 1:50 (with acceptable maximum of 1:40 for non-first-class football pitches). <u>Industrial development with limitations</u> (largely alignment of access road/delivery areas and loading bays). <u>Residential largely satisfactory.</u>
SLOPES STEEPER THAN	1:50 (=c.1°)	- ideal slopes for movement, drainage, playing fields, schools. <u>All types of development.</u>
SLOPES FLATTER THAN	1:50	- natural drainage difficulties begin to become apparent. <u>Special care with playing fields.</u> <u>All types of development satisfactory,</u> but possible need for care over invert levels of services; natural drainage or flooding if at low level.

District) in 1977, and eighteen houses affected by slips on the Hill Park estate (Fareham) in 1976 are typical of the scale of event involved. Part of the responsibility lies with geological susceptibility and part with the additional risks associated with nearby artificial slopes, particularly major road and rail cuttings. It may be that the landslip hazard has not been fully appreciated by county and district planners, and that greater constraint could be placed on developers. The use of preliminary slope mapping might be a useful first step towards designating vulnerable sites.

A more significant problem with extensive planning implications was the landslip in 1979-80 which threatened some thirty-four houses in Bryanston Road and Gainsford Road at Bitterne, a residential suburb of Southampton on the east bank of the River Itchen. Shallow slides were apparently confined to 3m of landfill and possibly 2-3m of superficial slope deposits overlying Bracklesham Beds, and were suggested (Barton, 1979) to relate to periodic slight rises of ground-water pressure at the foot of the slope or in several perched water tables within the mantle. Imminent substantial damage to properties valued at £120,000 was predicted, with ultimate damage to property worth £1 million if the slides were allowed to proceed unchecked. Remedial stabilisation works were designed by consulting engineers, and implemented during 1980.

In physical terms there is little that is particularly noteworthy about this event, but the social and economic repercussions produced intense local argument. A prolonged battle was fought between a local residents' association, the Southampton City Council and various insurance companies to decide responsibility for funding damage reinstatement and remedial works. Whether the city council could have been made legally liable for compensation is doubtful, though their case was not helped by the fact that in the early 1970s the Planning Department had refused permission for new buildings at the top of the slope, using the slope stability implications of tree felling as supportive argument. Later, however, planning permission was granted, so it might be argued that this confirmed that the planners had no substantial doubts about the stability of the site. The legal liability of the insurers was also unclear, and they categorically rejected the notion of 'moral obligation' applied to their responsibilities. After extensive argument, an agreed compromise left the city council paying £134,000 for remedial works, and the insurers meeting the bill for actual property damage. Since the issue was not fought in the courts, there was no definitive clarification of the real limits of responsibility of a local authority with respect to predicting and compensating natural hazard damage.

Building-foundation failure

Large landslips tend to be spatially and temporally restricted events, but their scale and lack of perceived warning often give them a brief 'headline' impact in public awareness. Damage to individual buildings by failure of foundations, either as a result of minor subsidence or clay swelling and shrinking, tends to be overlooked as a major environmental impact on urban areas, simply because it comprises a large number of small events rather than a few major problems. This general under-perception of the hazard received a severe jolt in 1975-6, when drought-induced clay shrinkage affected about one house per thousand in the UK to produce an estimated £100 million damage. This was perhaps five to eight times the average annual cost (Clark, 1980). Definitive data are unavailable, but a valuable secondary source is provided by records of insurance claims by householders for damage to their property. Thus the Sun Alliance Group listed 188 claims in Southern Hampshire and the Isle of Wight for the period 1971-

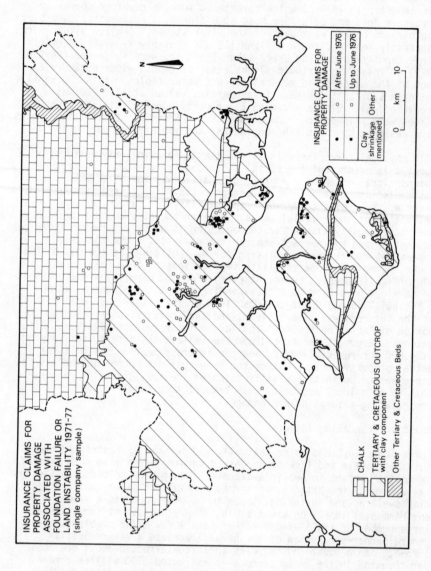

Figure 9.4 Insurance claims for property damage associated with
foundation failure and land instability, 1971–77.

Table 9.2

Insurance claims for house-foundation failure,
1971-76.

	Number of insurance claims per 100,000 dwellings		Rank in national scale of county severity of hazard	
	1971-75	1976	1971-75	1976
Hampshire	3.08	50.11	10th	11th
Isle of Wight	7.31	93.61	2nd	3rd

1977, of which 92 noted clay shrinkage as a contributory factor (Fig. 9.4).

Hampshire is placed in its national perspective in Table 9.2 by combining the 7000 insurance claims received by the Sun Alliance and Commercial Union companies, together representing about one-third of national claims. It can be clearly seen that foundation instability is a serious problem in the region as a whole as a result of geology (clay-rich foundations occupy about 32 per cent of the area of Hampshire and 58 per cent of the Isle of Wight) and climate (potential soil-moisture deficit for end-August 1976 was approximately 396mm in Hampshire and 405mm in the Isle of Wight - almost the highest in the country: Taylor, 1980). Figure 9.4 demonstrates that within the region there are very marked spatial variations in hazard impact. A major control of this pattern is the distribution of the housing stock, but additional concentration identifies areas of particular hazard susceptibility (for example, Bitterne and Fareham show strong clusters of claims, and both have already been mentioned in this consideration of land instability).

Whilst this aspect of the environment can be shown to have a very real impact on the urban fabric, it is too widespread to function as an effective location constraint. Rather, it could be argued that the 1975-76 drought highlighted the inadequacy of the British Standard for foundation design in clay-rich areas. Furthermore, since almost half the cases of damage are exacerbated by tree roots, a vigorous policy of guidance in the landscaping of new developments might be expected as a minimum response. It is both disappointing and surprising to find that, whilst building inspectors continue to check the traditional specification for foundations of new houses, it is still common to find developers being allowed to plant trees within a few metres of load-bearing walls, a practice tantamount to building in future foundation failures. There remains considerable scope for improvement in this aspect of environmental planning. The delicate issue of legal liability was brought sharply into focus in February 1980, when the High Court awarded damages of £5600 to a Southampton householder against Hampshire County Council on the grounds that subsidence damage to his house in 1976 had been caused by dehydration of the clay sub-soil by encroachment of the roots from a tree on a public roadside verge. In this instance, the damages were cancelled by the Appeal

Court in February 1981 on the basis that, since the clay outcrop did not appear on the geology map, the city council could not reasonably have foreseen the problem. Whether, as evidence of structural damage by trees mounts, it will continue to be possible for local authorities and developers to take refuge in a general plea of ignorance remains to be seen.

THE COASTAL ZONE

In geomorphological terms the coast of mainland Hampshire can be regarded (Clark, 1971) as the product of Pleistocene and post-glacial processes acting upon the varied Tertiary rocks preserved within the chalk-rimmed Hampshire Basin syncline, whilst the southern Isle of Wight displays an imposing coast cut in generally more resistant Cretaceous strata. A Pleistocene history of spasmodic sea-level fall produced a flight of concentric terraces (well preserved in the New Forest), across which an integrated regional drainage system (the "Solent River") was incised (Everard, 1954). Post-glacial marine transgression flooded and dismembered this system, breached the southern rim of Chalk, and initiated the estuarine drowning, cliff cutting and beach or spit building which today characterise the coast of Hampshire (Fig.9.5).

The immediate development implications are twofold. The drowned coast provided an admirable series of sheltered deep-water sites with port potential, including the harbours at Poole, Christchurch and Portsmouth, and the estuaries of the Medina at Cowes and the Solent-Southampton Water system. After a long tradition of maritime use, these sites have in recent decades achieved prominence in the regional growth process both through their ability to handle large deep-draught vessels (Fawley oil terminal, the Prince Charles container port), and through their national importance for yachting and water-based recreation in general.

Not surprisingly, coastal management problems have come to be regarded largely in terms of land-use pressure and conflict. An early review (National Parks Commission, 1967) recognised the general difficulties associated with recreational pressure, obtrusive land uses and very large retirement population. A programme of conservation and land-use management policies was initiated. Over the last decade this has been maintained and strengthened to culminate in the formulation of a coherent county policy for the coastal zone based largely on an amalgam of general planning strategies and powers (Hampshire County Council, 1979 and 1980). This initiative is to be welcomed environmentally in that it gives priority to landscape conservation and accepts the major ecological importance and sensitivity of many of the Hampshire wetlands. Understandably, the blanket protection provided is less than total (a major objective 'to enhance the beauty of the coast' is qualified significantly 'whilst meeting legitimate demands on its resources'), but the defined policy provides a valuable basis for constructive planning, albeit within an extremely complex inter-agency and multi-authority framework.

Almost inevitably, the management policies so far designated make negligible reference to physiographic problems in the region, largely

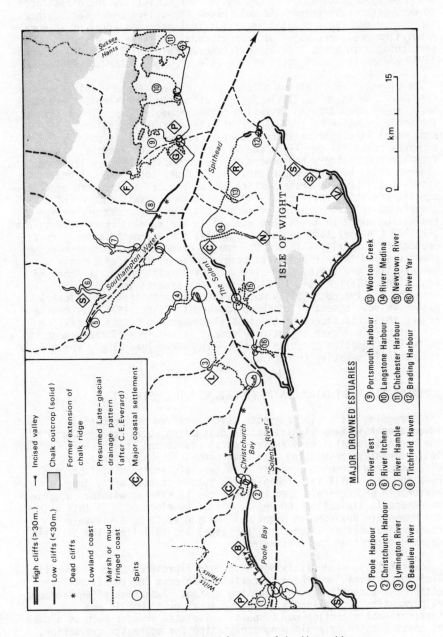

Figure 9.5 Main morphological features of the Hampshire coast

Legend:
- High cliffs (>30 m.)
- Low cliffs (<30 m.)
- Dead cliffs
- Lowland coast
- Marsh or mud fringed coast
- Spits
- Incised valley
- Chalk outcrop (solid)
- Former extension of chalk ridge
- Presumed Late-glacial drainage pattern (after C. E. Everard)
- Major coastal settlement

MAJOR DROWNED ESTUARIES

1 Poole Harbour
2 Christchurch Harbour
3 Lymington River
4 Beaulieu River
5 River Test
6 River Itchen
7 River Hamble
8 Titchfield Haven
9 Portsmouth Harbour
10 Langstone Harbour
11 Chichester Harbour
12 Brading Harbour
13 Wooton Creek
14 River Medina
15 Newtown River
16 River Yar

because such matters are regarded as coast protection responsibilities which fall (under the 1949 Coast Protection Act) to district rather than county control. The vulnerability of the Hampshire coast to erosion, produced by a combination of geological susceptibility and direct access to deep-ocean wave energy, is well known (May, 1964 and 1966). Since the consequent rapid coastal recession impinges upon areas of intense population pressure, major management conflicts have developed, particularly in areas such as Christchurch Bay (Phillips, 1973; Clark, 1974) and on the south coast of the Isle of Wight (Clark, 1978).

The planning implications of such problems have been widely discussed elsewhere, so there is little justification for repeating the arguments here, apart from drawing attention to two especially pertinent issues. The whole question of the balance of interests in coastal-zone management is yet to be satisfactorily resolved in this country, so that numerous potential conflicts can be identified (for example, between frontage householders and others in the community, between residents and other coastal resource exploiters, and between local and national interests). Some of these matters can be reduced to the form of cost-benefit analysis (Phillips, 1974), and it may be that the recent government-initiated review of such techniques for coast protection evaluation might be taken into account in the current reconsideration of the 1949 Coast Protection Act. Secondly, the approach taken by coast-protection authorities in the UK remains essentially short-term and reactive, and their range of strategy choice is still distinctly conservative and engineering-biased compared with the North American equivalent (Clark et al, 1976). Given the present impact of coastal hazards, and the potentially much greater impacts that could follow extensive development of offshore resources (Clark, 1977), it can be argued that this aspect of the coastal management system is still in its infancy, and that urgent development is required if management is to be in a position to guide development rather than simply reacting to its periodic negative impacts.

A PERSPECTIVE ON ENVIRONMENTAL POTENTIAL AND CONSTRAINT

The foregoing discussion suggests that perceived environmental advantages have been significant in triggering socio-economic growth in the region, and that many environmental attributes have been instrumental in permitting such development to proceed in a cost-effective and harmonious manner. In general, environmental concerns have now been built into the planning system in such a way that reasonable protection and enhancement can be offered without incurring unreasonable limitations on any aspect of development. To this extent, the Hampshire environment might well be judged to be a valuable resource as well as a treasured heritage, and on balance the potential seems greater than the constraint.

Nevertheless, some misgivings have been expressed above in specific limited contexts, and there is certainly no room for complacency in either the community or the planning system. Awareness of environmental parameters is distinctly uneven, so that great public and institutional attention may be paid to isolated impacts such as a case of coast erosion or a planning application for aggregate extraction, whilst the massive total regional repercussions of other matters such

as foundation instability or declining beach-sediment budgets are
relatively neglected. One reason is probably that, whilst slow progress
is now being made towards environmental forward planning, much of the
system remains dominated by a reactive response to present or imminent
events. A particular case in point is the obvious temptation to
encourage offshore aggregate exploitation in the hope that the
environmental repercussions will be acceptable, but in the knowledge
that if adverse impacts do occur, then they are likely to be long-term
rather than short-term. Concern could also be expressed that so much of
environmental decision-making is left to an institutional framework
which traditionally has had an overwhelmingly socio-economic focus. For
historical reasons, only water is treated as a physical resource
requiring large-scale management by professional specialists, whilst
other environmental systems (many of them lacking the financial
prospects of a conveniently saleable product such as water) may be
subject to a democratic, lay-dominated, decision-making hierarchy.
Despite these problems, Hampshire has been innovative in several aspects
of its adjustment to environmental priorities, and the overall
perspective for the next decade would seem to be challenging, but
generally encouraging.

REFERENCES

ALFORS, J T, BURNETT, J L and GAY, T E (1973), Urban geology master
          plan for California, California Division of Mines and Geology
          Bulletin, 198.

BARNARD, K C (1978), The Residential Geography of the Elderly: a
          Multiple-scale Approach (Unpublished PhD thesis, University of
          Southampton).

BARTON, M E (1979), Report on a Site Investigation at Bryanston and
          Gainsford Roads, Bitterne, Southampton (Unpublished technical
          report for Messrs E W H Gifford and Partners, Consulting
          Engineers).

BRUNSDEN, D, DOORNKAMP, J C, FOOKES, P G, JONES, D K C and KELLY, J M H
          (1975), Large-scale geomorphological mapping and highway
          engineering design, Quarterly Journal of Engineering Geology,
          8, 227-53.

CLARK, M J (1965), The Morphology of Chalk Slopes (Unpublished PhD
          thesis, University of Southampton).

CLARK, M J (1971), The coast of south-west Hampshire, in Clark, M J
          (ed.), Field Studies in South Hampshire (Southampton,
          Geographical Association), 98-106.

CLARK, M J (1974), Conflict on the coast, Geography, 59(2), 93-103.

CLARK, M J (1977), The relationship between coastal-zone management and
          off-shore economic development, Maritime Policy and
          Management, 4, 431-449.

213

CLARK, M J (1978), Geomorphology in coastal-zone environmental management, Geography, 63(4), 273-282.

CLARK, M J (1980), Building-foundation failure, in GREGORY, K J and DOORNKAMP, J C (eds) Atlas of Drought in Britain 1975-6 (London, Institute of British Geographers), 63-4.

CLARK, M J, RICKETTS, P J and SMALL, R J (1976), Barton does not rule the waves, Geographical Magazine, 48(10), 580-588.

COATES, D R (ed.)(1971), Environmental Geomorphology (Binghampton, State University of New York).

COATES, D R (ed.)(1976a), Urban Geomorphology (Boulder, Colorado; Geological Society of America).

COATES, D R (1976b), Geomorphic engineering, in COATES, D R (ed.) Geomorphology and Engineering (Stroudsberg, Pennsylvania; Dowden, Hutchinson and Ross), 3-21.

COLES, B J (1980), Theoretical and Experimental Observations on the Stability and Design of Chalk Slopes and Cuttings (Unpublished BSc Research Report, Department of Civil Engineering, University of Southampton).

COOKE, R U and DOORNKAMP, J C (1974), Geomorphology in Environmental Management (Oxford, Clarendon Press), 361.

DEAN, C (1981), Oil flows on the Dorset mainland, Geographical Magazine, 43(9), 576-580.

DEMEK, J (ed.)(1972), Manual of Detailed Geomorphological Mapping (Prague, Academia).

DEPARTMENT OF THE ENVIRONMENT, SCOTTISH DEVELOPMENT OFFICE, WELSH OFFICE (1975), Aggregates: the Way Ahead (London, HMSO).

DOORNKAMP, J C, BRUNSDEN, D, JONES, D K C, COOKE, R U and BUSH, P R (1979), Rapid geomorphological assessments for engineering, Quarterly Journal of Engineering Geology, 12, 189-204.

ELLIOTT, D J (1978), The Prevention and Control of Landslides (Unpublished BSc Research Peport, Department of Civil Engineering, University of Southampton).

EVERARD, C E (1954), The Solent River - a geomorphological study, Transactions of the Institute of British Geographers, 20, 41-58.

FLAWN, P T (1970), Environmental Geology (New York, Harper and Row).

GILMOUR, J and DEACON, C (1980), Introduction to onshore petroleum exploration in the United Kingdom, in HAMPSHIRE COUNTY COUNCIL, Onshore Oil Exploration and Development in Hampshire (Winchester, County Planning Department), 3-15.

HAMPSHIRE COUNTY COUNCIL (1969), South Hampshire Study (Winchester, Hampshire County Council),

HAMPSHIRE COUNTY COUNCIL (1977), Hampshire Facts and Figures 1977 (Winchester, Hampshire County Council).

HAMPSHIRE COUNTY COUNCIL (1979), The Hampshire Coast: Interim Report (Winchester, Hampshire County Council).

HAMPSHIRE COUNTY COUNCIL (1980), Coast and Countryside Conservation Policy (Winchester, Hampshire County Council).

HAMPSHIRE COUNTY COUNCIL (1981a), Oil and Gas Exploration and Exploitation in Hampshire (Winchester, Hampshire County Council), Strategic Planning Paper 9.

HAMPSHIRE COUNTY COUNCIL (1981b), Landscape and Development: Part I Survey and Analysis (Winchester, Hampshire County Council).

JOLLIFFE, I P (1974), Beach-offshore dredging: some environmental consequences, Proceedings of the 1974 Offshore Technology Conference, 2, 257-265.

KNILL, J (1970), Environmental geology, Proceedings of the Geologists' Association, 81(3), 529-537.

KWAMENA, F A (1980), Implications of offshore resources development for coastal management, in McCALLA, R J (ed.) Coastal Studies in Canadian Geography (Saint Mary's University Occasional Papers in Geography), 4, 9-31.

LAWRENCE, J R (1980), Survey and exploration - the first stages, in HAMPSHIRE COUNTY COUNCIL, Onshore Oil Exploration and Development in Hampshire (Winchester, Hampshire County Council), 21-26.

MAY, V J (1964), A Study of Recent Coastal Changes in South-east England (Unpublished MSc thesis, University of Southampton).

MAY, V J (1966), A preliminary study of recent coastal changes and sea defences in south-east England, Southampton Research Series in Geography, 3, 3-24.

MINISTRY OF TOWN AND COUNTRY PLANNING (1950), Report of the Advisory Committee on Sand and Gravel: Part 5 Wessex (London, HMSO), 10.

MITCHELL, J K (1976), Onshore impact of Scottish offshore oil: planning implications for the Middle Atlantic States, Journal of the American Institute of Planners, 42, 386-398.

NATURE CONSERVANCY COUNCIL (1976), Shetland: Localities of Geological and Geomorphological Importance (Newbury, Nature Conservancy Council).

NATIONAL PARKS COMMISSION (1967), The Coasts of Hampshire and the Isle
          of Wight (London, HMSO).

PHILLIPS, P H (1973), Coast Protection: Physiography and the Planning
          Process (Unpublished PhD thesis, University of Southampton).

PHILLIPS, P H (1974), Coastal stabilisation at Barton-on-Sea, Civil
          Engineering, 69, 47-53.

RITCHIE, W (1981), Giant oil terminal on Shetland farmland,
          Geographical Magazine, 53(8), 489-496.

RÓŻYCKA, W (1964), Physiographic research in town and country planning,
          Problems of Applied Geography II (Warzawa, PWN - Polish
          Scientific Publishers), Geographia Polonica 3.

SHEPPARD, D and ADAMS, J M (1971), A survey of drivers' opinions on maps
          for route finding, The Cartographic Journal, 8(2), 105-114.

STANDING CONFERENCE ON LONDON AND SOUTH EAST REGIONAL PLANNING (1971),
          Sand and Gravel extraction: Interim Reports.

STANDING CONFERENCE ON LONDON AND SOUTH EAST REGIONAL PLANNING (1980),
          Wessex Sand and Gravel Region - Sub-regional Commentary on
          Results of Annual Monitoring Exercise.

TAYLOR, J A (1980), Potential soil-moisture deficit and soil-water
          availability, in GREGORY, K J and DOORNKAMP, J C (eds) Atlas
          of Drought in Britain 1975-6 (London, Institute of British
          Geographers), 51-52.

THOMPSON, J R (1973), Ecological effects of offshore dredging and beach
          nourishment: a review, US Army Coastal Engineering Research
          Center, Miscellaneous Paper, 1.

TRICART, J (1973), La géomorphologie dans l'études intégrées
          d'amenagement du milieu naturel, Annales de Geographie, 82
          (449), 420-453.

WEST, I M (1980), Geology of Hampshire in relation to petroleum
          exploration, in HAMPSHIRE COUNTY COUNCIL, Onshore Oil
          Exploration and Development in Hampshire (Winchester,
          Hampshire County Council), 17-20.

YELVERTON, C A (1971), The role of local governments in urban geology,
          in NICOLLS, D R and CAMPBELL, C C (eds) Environmental
          Planning and Geology (Washington, US Department of Housing and
          Urban Development, and US Department of the Interior),
          CDPD-32, 76-81.

10 Hydrological Implications of Urban Growth

A M GURNELL, J BUTTLE AND C W PROWSE

The most important factor influencing changes in the hydrology of
Hampshire during the period 1960 to 1980 has been the marked expansion
in the size of the population and industrial base. Figure 10.1 shows
that within the Hampshire River and Water Division (the limit of the
study area for this essay) of the Southern Water Authority (SWA), there
has been a steady increase in the total demand for water throughout the
twenty-year period. This increasing requirement is compounded from two
separate demand categories, namely those for metered and unmetered
water. An examination of the detailed trends shown in Figure 10.1 helps
to explain some of the special local factors which may be important with
respect to adjustments in local hydrology.

It is difficult to categorise precisely the nature of water users who
are supplied with metered or unmetered supplies, but in general metered
supplies are associated with large industrial premises, agricultural
concerns and small businesses with an unusually heavy demand for water
(e.g. launderettes). In contrast, the majority of unmetered users are
domestic consumers, although small industrial firms and many other
commercial premises may also receive an unmetered water supply. Thus
the trend in the unmetered supply reflects population growth in the area
but in addition there has also been an increase in per capita water
consumption from 228 litres/capita/day in 1961 to 268 litres/capita/day
in 1979. This increase partly results from a genuine increase in per
capita water use, but it also contains some losses in distribution
which, over the whole of the SWA area, are estimated at approximately 22
per cent of the total unmetered demand (SWA, pers. comm.). Of
particular interest is the contrast between the effect of the hosepipe-
ban in reducing unmetered demand in 1976 and the increase in metered

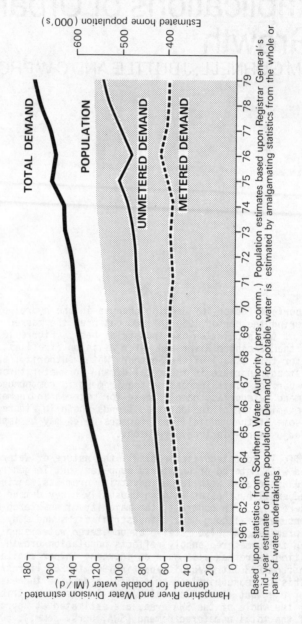

Figure 10.1 Trends in water demand and population growth in
the HRWD, 1960 – 80.

demand in the same year. Interestingly there had been a markedly higher
unmetered demand in the preceding dry summer of 1975, when a hosepipe-
ban had not been imposed. Associated with the population growth, there
has been considerable industrial expansion and as a result, metered as
well as unmetered demand has grown considerably within the area.

The increase in demand for water has been met almost entirely from
local water resources. Between 60 and 70 per cent of the water
abstracted annually in the Hampshire River and Water Division (HRWD) for
public water supply is derived directly from groundwater sources.
Surface water is abstracted at two sites, from the river Itchen at
Otterbourne and from the river Test at Testwood, and in addition, a
substantial quantity of non-potable water is supplied to one industrial
concern from the Testwood pumping station (Fig.10.2). Since flows in
both the rivers Itchen and Test have a large groundwater component
(perhaps 70 to 80 per cent of the flow in these rivers is derived from
the Chalk aquifer), it is clear that the development and careful
management of the water resources of the Chalk is crucial to all aspects
of water supply in the HRWD area.

The major hydrological implication of this demographic and economic
growth and its related water demand is that the extended urban area has
had significant repercussions on both runoff dynamics and water quality.
In addition, the increasing demand for water has led to a great
concentration in research effort by the SWA into improving understanding
of the natural hydrology of the Chalk aquifer and into devising methods
by which the resource might best be developed and managed. This essay
will, therefore, concentrate on three specific aspects of local
hydrology. The first two aspects concern some of the hydrological
effects of urbanising drainage basins (Fig.10.3). The first section
focuses upon adjustments in runoff dynamics in a recently-developed
area of medium-density housing, and the second concentrates upon water-
quality changes in relation to residential and industrial development
in a drainage basin to the north of Southampton. The third aspect
concerns the development of the Chalk aquifer to meet the increasing
water demands, with particular reference to the research being carried
out by the SWA into new techniques of groundwater management.

RESIDENTIAL DEVELOPMENT AND ITS EFFECT ON RUNOFF DYNAMICS

Figure 10.3 illustrates the extensive impact of urban development on
the flow of water through a drainage basin. The expanding population
in Hampshire has resulted in considerable housing development, and the
hydrological effects of this have been monitored in three small
catchments in the northern suburban fringe of Southampton (Fig.10.4A).
The flood hydrograph generated by a catchment in response to a given
input of precipitation is the product of the interaction of many flow
processes (Fig.10.4B). Many workers have identified the total effect
of urban development on the flood hydrograph in relation to different
types of urban development (James, 1965; Leopold, 1968; and Anderson,
1970), different stages of urban development (Carter, 1961; Anderson,
1970; Van Sickle, 1968) and the trends in the hydrograph during
development (Gregory, 1974; Hollis, 1977). But here an attempt will be
made to identify the effect of residential development on the relative

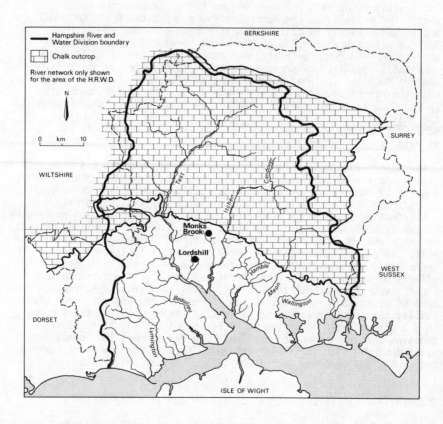

Figure 10.2   Location of study sites within the HRWD.

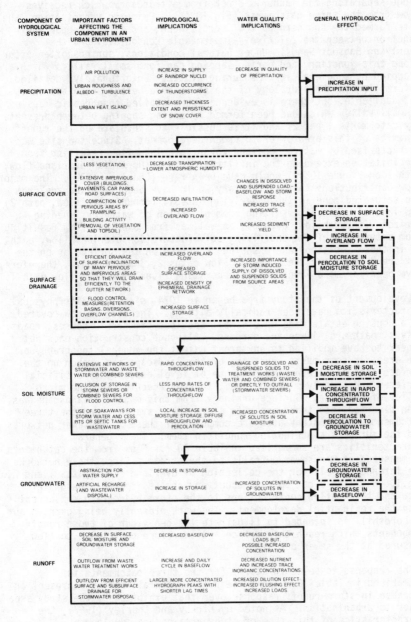

COMPONENT OF HYDROLOGICAL SYSTEM	IMPORTANT FACTORS AFFECTING THE COMPONENT IN AN URBAN ENVIRONMENT	HYDROLOGICAL IMPLICATIONS	WATER QUALITY IMPLICATIONS	GENERAL HYDROLOGICAL EFFECT
PRECIPITATION	AIR POLLUTION	INCREASE IN SUPPLY OF RAINDROP NUCLEI	DECREASE IN QUALITY OF PRECIPITATION	INCREASE IN PRECIPITATION INPUT
	URBAN ROUGHNESS AND ALBEDO - TURBULENCE	INCREASED OCCURRENCE OF THUNDERSTORMS		
	URBAN HEAT ISLAND	DECREASED THICKNESS EXTENT AND PERSISTENCE OF SNOW COVER		
SURFACE COVER	LESS VEGETATION	DECREASED TRANSPIRATION - LOWER ATMOSPHERIC HUMIDITY		
	EXTENSIVE IMPERVIOUS COVER (BUILDINGS, PAVEMENTS, CAR PARKS, ROAD SURFACES)		CHANGES IN DISSOLVED AND SUSPENDED LOAD - BASEFLOW AND STORM RESPONSE	DECREASE IN SURFACE STORAGE
	COMPACTION OF PERVIOUS AREAS BY TRAMPLING	DECREASED INFILTRATION	INCREASED TRACE INORGANICS	
	BUILDING ACTIVITY (REMOVAL OF VEGETATION AND TOPSOIL)	INCREASED OVERLAND FLOW	INCREASED SEDIMENT YIELD	INCREASE IN OVERLAND FLOW
SURFACE DRAINAGE	EFFICIENT DRAINAGE OF SURFACE (INCLINATION OF MANY PERVIOUS AND IMPERVIOUS AREAS SO THAT THEY WILL DRAIN EFFICIENTLY TO THE GUTTER NETWORK)	INCREASED OVERLAND FLOW	INCREASED IMPORTANCE OF STORM INDUCED SUPPLY OF DISSOLVED AND SUSPENDED SOLIDS FROM SOURCE AREAS	DECREASE IN PERCOLATION TO SOIL MOISTURE STORAGE
		DECREASED SURFACE STORAGE		
		INCREASED DENSITY OF EPHEMERAL DRAINAGE NETWORK		
	FLOOD CONTROL MEASURES (RETENTION BASINS, DIVERSIONS, OVERFLOW CHANNELS)	INCREASED SURFACE STORAGE		
SOIL MOISTURE	EXTENSIVE NETWORKS OF STORMWATER AND WASTE WATER OR COMBINED SEWERS	RAPID CONCENTRATED THROUGHFLOW	DRAINAGE OF DISSOLVED AND SUSPENDED SOLIDS TO TREATMENT WORKS (WASTE WATER AND COMBINED SEWERS) OR DIRECTLY TO OUTFALL (STORMWATER SEWERS)	DECREASE IN SOIL MOISTURE STORAGE
	INCLUSION OF STORAGE IN STORM SEWERS OR COMBINED SEWERS FOR FLOOD CONTROL	LESS RAPID RATES OF CONCENTRATED THROUGHFLOW		INCREASE IN RAPID CONCENTRATED THROUGHFLOW
	USE OF SOAKAWAYS FOR STORM WATER AND CESS PITS OR SEPTIC TANKS FOR WASTEWATER	LOCAL INCREASE IN SOIL MOISTURE STORAGE, DIFFUSE THROUGHFLOW AND PERCOLATION	INCREASED CONCENTRATION OF SOLUTES IN SOIL MOISTURE	DECREASE IN PERCOLATION TO GROUNDWATER STORAGE
GROUNDWATER	ABSTRACTION FOR WATER SUPPLY	DECREASE IN STORAGE		DECREASE IN GROUNDWATER STORAGE
	ARTIFICIAL RECHARGE (AND WASTEWATER DISPOSAL)	INCREASE IN STORAGE	INCREASED CONCENTRATION OF SOLUTES IN GROUNDWATER	DECREASE IN BASEFLOW
RUNOFF	DECREASE IN SURFACE SOIL MOISTURE AND GROUNDWATER STORAGE	DECREASED BASEFLOW	DECREASED BASEFLOW LOADS BUT POSSIBLE INCREASED CONCENTRATION	
	OUTFLOW FROM WASTE WATER TREATMENT WORKS	INCREASE AND DAILY CYCLE IN BASEFLOW	DECREASED NUTRIENT AND INCREASED TRACE INORGANIC CONCENTRATIONS	
	OUTFLOW FROM EFFICIENT SURFACE AND SUBSURFACE DRAINAGE FOR STORMWATER DISPOSAL	LARGER, MORE CONCENTRATED HYDROGRAPH PEAKS WITH SHORTER LAG TIMES	INCREASED DILUTION EFFECT, INCREASED FLUSHING EFFECT, INCREASED LOADS	

Figure 10.3 The effects of urban development on the hydrological cycle of the drainage basin.

221

magnitude and timing of the different flow processes, which together control the form and magnitude of the flood hydrograph.

The study catchments are located on the southern portion of a low ridge separating the Tanner's Brook from a tributary which receives flow from the three catchments (Fig.10.4A). Prior to urbanisation, the site formed the southern part of Lord's Wood, and it rests upon the junction between the relatively-impermeable London Clay and the overlying Bagshot Sands. Under natural conditions, springs often occur along this junction, and spring-sapping can form small valleys which are occupied by ephemeral streams during winter. Unfortunately, detailed information on the hydrology of the study area before urbanisation is not available, but there is evidence from detailed topographic maps of a small valley which had been formed by spring-sapping between present-day catchments 1 and 2, and it is possible to speculate on the runoff dynamics of this area prior to urban development. Since the site was characterised by mature woodland cover, overland flow resulting from precipitation exceeding the infiltration rate (Hortonian overland flow, path 1 on Figure 10.4B) would have been rare (Chorley, 1978). The major flow contributions to the tributary would have been from seepage from the saturated zone in the underlying subsoil (groundwater flow, path 2) and lateral drainage resulting from diversion of water by impeding horizons (throughflow, path 3), as well as from overland flow resulting from saturation of the underlying soil (saturation overland flow, path 4) in those locations where springs occurred on the surface or on the wet areas bordering the stream. Flow paths 2, 3 and 4 would, therefore, have been far more important in generating river flow than flow path 1.

Development of the study area began in 1974, since when its physical characteristics have been radically altered. The site is now covered by a housing estate made up of small sections of "row" houses, roads, drives, pathways, lawns and gardens. Although construction does not appear to have modified to any great extent the general topography of the area, in some parts terracing of the landscape has broken up the surface into an alternating sequence of level expanses of artificial surfaces and steeply-sloping lawns, thereby accentuating the micro-relief of the site. Surface drainage from this modified landscape has been diverted into three separate storm-sewer systems, and the three catchments in the study area are composed of these storm-sewer networks and the surfaces contributing runoff to them. Their general characteristics are summarised in Table 10.1. Flow from the catchments is measured at the sewer outfalls to the stream. Since these networks are intended solely for the collection of overland flow (paths 1 and 2, Fig.10.4B), little can be said about any changes in the groundwater flow and throughflow contributions to the storm hydrograph consequent upon the residential development. The work presently being carried out at Lordshill is intended to illustrate the behaviour of those runoff components which reach the surface and therefore contribute to flow measured at the sewer outfall.

The response to selected storms for the three catchments is summarised in Table 10.2 and these runoff/rainfall ratios represent an increase in storm-runoff response over that exhibited by the study area prior to urbanisation. As noted by Kirkby and Chorley (1967), the characteristics of this type of study area before development (appreciable soil and vegetation, with a humus or litter cover) only

222

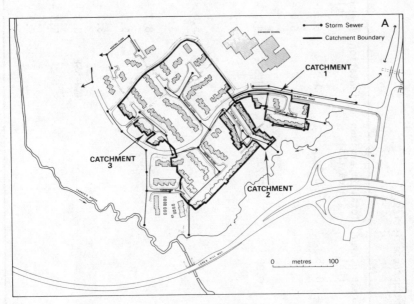

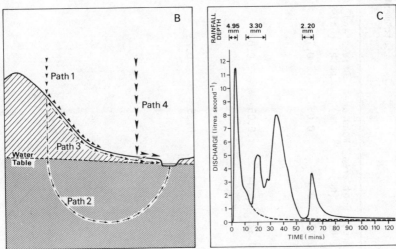

Figure 10.4 Flow paths and runoff from the Lordshill catchments:

A The Lordshill catchments

B Possible flow paths of water moving downhill (after Dunne, 1978)

C Runoff response to rainfall in catchment 2, 20th. October 1977.

Table 10.1

Catchment characteristics.

Catchment	Area (ha)	Roof area (ha)	Road area (ha)	Drives and paths (ha)	Grassed area (ha)	Total impervious area (ha)	Orientation	Average ground slope (%)
1	0.43	0.10	0.08	0.10	0.15	0.28	NW-SE	6.3 - lower portion 5.0 - upper portion
2	0.32	0.11	0.05	0.08	0.08	0.24	NNW-SSE	9.1 - lower portion 5.3 - upper portion
3	3.18	0.67	0.35	0.23	1.93	1.25	NNE-SSW	5.6 - lower portion 3.4 - upper portion
							N-S	8.3 - lower portion 5.0 - middle portion 3.3 - upper portion
							NNW-SSE	8.3 - lower portion 5.3 - middle portion 2.9 - upper portion

224

Table 10.2

Runoff response to selected storm events, Lordshill catchments.

Catchment	Area (ha)	Artificial surfaces (%)	Event	Rainfall (mm)	Runoff (mm)	Runoff/ rainfall
1	0.43	65.1	2	4.19	2.35	0.56
			3	8.40	3.63	0.43
			4	3.69	1.64	0.45
			5	6.47	3.10	0.48
			6(1)	2.36	0.72	0.31
			6(2)	2.37	0.97	0.41
			7	2.21	1.14	0.52
			8	3.18	2.33	0.73
			9	9.68	6.67	0.69
			10	3.71	1.77	0.48
			11	9.97	7.05	0.71
			12	8.13	7.23	0.89
			13	4.02	3.44	0.86
			14	3.12	1.40	0.45
			15	4.52	2.89	0.64
			16	2.00	0.81	0.41
			18	4.73	1.77	0.37
			19	2.34	0.89	0.38
			21	2.00	0.33	0.17
2	0.32	75.0	7	2.21	0.89	0.40
			8	3.18	1.52	0.48
			9	9.68	5.02	0.52
			10	3.71	1.47	0.40
			11	9.97	5.20	0.52
			12	8.13	4.47	0.55
			13	4.02	2.34	0.58
			14	3.12	1.52	0.49
			15	4.52	2.51	0.56
			16	2.00	0.91	0.46
			17	11.52	5.95	0.52
			18	4.73	2.30	0.49
			19	2.34	1.05	0.45
			20	3.57	2.39	0.67
3	3.18	39.3	1	2.00	0.31	0.16
			2	3.50	0.61	0.17
			3	5.00	0.90	0.18

produce substantial amounts of overland flow under the most extreme storm conditions. Any surface runoff, which would for the most part have been in the form of saturation overland flow, would appear to have been confined to a narrow zone beside the stream and to local seepage areas,and so would probably have resulted in runoff coefficients in the range 0.0 to 0.27 as were measured by Dunne (1969) for a rural catchment in the northeastern United States where the storm hydrograph was dominated by saturation overland flow. In contrast, the introduction of artificial surface cover over the study area means that the production of stormflow is no longer localised. There has also been an increase in the density of ephemeral channels which can convey this runoff to the catchment outlet. Whereas prior to urbanisation there do not appear to have been any channels in the study area, the ephemeral channels represented by the roadside gutters now present result in drainage densities of 0.05, 0.04 and 0.03m/m^2 for catchments 1, 2 and 3 respectively. When it is considered that individual roofs are also directly connected to the storm-sewer system, then the great expansion in the amount of the study area capable of contributing runoff to the stream within a few hours of a rainfall event can be appreciated.

Most of the increased hydrological response of the study area is the result of the increased production of Hortonian overland flow (path 1, Fig.10.4B) by the artificial surfaces in the three catchments and its rapid collection by the improved drainage networks. This is the single largest change in the runoff dynamics of the study area, since an increase in surface runoff must lead to a decrease in both groundwater flow and soil-moisture storage and thus throughflow through the soil matrix (Douglas, 1976). Prior to development, groundwater flow and throughflow would have dominated flow contributions from the site.

A closer examination of Table 10.2 reveals that the amount of artificial surface cover in the catchments does not entirely account for their runoff response. Rather, it suggests that their runoff dynamics may be slightly more complex. There is a great range in the runoff/ rainfall ratios, particularly for catchments 1 and 2 and, in all but a few events for catchment 1, the runoff coefficient is less than the percentage artificial cover. Part of the reason for this is the loss of water that occurs even on 'impervious' surfaces; this explains why the runoff coefficient of a road or roof never reaches 1.0. Many workers have considered losses on these artificial surfaces to be quite small (Viessman, 1966; Brater and Sangal, 1969; Falk and Niemcyznowicz, 1978), while others have found the losses to be substantial depending upon the type and age of surface (Van der Klout, Van der Wal and Zondervan, 1977). Linked with this is the concept of 'hydraulic connectivity' (Luckman, pers. comm.). Not all artificial surfaces may contribute to stormflow measured at the sewer outfall, because the runoff generated by them flows onto pervious surfaces, such as lawns and gardens, and thus infiltrates before reaching the storm-sewer inlet. This is particularly the case with many of the drives and paths in the study area. However, it is felt that both the amount of artificial surface directly contributing runoff and the processes of initial wetting, depression storage and infiltration detracting from the contributions of such 'impervious' surfaces would not be sufficiently variable from event to event to account for the wide range in the runoff/rainfall ratios, particularly those coefficients exceeding the percentage of the catchment area covered by artificial surfaces. Two other mechanisms appear to be operating, and may account for this behaviour.

The first of these is Hortonian overland flow produced by pervious areas within the catchments. Kelling and Peterson (1975), employing a sprinkling infiltrometer on urban lawns, found that large disruptions of the soil profile during building and lawn construction reduced infiltration to about 35 per cent of that for a lawn with an undisturbed profile. The reduced infiltration capacity of urban lawns implies that they may contribute runoff under intense storm conditions, and even when the rainfall intensity is lower than the soil's theoretical infiltration capacity, the presence of artificial surfaces upslope of the lawn may result in the production of Hortonian overland flow. Runoff from a drive or path may rapidly saturate the lawn immediately adjacent to it, which in turn will produce runoff that progressively saturates grassed areas downslope. In this way, not only may lawns generate overland flow, but those impervious areas considered hydraulically remote from the storm-sewer system for small storms may contribute runoff for medium- to large-scale events. In either case, the result is an increase in the proportion of the catchment generating runoff, and consequently an increase in the runoff coefficient.

A second process, which may account for some of the observed variation in runoff response, is the occurrence of saturation overland flow on some pervious areas within the catchments, due to the disruptive effects urbanisation has upon subsurface flow paths. This impact is of local importance in the case of the Lordshill site, because of the large numbers of springs which were present in the area along the junction of the Bagshot Sands and underlying London Clay prior to urbanisation. There are several locations where seepage from pervious areas runs over drives and paths to reach the storm-sewer inlets following large rainfall events during the winter. In one case, appreciable amounts of runoff were emerging from the back gardens between Osprey Close and Turnstone Gardens four days after a large winter rainstorm. However, the general decrease in soil wetness that accompanied the onset of spring meant that a large event in April, 1981 produced no saturation overland flow at all.

Superimposing these temporally- and spatially-variable runoff contributions from pervious areas upon the relatively constant proportion of rainfall translated into stormflow by the hydraulically-connected impervious areas within the catchments produces a picture of an area contributing runoff to the storm sewer, which seemingly expands and contracts in response to storm characteristics and antecedent wetness conditions in a similar fashion to the variable source-area model for natural basins described by Hewlett and Hibbert (1967). This is borne out by data from the Institute of Hydrology (Kidd and Lowing, 1979) for the Lordshill catchments, which suggest that for catchment 1, and to a lesser extent catchment 2, there is an increase in percentage runoff (and hence contributing area) with an increase in catchment wetness. Unfortunately, little information is presently available for catchment 3, but the general relationship between runoff response and catchment wetness is consistent with field observations. These indicate a larger saturated pervious area and a higher occurrence of saturation overland flow during the winter months, when evapotranspiration is at its lowest and soil-moisture content at its highest.

This variable behaviour of urban catchments has been observed elsewhere. Taylor and Roth (1979), studying a small catchment undergoing suburban development in Peterborough, Canada, found an increase in the runoff/rainfall ratio from summer, through autumn, to spring. The increase coincided with a general increase in catchment wetness, which in its turn (along with storm magnitude) determined how far those construction surfaces capable of readily generating runoff were integrated into the basin's active runoff contribution zone. Changes in the runoff response of urban catchments on a storm-by-storm basis were also noted by Macrae, Rodger and Luckman (1979), who found a positive correlation between the size of the rainfall event and the corresponding runoff coefficient for a completely urbanised catchment in London, Canada. This they related both to initial detention effects and a widening contributory area as the storm continued.

Table 10.3

Changes in runoff response during a rainstorm, 20th October 1977.

Catchment 2, Lordshill	Pulse		
	1	2	3
Rainfall amount (mm)	4.95	3.3	2.2
Runoff depth (mm)	0.84	1.45	0.35
Runoff/rainfall	0.17	0.44	0.16

It is argued that the observed increase in percentage runoff (and thus in the size of the contributing area) with increasing catchment wetness is a consequence of the two forms of pervious-area contribution previously noted, since the two runoff processes are positively correlated with catchment wetness as well as with increasing rainfall amount and intensity. The variable source-area model developed for rural drainage basins may, therefore, be applicable to the behaviour of urban catchments. The contributing area appears to expand and contract in size, not only between individual storm events but also during them, as shown by the change in runoff response during the course of a multiple-peaked event for catchment 2 (Fig.10.4C). The ratios of the volumes of runoff produced in response to the size of individual rain-fall pulses suggest that once initial abstractions are satisfied by rain falling early in the storm, the runoff coefficient and the size of the contributing area become more responsive to subsequent rainfall pulses (Table 10.3).

The view that "urban runoff from an event of a given magnitude is controlled by the extent both of the impervious surface and the storm-drain network in a fairly consistent way" (Taylor, 1977) appears to be too simple in the case of the Lordshill study area. The contributing area of these catchments is both spatially- and temporally-dynamic, and the changes in runoff response resulting from this behaviour may account for some of the observed non-linearities in the urban-runoff process. Such responses represent an important hydrological implication of the development process, not only for their explanatory value, but also as significant criteria for the design of urban storm-drainage networks.

THE IMPACT OF URBANISATION ON WATER QUALITY

In addition to their effects on runoff dynamics, urban areas may effect changes in river-water quality in a number of ways including the discharge of raw domestic or industrial sewage, final effluent from treatment works and surface storm-water drainage. The obvious detrimental effects of raw sewage have been well documented (Owens, 1970; Whipple, 1975). Similarly, treatment plant effluents have been investigated for their pollution potential (Sawyer, 1947; Smith, 1976), although the importance of wet-weather overflows is still a matter of some debate. Only in recent years has it been realised that storm-sewer discharges may be as poor, and often much poorer, in quality than treatment works effluent (Cordery, 1977).

As part of a comprehensive study of catchment-wide water quality variations, the Monks Brook (Chandler's Ford) has been monitored since January 1979 in order to identify water-quality changes related to urban growth (Fig.10.5A). There are no combined sewers or effluent outlets of any kind within the catchment, and all urban influences are restricted to surface storm-sewer runoff. It is supposed, therefore, that the river-water quality at site SP1, if different from the quality at site SP7, is largely the result of storm-sewer runoff from the extensive urban development between the two sites. Thus, spatial comparisons between water quality at site SP1 (a rural catchment area modified by urban development) and at site SP7 (a rural catchment area) can be used to infer the water-quality changes consequent upon urban growth. A complicating factor needing to be taken into account is the building activity which has taken place immediately upstream of SP7. This began in July 1979, so that SP7 must be recognised as having different catchment characteristics before and after that date.

Water-quality changes may best be determined first by analysing baseflow data and then by monitoring differences in storm response between selected sites. Standard methods were employed to determine the concentrations of anions (selective-ion electrodes and titrations) and cations (atomic absorption spectrophotometry) which together provide a measure of water quality.

Changes in baseflow response

Because the majority of urban runoff is effected during storms, baseflow response has received very little attention, even though the majority of storm sewers remain contributory during dry periods and non-point source drainage is also present. The term 'urban baseflow drainage' (UBD) is used here to include all dry weather flow.

The quality of UBD appears to be most seriously affected by construction. Along with the vast increases in sediment discharge from construction sites (Wolman, 1967), nutrients may be mobilised to contaminate ground and surface waters (Uttörmark et al, 1974). Differences between rural and established urban areas are less obvious. Walling and Webb (1975) describe nitrate removal as a function of soil disturbance and fertiliser application. This suggests that urban areas

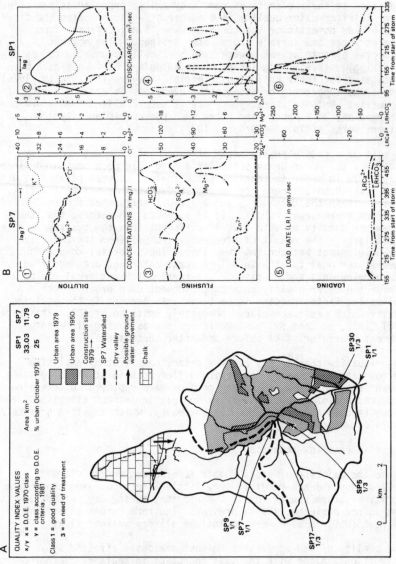

Figure 10.5   Storm hydrograph and chemographs for the
Monks Brook catchment:

A   The Monks Brook catchment

B   A storm hydrograph and selected chemographs at Sites SP1
and SP7, 25th. October 1979.

would display decreased nitrate levels, a point supported by Owens' data (1970) which showed that established urban areas produced only as much nitrate as rough-grazing land. Nevertheless, such levels of nutrients in river water would still be sufficient for substantial algal growth, leading to marked diurnal fluctuations in oxygen levels (Bedient et al, 1980); these fluctuations may be further accentuated by thermal pollution (Smith, 1980). Depending upon the basin dynamics and rainfall regime, established urban areas may exhibit lower (Wolman, 1967) or higher (Williams, 1976) 'total suspended solids' (TSS) concentrations than levels prior to construction. Finally, UBD may well provide high loadings of heavy metals derived from the urban environment, as for example zinc and lead from motor vehicles. These metals are normally flushed out in storm conditions, but UBD does exhibit their increased presence (Field et al, 1977). It would appear, therefore, that UBD may be distinguished from rural drainage by changes in the concentrations of nutrients, oxygen, sediment and heavy-metals. Simple averages of weekly-sampled aggregated data (mainly baseflow observations) from the Monks Brook are suggestive of some distinguishing properties (Table 10.4). Although all sites have a substantial part of their catchment areas under rural land uses, SP1 also represents urban land use, SP9 is a totally rural catchment, whilst SP7 is, at least in part, indicative of urban construction for the study period, July 1979 to January 1981. No data for TSS exist for SP9, so this leaves the interpretation of values for SP1 and SP7 rather open. Either the established urban area is exhibiting lower TSS levels (supported by field observation notes repeatedly remarking upon the clarity of UBD) or SP7 is exhibiting the influence of building activity in leading to increased levels. The oxygen data show very little difference between the three sample points. This suggests that the overall effect of urbanisation, both in terms of construction and of established urban areas, is negligible, in that all percentage saturation values are capable of supporting life. Dissolved oxygen data from site SP17, situated on a tributary draining livestock-farming land, suggest that areas of urbanisation may actually display improved oxygen levels. Site SP17 has an average oxygen saturation of only 48 per cent and is the only sample point within the basin regularly to infringe the European Economic Community drinking standard.

The nitrate levels display a clearer picture (Table 10.4). SP1 has a lower average concentration than SP9 and, although the difference is slight, it could be showing the importance of land disturbance, as mentioned by Walling and Webb (1975). Certainly the average value for SP7 is significantly greater than both those for SP1 and SP9. At SP7 the NO3-N value is, on average, nearly twice the World Health Organisation (WHO) drinking-water standard of 11.3mg/l (associated POLLNO3D equals 1.9). This lends some support to the idea of increased nutrient removal during construction (Uttörmark et al, 1974).

The heavy-metal concentrations indicate the importance of Zn^{2+} as an urban pollutant and the possibility of the emergence of Cu^{2+} and Cd^{2+} in UBD (Table 10.4). However, Pb^{2+} is noticeably unchanged and Sr^{2+} remains at similar levels suggesting that it is not land-use specific. A further quality variable to note is oil. The oil index used in Table 10.4 is based upon the number of days that oil was observed on the water (as a rough guide if OIL = 1.0, oil would be expected to be present more than 50 per cent of the time). The rural catchment has

Table 10.4

Mean values for selected water-quality variables.

Sample point	Status	TSS	OXY% SAT	DO	NO$_3^-$	Cu^{2+}	Cd^{2+}	Sr^{2+}	Cr*	Pb^{2+}	Zn^{2+}	OIL	Temp (°C)	POLLNO3D	POLLZND
				(	m i l l	i g r a	m m e s	p e r	l i t	r e	)				
SP1	Urban	215	91	10.2	14.8	.04	<.02	.17	<.01	<.01	.1	.46	10.1	1.3	.02
SP9	Rural	-	88.4	9.8	16	<.01	<.01	.2	-	<.01	<.01	.04	10.9	1.4	.002
SP7	Rural/ Construction	303	94	10.7	21.4	<.01	<.01	.17	<.01	<.01	.054	.02	10.1	1.9	.01

Notes: TSS = Total suspended solids.
OXY%SAT = Percentage oxygen saturation.
DO = Dissolved oxygen.
NO$_3^-$ = Nitrate expressed as NO$_3$-N.
OIL = Index of incidence of oil on stream.
Temp = Stream water temperature.
POLLNO3D = Index of nitrate pollution; if >1.0 the stream nitrate level may normally be expected to exceed WHO limit of 11.3mg/l.

POLLZND = Index of zinc pollution; if >1.0 the stream zinc level may normally be expected to exceed WHO limit of 5.0mg/l.

* = Ionic species uncertain.

almost no oil at all, whereas the urban section is often covered in oil. As will be shown later, this oil is often produced by single polluting events.

Changes in the quality of baseflow drainage may also be highlighted using an index of quality such as that employed by the Department of the Environment (DoE, 1970). Their 1970 survey showed the Monks Brook as having only one tributary of poor water quality (doubtful quality), this being the stream draining the established urban area of Chandler's Ford. The numbers below the site identifiers on Figure 10.4A refer to quality classes in 1970 and 1981, using DoE criteria. The 1981 survey shows that the rural drainage at SP17 is in class 3 because its oxygen level is so low. It is possible that SP5 is also in class 3 (certainly class 2), due to a series of polluting events, whilst SP30 is arguably also in class 3 because of rare, but serious polluting events. Either the DoE in its 1970 survey omitted some tributaries or missed out some information, or alternatively major changes have taken place in the last ten years.

In conclusion, these baseflow observations suggest that urbanisation might be accompanied by (i) increasing sediment and nutrient discharges associated with construction, (ii) lower nutrient and sediment discharges from established urban areas and (iii) the appearance of certain heavy metals. It also appears that the oxygen regime may not be adversely affected, although serious polluting events, including the emergence of oils, could lead to environmental problems.

Changes in stormflow response

The importance of both sewer-point sources (Randall et al, 1977) and non-point sources (Colston and Tafuri, 1975) in changing the storm response of urban areas becomes evident when examining particular chemograph changes. With increased discharge and hydrograph peakedness (Hollis, 1974), urban areas might well be expected to provide increased sediment yield (Dawdy, 1967). Such increased yields were observed by Douglas (1975), and have been linked to the presence of absorbed ions (especially heavy metals on suspended-sediment particles) which, in small catchments, may well peak before discharge (Ellis, 1975). First flushes of heavy metals (e.g. Pb^{2+}, Zn^{2+}, Cu^{2+}) from urban areas were noted by Wilbur and Hunter (1975), who also recorded that 86 per cent of all lead in two small catchments was removed by surface drainage. Increased total loads and significant flushes of sediment and metals appear to be characteristic of urban chemographs. In addition, urban storm responses often show oil chemographs (Hunter et al, 1975) and flushes of sodium chloride (Cherkauer, 1975) associated with road-use practices, such as petrol spillages and salt applications in winter. Such storm responses might be expected for sediment, metals, oil and salt, all of which have specific urban sources. However, ubiquitous materials also display particular urban characteristics. These may be manifested as increased dilution, flushing effects and high loads (Prowse, 1981).

Many of these quality characteristics of urban storm water observed elsewhere may be highlighted in the Monks Brook, using data from a storm event on 25th October, 1979, when 10mm of rain fell over a 5 hour period. This is achieved by contrasting the discharge and water-quality responses at sites SP7 and SP1 (Fig.10.5B). Graphs 1 and 2 show the increased discharge volume and peakedness of the urban section of the Monks Brook. The amount of urban expansion above SP7 by this date was minimal, so it is assumed that SP7 displayed an essentially rural response. The urban area exhibited more intense dilution, as exemplified by the chemographs for Mg^{2+} and Cl^-. The importance of this hydrological control is highlighted by the response of K^+, which shows the 'normal' concentration through the discharge peak at the rural point (SP7), but a definite dilution at point SP1. This also supports the idea that the clay fraction of soils is the source of K^+ (Loughran and Malone, 1976), since such soils are poorly exposed in the urban area. Although not well defined in graphs 1 and 2, there seems to be a downstream reduction in the lag time of the solute trough after the hydrograph peak.

Graphs 3 and 4 exhibit two major flushing regimes (Fig.10.5B). The urban area appears to have concentrated and released certain ions faster than the rural area, bearing in mind that the antecedent conditions were identical. Both SO_4^{2-} and HCO_3^- flushed in this way and preceded peak discharge; Cl^- also showed this tendency in graph 2. Flushing before peak discharge can be explained in terms of the rapidity of the movement of readily-available material by overland flow in the urban area, the movement early in the storm being sufficiently large not to be overwhelmed by the peak of the flood wave. The rural area, which incorporates the majority of material during slower throughflow or saturated overland flow, did not show any signs of this first flush. In contrast, it showed a second main flushing regime, that of a late pulse exemplified by the chemographs for Mg^{2+} and HCO_3^-. This rural phenomenon relates more to spatial influences on storm response associated with different source areas (Prowse, 1981), as also stressed by Walling and Webb (1980).

A subsidiary flushing phenomenon is evident in graph 4 which relates to heavy metals (Fig.10.5B). In the Chandler's Ford area the flushing of Zn^{2+} may be explained in terms of its presence in rainfall. Similar links between urban environments and high Zn^{2+} concentrations in both precipitation and atmospheric fall-out have been found by other workers (e.g. Pilegaard, 1979). Material entering the basin from the atmosphere during a storm is likely to be very closely linked to the passage of the flood wave. Assuming that the solutes travel at about 75 per cent of the velocity of the flood wave (Glover and Johnson, 1974), the Zn^{2+} could be expected to have peaked after discharge and at the same time as other ions reached their minimum concentrations. The peakedness of the Zn^{2+} chemograph may reflect a process of atmospheric flushing and rapid exhaustion, as material is washed to the ground at the start of rain. Another explanation could be that Zn^{2+} is associated with contributory areas in the urban basin which only become effective at a certain rainfall intensity or after a certain rainfall volume has been reached and according to the antecedent conditions.

The increased dilution associated with urban areas does not necessarily mean that urban areas are not significant sources of certain ions. Graphs 5 and 6 show how the loads of Ca^{2+} (LRCA^{2+}) and HCO_3^- (LRHCO$_3^-$) were five times greater at SP1 than at SP7, in accordance with the differences in discharge (Fig.10.5B). Table 10.5 shows how the urban loads per unit area may be greater than those in

Table 10.5

Total loads of Ca^{2+} and HCO_3^- generated from the urban and rural catchments for the storm, 25th October 1979.

Sample point	Status	Ca^{2+} (kg/km^2)	HCO_3^- (kg/km^2)
SP1	Whole basin	12.4	43.05
SP1	Urban component only	12.8	49.7
SP7	Rural	11.7	31.0

rural areas. SP1 (urban) values were estimated by taking the difference between SP1 (whole basin) and SP7 (rural). This high loading from the urban area reflects a dual process of rapid accumulation and rapid cycling or transportation of material. Luckman (1979) found that urban areas could accumulate enough material to exhibit flushing within a day or so of a previous rainstorm. In any event, preceding accumulations of material control loading response.

These data for just one storm in the Monks Brook bring to light a series of ways in which urban areas modify rural storm water quality response:

(i)   intensification of the dilution of some constituents and reduction of lag time;

(ii) rapid flushing of material as a result of enhanced overland flow and of the availability of metals perhaps related to specific urban sources, and

(iii) increased loads of some constituents which have accumulated quickly on urban surfaces.

The importance of hydrological parameters is stressed in that increased dilution is a function of higher runoff ratios, while higher loadings are a function of antecedent conditions (accumulation rates) and flushing is a function of both greater overland flow and antecedent conditions.

Environmental impact

It is believed that these changes in the water quality of the Monks Brook are typical of any urbanising catchment in which storm sewers and non-point source pollution predominate. In terms of environmental impact, two distinct problems can be identified. The first relates to the repeated discharge of potentially-harmful materials, most often heavy metals related to suspended sediments. Although not evident in Table 10.4, under the right conditions (such as very long spells between intense storms), storm sewers may introduce levels of such toxic chemicals as Pb^{2+}, Cu^{2+}, Cd^{2+}, and Cr in excess of the WHO drinking standard or the European Economic Community bathing standards, which are 0.01, 0.05, 0.01, 0.05 and 0.1, 1.0, 0.01, 0.05mg/l respectively. The maximum recorded values at SP1 are 0.2, 0.4, 0.19 and 0.18mg/1 respectively. The short-term effect of such pollution is probably negligible, especially over the period of a storm, but it is not known how such repeated discharges of toxic materials will affect the stream environment in the long term. It is also significant, particularly where water is abstracted for domestic use, that the WHO includes Cd^{2+}, Cr, Pb^{2+} and NO_3^- in its list of elements which have a potential long-term effect on health.

The second environmental impact could be viewed as even more serious. Infrequent discharges of industrial pollutants may be severe enough to sterilise a watercourse over a period of only a few hours, after which recovery may take many months or even years. The Monks Brook has suffered at least two such debilitating incidents in the past two years, namely at SP6 (February 1979) and at SP30 (February 1981). In the first case, a severe oil spillage caused widespread damage; oil remained in the bed sediments and vegetation for many months. In the second case, approximately 1000 fish were killed by a discharge of a highly-toxic chemical; the incident was reported in the Southern Evening Echo (6.2.81) as "a severe setback". The offending manufacturers have subsequently been fined and ordered to re-stock the Brook with fish (Southern Evening Echo, 1.6.81).

It is clear that careful management practices, including monitoring and modelling stormflow discharges and implementing legal constraints on effluent discharges, are an essential step in maintaining the quality of urban stream environments. Perhaps a more positive approach to the way in which water resources are viewed is even more important. Recent work by Field and Fan (1981) has shown how urban storm water may be reclaimed as an industrial sub-potable supply and, at the same time, used to reduce pollutant discharges, to improve drainage and to create recreational ponds. A change in attitude towards storm-water drainage, from viewing it as a nuisance to seeing it as a useful resource, could be the key to efficient urban planning and water management.

THE ESTIMATION, MANAGEMENT AND DEVELOPMENT OF GROUNDWATER RESOURCES

The expansion of Hampshire's population and the extension of its urban area have not only effected changes in local water discharge and quality dynamics, but they have also encouraged a great deal of research into local water resources and into possible methods by which these might be managed and developed.

Chalk underlies a large area of the land surface in the HRWD area and the aquifer is of considerable thickness (Fig.10.2). As a result, it is able to receive water over a large area, to store it and to provide reliable groundwater-flow components to discharge in many of the local rivers. Over the last fifteen years, attention has been directed particularly towards the understanding and management of this aquifer and the SWA (and previously the Hampshire River Authority) has placed considerable emphasis on research into groundwater management. The general structure of the Chalk outcrop in Hampshire is fairly simple, consisting mainly of Upper Chalk, with two small inliers of Middle and Lower Chalk and an outcrop of Middle Chalk in the north of the area. The Upper Chalk is gently folded along east-west axes, the small folds becoming less marked towards the west. These minor folds, in conjunction with layers of varying permeability within the Chalk, have a strong effect on the occurrence and movement of groundwater and result in local features, such as the presence of artesian springs around Alresford and Micheldever (Headworth, 1978) and the variable positions of some catchment watersheds (vide infra).

Well-level records provide a primary source of information for understanding the behaviour of water in the aquifer and approximately 500 wells are used to observe water-table levels twice a year (in March and October) within the HRWD area. These data show the considerable differences between the highest water-table levels in March and the lowest levels in October, and they also reveal the major deviations between some groundwater and topographic catchment areas. The river Itchen catchment illustrates this problem well, since the groundwater catchment area (approximately $124km^2$) is 35 per cent larger than the topographic catchment and may vary by up to $21km^2$ seasonally. In spite of the short period of records (few wells have records before 1950), it seems that the water table is relatively stable from year to year, and there is only very localised evidence of a decline in water-table levels.

Useful information may be gained if well levels are recorded at very frequent intervals. Headworth (1972), using continuous records from twelve wells in the HRWD area, has demonstrated how such data might be used to evaluate aquifer characteristics. None of these wells was affected by pumping, and Headworth has provided methods for calculating the rate of recession, the recession constant, the rate of apparent percolation and an estimate of the coefficient of transmissibility. Such parameters give an indication of gross trends in water flow through the aquifer and form a very useful basis for water management. However, the results are generalised and throw little light upon the ways in which water moves through the aquifer, but this has been studied using other types of field measurements.

There is little agreement on the relative importance of different modes of water movement through the Chalk, probably because this is very variable; certainly research in the local area has underlined this variability from site to site. Tate et al (1970) recorded water temperature, electrical conductivity and inflow velocity at different levels in a borehole near Newbury fed by seepage from Chalk. They were able to identify significant individual inflows, presumably resulting from drainage along fissures. Much recent research on the modes of flow of groundwater has attempted, using tracers, to establish the relative importance of fissure flow as opposed to seepage through the inter-granular spaces in the solid rock. Naturally-occurring tritium, a by-product of thermo-nuclear explosions which is present in rain water, is particularly useful. Since thermo-nuclear explosions started in 1954, the concentration of tritium at different depths in the Chalk can provide data on rates of water movement and possible mechanisms for that movement. A local example of such research is provided by Downing et al (1978). Their study of three wells near Brighton showed that groundwater recharge occurred both by rapid fissure flow and by much slower piston displacement of water through microfissures. They also discovered that about 10 per cent of recharge of the saturated zone was a result of rapid water movement through the unsaturated zone, although

237

this was very variable from site to site and tended to occur mainly after heavy rainfall.

The relative importance of fissure flow and piston displacement of water in the unsaturated zone has also been studied in connection with modelling solute movements in the Chalk. The movement of nitrate has caused particular concern, because concentrations well above the WHO's recommended limits for drinking water have been discovered in the Chalk, especially in the upper levels of the unsaturated zone. In the study area, several workers have observed and analysed nitrate concentration in groundwater, notably at Bridget's Farm, near Winchester (Young et al, 1976; Young and Gray, 1978; Wellings and Bell, 1980). Solutes seem to move vertically downward through the unsaturated zone, although opinions vary as to whether this is governed mainly by piston flow (Wellings and Bell, 1980) or by diffusion of solutes into interstitial water from fissure flow (Young et al, 1976). Regardless of the flow mechanism, observations of average rates of movement of solutes are remarkably consistent and are of the order of one metre/year in the unsaturated zone. Nitrate seems to move downwards at a steady rate with some limited attenuation in peak concentrations. The nitrate concentration is apparently related to land use, with the highest levels being leached from fertilised arable fields and the lowest levels being associated with unfertilised pasture. Young et al (1976) suggest that there may be biological activity within the unsaturated zone, leading to some denitrification and thus improvement in water quality with depth.

Information on the hydrology of the Chalk has formed a firm basis for research into new methods of developing the resource. The SWA, in conjunction with other organisations, is currently involved in three major research projects into different methods of developing groundwater: the Hardham artificial recharge scheme, the South Downs investigation and the Candover pilot scheme. The Hardham artificial recharge scheme is not on the Chalk, but is a study of the possibility of augmenting groundwater abstraction at Hardham, Sussex by artificially recharging the Folkestone Sands through lagoons (Ellson, 1973). The South Downs investigation encompasses detailed studies of the hydrology of the Brighton, Worthing, Chichester, Eastbourne and Seaford Chalk blocks to enable further development of the Chalk aquifer by extending controlled pumping, whilst minimising saline intrusion. The project aims to model mathematically the behaviour of the aquifer so that the effects of different levels and patterns of pumping can be assessed in relation to water yields and salinity (SWA, pers. comm.; Monkhouse and Fleet, 1975). The Candover pilot scheme is the only one of these three research projects to be based in the study area and so warrants a more detailed discussion.

The Candover pilot scheme was carried out in the northern part of the Itchen catchment in a valley drained by the Candover stream (Fig.10.2). The aim was to assess the feasibility of seasonally-augmenting flows in the river Itchen by the abstraction of groundwater to be diverted into the river system. This method of water management has many advantages, the most important of which is that it increases river flows in summer, when water demand would normally be high and river levels low. This is achieved at the expense of groundwater resources, so that when groundwater pumping ceases in the winter, there is surplus capacity in

238

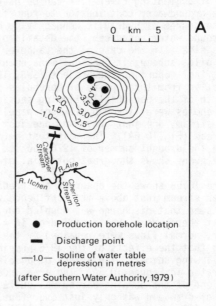

A

0   km   5

2.0
1.5
4.0
3.5
3.0
2.5
1.0

Candover Stream

R. Aire

R. Itchen

Cherton Stream

● Production borehole location

▬ Discharge point

—1.0— Isoline of water table depression in metres

(after Southern Water Authority, 1979)

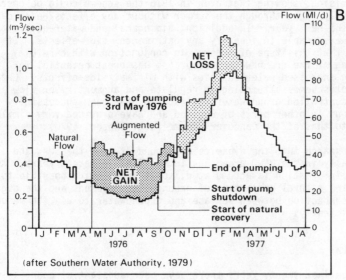

B

Flow (m³/sec)

Flow (MI/d)

1.2
1.0
0.8
0.6
0.4
0.2
0

110
100
90
80
70
60
50
40
30
20
10
0

NET LOSS

Start of pumping 3rd May 1976

Augmented Flow

Natural Flow

NET GAIN

End of pumping

Start of pump shutdown

Start of natural recovery

J F M A M J J A S O N D J F M A M J J A
1976   1977

(after Southern Water Authority, 1979)

Figure 10.6 The Candover catchment:
A   Depression of the water table after 130 days of pumping.
B   Augmented and estimated natural flows at Borough Bridge, 1976–77.

groundwater storage. This results in a larger proportion of winter precipitation percolating to groundwater storage, thus prompting a depression of river levels when they would normally be high. This method of augmenting river flow can be used in any drainage basin with a large groundwater contribution to runoff, but since the method depends upon the degree of hydraulic connectivity between surface and underground water resources, the details of the technique vary from site to site. In the case of the Candover stream, a full description of the pilot scheme, its design, management and side-effects, is given in the final report on the project (SWA, 1979). It was based upon abstraction from three pairs of boreholes sunk in dry valleys well to the north of the perennially-flowing section of the Candover stream. The boreholes were linked by 13km of pipeline to two discharge points on the stream, one just above and one just below the perennial head of the stream (Fig.10.6A). The main test period for the pilot scheme ran through the drought summer of 1976 and its effectiveness during this extreme event shows the great potential of the method.

Figure 10.6B shows the observed and predicted discharge of the Candover stream just above its confluence with the river Itchen. It can be seen that discharge was doubled during the main pumping period and that there was a substantial drop in flows after pumping. However, normal flows were regained by the end of April 1977, thus showing that the effects of the 1976 pumping did not carry over into the following summer. The effect of pumping on the water table is illustrated in Figure 10.6A. The area undergoing water-table drawdown at the end of the pumping period was quite large, but the maximum amount of drawdown was only just over four metres. These results are very promising, showing that even in 1976 the scheme could be operated successfully right through the summer without any effects being carried over to the next year. In addition, biological and water-quality studies were unable to identify any detrimental side-effects. It is apparent that this type of scheme, in conjunction with careful monitoring of the groundwater resources, has great potential for providing increased water supplies with minimal side-effects. Certainly many pilot schemes attempting to regulate and augment river flow through controlled groundwater abstraction have been successfully carried out in other parts of England and have provided very similar results to that of the Candover Scheme (e.g. Ineson, 1970).

Thus research into the dynamics of groundwater in the SWA, and specifically in the HRWD area, has intensified in recent years. As detailed information is accumulated, so it is becoming possible to exploit the natural properties of groundwater movement and the degree of interconnection between surface and groundwater to use the resource more efficiently.

CONCLUSION

During the last twenty years there have been substantial changes in the hydrology of the Hampshire River and Water Division area. This essay has highlighted the effects of population growth and urban expansion, particularly the alteration of runoff and water-quality dynamics and the generation of an increased demand for water supply. These, in their turn, have stimulated research into the understanding and

management of water resources. Three locations of local significance
have been used to illustrate these aspects of change, but the local
results are representative of more widely-observed effects of urban
development and of general trends in the evaluation and management of
groundwater resources.

REFERENCES

ANDERSON, D G (1970), Effects of urban development on floods in northern
        Virginia, United States Geological Survey, Water Supply Paper,
        2001-C.

BEDIENT, P B, LAMBERT, J L and MACHADO, P (1980), Low flow and
        stormwater quality in urban channels, American Society of
        Civil Engineers, Journal of the Environmental Engineering
        Division, 106, 421-436.

BRATER, E F and SANGAL, S (1969), Effects of urbanisation on peak flows,
        in MOORE, W L and MORGAN, C W (eds), Effects of Watershed
        Changes on Streamflow (Texas, University of Texas), 201-214.

CARTER, R W (1961), Magnitude and frequency of floods in suburban areas,
        United States Geological Survey, Professional Paper, 424-B,
        B9-B11.

CHERKAUER, D S (1975), The hydrologic response of small watersheds to
        suburban development: observations and modelling, in WHIPPLE,
        W (ed.), vide infra, 110-119.

CHORLEY, R J (1978), The hillslope hydrological cycle, in KIRKBY, M J
        (ed.) Hillslope Hydrology (London, Wiley), 1-42.

COLSTON, N V and TAFURI, A N (1975), Urban land runoff considerations,
        in WHIPPLE, W (ed.) vide infra, 120-127.

CORDERY, I (1977), Urban stormwater - a major contribution to water
        pollution, in MOREL-SEYTOUX, M J et al (ed.), Surface and
        Subsurface Hydrology (Fort Collins, Water Resources
        Publications), 601-619.

DAWDY, D R (1967), Knowledge of sedimentation in urban environments,
        American Society of Civil Engineers, Journal of the Hydraulics
        Division, 93, 235-245.

DEPARTMENT OF THE ENVIRONMENT AND WELSH OFFICE (1970), Report of a River
        Pollution Survey of England and Wales (London, HMSO), 1.

DOUGLAS, I (1975), Flood Waves and Suspended Sediment Pulses in
        Urbanized Catchments (Armidale, Australian Institution of
        Engineers).

DOUGLAS, I (1976), Urban hydrology, Geographical Journal, 142, 65-72.

DOWNING, R A, SMITH, D B and WARREN, S C (1978), Seasonal variations of tritium and other constituents in groundwater in the Chalk near Brighton, England, Journal of the Institution of Water Engineers and Scientists, 32, 123-136.

DUNNE, T (1969), Runoff Production in a Humid Area, unpublished Ph.D. Dissertation, Department of Geography, John Hopkins University, Baltimore, Maryland.

DUNNE, T (1978), Field studies of hillslope processes, in KIRKBY, M J (ed.), Hillslope Hydrology (London, Wiley), 227-293.

ELLIS, J B (1975), Urban stormwater pollution, Middlesex Polytechnic Research Report, 1.

ELLSON, T R (1973), Artificial recharge investigations of Folkestone Sands - Hardham, Sussex, Journal of the Institution of Water Engineers and Scientists, 27, 163-174.

FALK, J and NIEMCYZNOWICZ, J (1978), Characteristics of the above-ground runoff in sewered catchments, in HELLIWELL, P R (ed.), International Conference on Urban Storm Drainage (London, Pentech), 11-14.

FIELD, R and FAN, G-Y (1981), Industrial reuse of urban stormwater, American Society of Civil Engineers, Journal of the Environmental Engineering Division, 107, 171-189.

FIELD, R, TAFURI, A N and MASKERS, H E (1977), Urban runoff pollution control technology overview, Environmental Protection Agency, USA, Technical Series, 00/2-77-047.

GILPIN, A (1976), Dictionary of Environmental Terms (London, Routledge and Kegan Paul).

GLOVER, B J and JOHNSON, P (1974), Variations in the natural chemical concentration of river water during flood flows and the lag effect, Journal of Hydrology, 22, 303-316.

GREGORY, K J (1974), Streamflow and building activity, in GREGORY, K J and WALLING, D E (eds), Fluvial Processes in Instrumented Watersheds (Institute of British Geographers Special Publication), 6, 107-122.

HEADWORTH, H G (1972), The analysis of natural groundwater level fluctuations in the Chalk of Hampshire, Journal of the Institution of Water Engineers and Scientists, 26, 107-124.

HEADWORTH, H G (1978), Hydrological characteristics of artesian boreholes in the Chalk of Hampshire, Quarterly Journal of Engineering Geology, 11, 139-144.

HELVEY, J D, HEWLETT, J D and DOUGLASS, J E (1972), Predicting soil moisture in the Southern Appalachians, Proceedings of the Soil Science Society of America, 36, 954-959.

HEWLETT, J D and HIBBERT, A R (1967), Factors affecting the response of small watersheds to precipitation in humid regions, in SOPPER, W E and LULL, H W (eds), Forest Hydrology (Oxford, Pergamon), 275-290.

HOLLIS, G E (1974), The effect of urbanization on floods in the Canon's Brook, Harlow, Essex, in GREGORY, K J and WALLING, D E (eds), Fluvial Processes in Instrumented Watersheds (Institute of British Geographers Special Publication), 6, 123-139.

HOLLIS, G E (1977), Water yield changes after the urbanization of the Canon's Brook catchment, Harlow, England, Hydrological Sciences Bulletin, 22, 61-75.

HUNTER, J V, YU, S L and WHIPPLE, W (1975), Measurement of urban runoff petroleum, in WHIPPLE, W (ed.), vide infra, 162-168.

INESON, J (1970), Development of ground water resources in England and Wales, Journal of the Institution of Water Engineers and Scientists, 24, 155-177.

JAMES, L D (1965), Using a digital computer to estimate the effects of urban development on flood peaks, Water Resources Research, 1, 223-234.

KELLING, K A and PETERSON, A E (1975), Urban lawn infiltration rates and fertiliser runoff losses under simulated rainfall, Proceedings of the Soil Science Society of America, 39, 348-352.

KIDD, C H R and LOWING, M J (1979), The Wallingford urban subcatchment model, Institute of Hydrology Report, 60.

KIRKBY, M J and CHORLEY, R J (1967), Throughflow, overland flow and erosion, Bulletin of the International Association of Scientific Hydrology, 12, 5-21.

LEOPOLD, L B (1968), Hydrology for urban land planning: a guidebook, United States Geological Survey Circular, 554.

LOUGHRAN, R J and MALONE, K (1976), Variations in some stream solutes in a Hunter Valley catchment, University of Newcastle, New South Wales, Research Papers in Geography, 8.

LUCKMAN, B H (ed.)(1979), Urban runoff and water quality monitoring in the Carling Street catchment, London, Ontario, Department of Geography, University of Western Ontario, Geographical Papers, 39.

MACRAE, C R, RODGER, D and LUCKMAN, B H (1979), Hydrologic characteristics, Department of Geography, University of Western Ontario, Geographical Papers, 39, 15-42.

MONKHOUSE, R A and FLEET, M (1975), A geophysical investigation of saline water in the Chalk of the South Coast of England, Quarterly Journal of Engineering Geology, 8, 291-302.

OWENS, M (1970), Nutrient balances in rivers, Water Treatment and Examination, 19, 239-252.

PILEGAARD, K (1979), Heavy metals in bulk precipitation and transplanted Hypogymnia Plysodes and Dicranoureisia Girrata in the vicinity of Danish steelworks, Water, Air and Soil Pollution, 11, 77-91.

PROWSE, C W (1981), Urban effects on storm water quality, Wessex Geographer, 16, 2-11.

RANDALL, C W, GARLAND, J A, GRIZZARD, T J and HOEHN, R C (1977), The significance of stormwater runoff in an urbanizing watershed, Progress in Water Technology, 9, 547-502.

SAWYER, C N (1947), Fertilization of lakes by agricultural and urban drainage, New England Water Works Association, 41, 109-127.

SMITH, K (1976), Nutrient budget of the River Main, County Antrim, Ministry of Agriculture, Fisheries and Food, Research Report, 32, 315-339.

SMITH, K (1980), Temperature characteristics of British rivers and the effects of thermal pollution, in HOLLIS, G E (ed.), Man's Impact on the Hydrological Cycle in Great Britain (Norwich, Geoabstracts), 229-242.

SOUTHERN WATER AUTHORITY (1979), Itchen Groundwater Regulation Scheme. Final Report on the Candover Pilot Scheme (Worthing, Directorate Resource Planning).

TATE, T K, ROBERTSON, A S and GRAY, O A (1970), The hydrogeological investigation of fissure-flow by borehole logging technique, Quarterly Journal of Engineering Geology, 2, 195-215.

TAYLOR, C H (1977), Seasonal variations in the impact of suburban development on runoff response: Peterborough, Ontario, Water Resources Research, 13, 464-468.

TAYLOR, C H and ROTH, D M (1979), Effects of suburban construction on runoff contributing zones in a small Ontario drainage basin, Hydrological Sciences Bulletin, 24, 289-301.

UTTÖRMARK, P D, CHOPIN, J D and GREEN, K M (1974), Estimating nutrient loadings of lakes from non-point sources, United States Environmental Protection Agency Report, 660/3-74-020.

VAN DER KLOUT, P, VAN DER WAL, M and ZONDERVAN, J G (1977), Calculation of instantaneous unit hydrograph in an urban area, International Association of Hydrological Sciences Publication, 123, 124-143.

VAN SICKLE, D R (1968), Experience with the evaluation of urban effects for drainage design, in MOORE, W L and MORGAN, C W (eds) Effects of Watershed Changes on Streamflow (Texas, University of Texas), 229-254.

VIESSMAN, W (1966), The hydrology of small impervious areas, Water Resources Research, 2, 405-412.

WALLING, D E and WEBB, B (1975), Spatial variations of river water quality: a survey of the River Exe, Transactions of the Institute of British Geographers, 65, 155-172.

WALLING, D E and WEBB, B (1980), The spatial dimension in the interpretation of stream solute behaviour, Journal of Hydrology, 47, 129-149.

WELLINGS, S R and BELL, J P (1980), Movement of water and nitrate in the unsaturated zone of the Upper Chalk near Winchester, Hampshire, England, Journal of Hydrology, 48, 119-136.

WHIPPLE, W (ed.)(1975), Urbanisation and Water Quality Control (Minneapolis, American Water Research Association), 20.

WILBUR, W G and HUNTER, J V (1975), Contributions of metals resulting from stormwater and precipitation in Lodi, New Jersey, in WHIPPLE, W (ed.), ibid, 45-54.

WILLIAMS, P W (1976), Impact of urbanization on the hydrology of the Wairau Creek, North Shore, Auckland, Journal of Hydrology (N.Z.), 15, 81-99.

WOLMAN, M G (1967), A cycle of sedimentation and erosion in urban river channels, Geografiska Annaler, 49A, 385-395.

YOUNG, C P and GRAY, E M (1978), Nitrate in groundwater, Water Research Centre, Technical Report, 69.

YOUNG, C P, HALL, E S and OAKES, D B (1976), Nitrate in groundwater - studies in the Chalk near Winchester, Hampshire, Water Research Centre, Technical Report, 31.

Acknowledgements   To the Southern Water Authority for supplying the data for Figure 10.1 and for permission to reproduce Figure 10.6A and B; to John Wiley and Sons for permission to reproduce Figure 10.4B.

11 Changing Views of the Countryside

B P BIRCH

To many, as W H Hudson (1910) long ago remarked of its larger
neighbour, Wiltshire, the countryside of Hampshire "never appears to be
a favourite." For most people it is an undramatic area of gentle
scenery, of downland and heath, woodland and farms, an area one passes
through on the way to somewhere else. Yet for others, as another
country-writer has more recently noted (Dutton, 1970), Hampshire is a
county "which has inspired great affection in those who have known it
well." That same writer also felt it necessary to pose the question,
"for how long, one wonders, will the county be allowed to retain the
quiet beauty which is so appealing?" Geographers, wary of
distinguishing between 'appealing' and 'outstanding' landscape
features, have, like the passing travellers, largely ignored
Hampshire's countryside and have little considered the current threats
to its landscapes. One must turn then to travel writers, both past and
present, and to planners in order to see how Hampshire's countryside
has been viewed and to appreciate how change now threatens some of its
appeal.

EARLY VIEWS OF RURAL HAMPSHIRE

Most of the early accounts of Hampshire, until the beginning of the
nineteenth century, focused on its general agricultural importance and
on individual features of the countryside around the main towns. They
paid little attention to the various physiographic units of the county
beyond distinguishing between the broad central block of Chalk with its
sheep and arable farms, the more wooded, lower country to the south and
the attractive landscapes and coastal areas of the Isle of Wight.

There are several reasons why the early topographers showed a lack of interest in, and understanding of, the varied landscapes within the county. First, although the Hampshire Basin, with its rich fossil record and diverse scenery, was an attractive area to the early geologists, little of it had been examined before the 1820s. The debate on the structural relationships between the Weald, the Hampshire Basin and the Chalk was still continuing, so that the overall pattern of the major physical units of the region was still unclear. Secondly, as the first Ordnance Survey map of the southern part of the county did not appear until 1810 (the first for the centre and north coming seven years later), this re-emphasised the lack of a proper base on which to detail the physiographic units. One finds, as a result, that the districts of Hampshire were delimited and often described in the earliest county surveys more on the basis of the administrative units, or hundreds, than by their distinctive landscapes. Even one of the later surveys, the Victoria County History (1900), took the same approach. In that part of his 'New Survey of England' devoted to Hampshire, Salmon (1731) for example made little reference to the county's varied physique, beyond describing in turn each of the thirty hundreds, the large number of which he noted as reflecting the considerable labour requirements of the agricultural economy. Cook's topographical account of the county, produced in several editions during the early 1800s, adopted a similar line.

Even the writers of the early agricultural surveys of the county generally found it difficult to pay sufficient regard to the various physical districts as a framework for better explaining the agricultural conditions. The brief report to the Board of Agriculture in 1794 by Abraham and William Driver pointed out that the New Forest and "the southern foot of the chalk hills" were the only districts "tolerably well defined." The county's other areas, namely the northern lowland adjacent to the Thames Basin in Berkshire, the eastern heath-lands adjoining those of Surrey and Sussex, and the great central block of Chalk which runs on into Wiltshire, were held to be mainly extensions of districts better developed in those other counties, and hence deserving less attention in a report on Hampshire. Whether their survey lacked this essential detail, and dealt instead mainly with the large area of wasteland in the county, because the Driver brothers were foresters rather than agriculturalists, or because they had been robbed of the notes for their report during their tour, is not relevant here. What is important is that in its place, Vancouver's report (1810) was commissioned by the Board and so provided the first, albeit very generalised, attempt to survey and regionalise, in this case for agricultural purposes, the districts of the county. In basing his divisions mainly on the soil and climatic characteristics of each area, and to a lesser extent on farming conditions and woodland cover, Vancouver identified five main areas (and three more on the Isle of Wight) and provided a level of detail about the landscapes of the county found neither in any of the earlier surveys nor in some that came later (Fig.11.1A). Not only, for example, had Marshall's account of the agriculture of Hampshire in 1798 completely ignored the New Forest and southern parts of the county, but even Cobbett (1830), in his colourful and perceptive reports based on his rides through rural Hampshire, never attempted to provide a systematic coverage of the county and its various districts. Similarly, Caird's survey (1852), compiled forty years after Vancouver's report, noted the diversity of soils, but presented only a simplistic view of the county and its farming areas, dividing Hampshire into no more than a central ridge of chalk, a southern district and a northern border area where "the clay and gravel substratum of the southern district again presents itself."

What compounded this common lack of a clearer overview of the varied landscapes and districts of the county by the agricultural writers and topographers, at least until the early decades of the last century, was a marked imbalance between the northern and southern halves of the county in terms of what was known and what was considered worth reporting. The considerable amount known and written about the more densely-settled and accessible Tertiary basin, along with the Isle of Wight, stemmed from the fact that it was considered to have more appeal to the tourist. This contrasted with the little attention paid by writers and visitors to the extensive, but less accessible downlands to the north. If we take the period up to the 1830s, when the London-Southampton railway was under construction across the Chalk areas, and only two decades after Vancouver's attempt at defining the county's agricultural districts, we find that numerous local guidebooks and other accounts had for long been in circulation about the various southern districts of the county and the Isle of Wight. Yet little had been published about the extensive downland areas. The descriptions of the southern districts took various forms. For the New Forest, they ranged from very early accounts of the history and administration of this Royal Forest, like that by Manwood in 1615, through to the first systematic guide to its scenery by William Gilpin in 1791. Several town guides had appeared for Southampton, Portsmouth, Lymington and Winchester by the early 1800s. For Southampton, for example, these included 'A walk through Southampton' (Englefield, 1801) and 'A companion in a tour round Southampton' (Bullar, 1801). Several of these guides ran into numerous editions, like that by Skelton which reached its twenty-third by 1818. As most of these guides were intended for the gentleman-visitor, who would base himself temporarily in the town and tour out from there, descriptions were also provided of the New Forest, the coast, various country estates and other points of interest in the environs of Southampton. Yet few of these tour descriptions penetrated the Chalk country north of Winchester, and similarly the Winchester city guides of the period made scant reference to the surrounding downland areas.

The little that was published before the 1830s about the downlands of the county provided only the most general information on the scenery and the agriculture. This would have been of little value to the tourist or the more serious topographer and was often indicative of the tour-writer's lack of familiarity with the nature and extent of the Chalk district. One anonymous writer for example, referred in 1764 to the higher parts of the Hampshire Downs as "barren and fit only for sheep", although he did admit that around Winchester "the plains and downs ... continue with few intersections of rivers and vallies for about fifty miles (which) renders this country very pleasant to those who are fond of an open situation and extensive prospect." Another writing about the county in 1769 praised the air of Hampshire as "pure and healthy, especially on the fine downs", but found little else to say of them. The agricultural writer, Marshall (1798), also pointed to their "extensive prospects ... by which few minds are not exhilarated if not enlarged." He noted that the west of the county "abounds in picturable scenery", yet that most famous exponent of the picturesque, William Gilpin, found little to impress him. Whereas at the start of his western tour in 1798 he had commented that the narrow Cretaceous rampart of the Surrey 'hog's-back' was "singular" in appearance, further along his route on the Hampshire Chalk he noted "little that excites attention ... where the downs begin to open they are heavy, uninteresting swells of ground." Although he found towards the Wiltshire border rather more of scenic interest, where the downs "often fold beautifully over each other", yet his overall impression of chalkland scenery was not favourable. As he later wrote of the Sussex downs (Gilpin, 1804) "chalk disfigures every landscape."

Because of its farming value, Cobbett (1830), like other agricultural writers, took a more practical view of the North Hampshire Chalk. He noted that it produced "some of the best wheat in England. All these high, and indeed, all chalky lands are excellent for sheep", yet he recognised that his liking for these downs was "notwithstanding their everlasting flints." A later agricultural writer, James Caird (1852), who also saw the farming value of the chalklands, similarly found them wanting in landscape appeal in comparison with the southern, lower part of the county. To him, the downs had "a bare landscape ... the trees being scanty and of stunted growth, the arable land in large fields frequently unenclosed and the wide refreshing streams which drain the lower country being exchanged for meagre rivulets."

Writing in this way, Caird was almost the last to make such comparisons, for if we are to believe that what the topographers wrote either was influenced by, or shaped, the attitudes of their readers, we can discern a major re-evaluation of the scenic qualities of the Chalk landscape of Hampshire underway by the late 1830s. One event more than any other seemed to account for this change, the opening of the London-Southampton railway in 1840. Starting a year or so before the line took its first passengers, a series of travel guides appeared over the next few decades encouraging tourists to explore the newly-accessible downland areas, as well as other places along the line, by stopping off at the principal stations. One handbook published in 1858 laid out a seven-week touring itinerary intended to cover all points of interest along the route between Surrey and the Isle of Wight. For the first time, the topographers and tour-guide writers began to outline the main areas and major features of interest within the downlands just as other writers, a half-century before, had detailed the features of the countryside to the south. For the first time also, the valleys of the Test and Itchen came into prominence as areas of scenic quality. As late as 1831 Kendall could only state that "from the neighbourhood of Basingstoke a beautiful valley extends in direction mainly south-west to a short distance from Southampton", whereas but seven years later Mudie (1838) was devoting the first book of his three-volume topography of Hampshire to the Test and Itchen valleys alone. At about the same time Duthy (1839) focused much of his 'Sketches of Hampshire' on the Itchen valley, detailing six rambles based on Alresford.

In becoming more accessible, an accessibility enhanced later in the century as other railway lines were opened, the Hampshire downs and valleys were over the next few decades appreciated as much for their scenery as they had for long been for their agriculture, such that by the end of the century, in many minds, they rivalled the more fashionable southern areas. W H Hudson (1923), perhaps the greatest proponent of the countryside of the southern counties, clearly found the Hampshire chalklands as appealing as the New Forest in the early years of the present century:

> "There are no more refreshing places in Hampshire, one might almost say in England, than the green level valleys of the Test and Itchen that wind, alternately widening and narrowing, through the downland country to Southampton Water ... They are not long rivers ... but long enough for men with unfevered blood in their veins to find sweet and peaceful homes on their margins ... I think I know quite a dozen villages ... in any one of which I could spend long years in perfect contentment ... These are, indeed, among the most characteristic Hampshire villages ... as natural and one with the scene as chalk down and trees and green meadows, and have an air of immemorial quiet and human life that is part of nature's life, unstrenuous, slow and sweet..."

A RECENT DIVERSITY OF VIEWS

As Hudson's words might suggest, it was not only that the downlands of the county had come clearly into vogue as a preferred landscape. But beginning more than half a century ago, there was an increasing appreciation by a growing number of visitors and local people of the more diverse appeals of the countryside - its scenery, its wildlife, its customs, its sense of oneness. This in turn called forth fresh approaches to the art of travel writing. The guide book of the earlier decades which laid out a detailed tour itinerary, whether it be followed in a carriage (with a Claude glass in hand as with the seekers after the picturesque) or taken along in the train, was now joined by a more diverse family of country books. Some of these attempted to provide a more complete coverage of the county's topography, wildlife, customs and economy to suit the varied interests of the new and more varied breed of tourist. At this time also, the first geographic inter-pretations appeared of parts of the region (Crawford, 1922; Dent, 1924). Others were little more than personalised meanderings around parts of the Hampshire countryside. But all, unlike their predecessors, left the reader much more to choose his own tour and stopping places. The New Forest, for example, about a century ago, provided many a travel writer with the opportunity to develop a fresh approach, with titles like 'The New Forest: its Traditions, Inhabitants and Customs' (de Crespigny, 1895). Several books considered its wildlife and conservation needs (Cornish, 1895), while two novelists used the Forest as a setting for their stories (Marryat, 1847; Blackmore, 1866).

To give some of this diverse style of country book the coherence enjoyed by the older guides, several writers attempted to more clearly regionalise the county into units of a size smaller and more practicable than the three or four major areas that largely defined themselves. But since nature and its landscapes provided few clues as to what these units should be and where their boundaries might be drawn, different writers adopted markedly different approaches to regionalisation. In

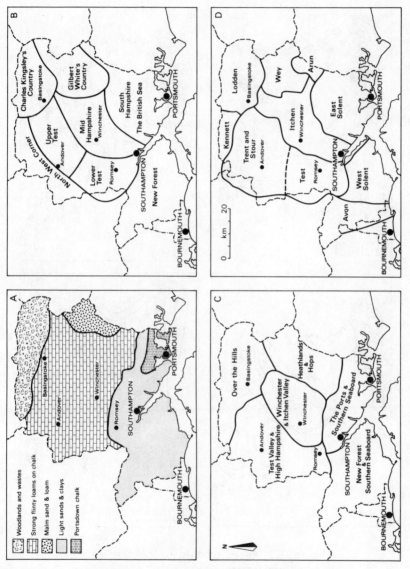

Figure 11.1 Historic subdivisions of Hampshire:
    A Vancouver's agricultural districts, 1810
    B Dewar's regionalisation, 1900.
    C Dutton's districts, 1970.
    D Townsend's botanical districts, 1883.

251

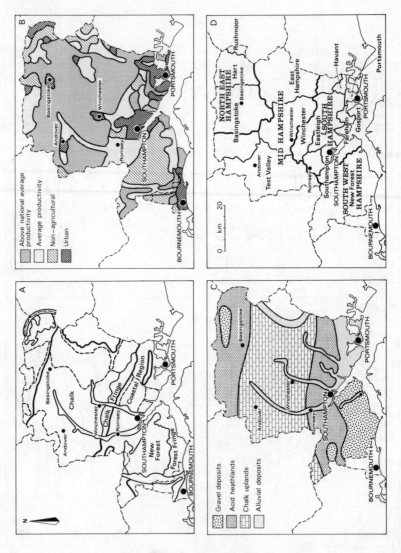

Figure 11.2 Recent subdivisions of Hampshire:
A Green's land-use regions, 1940.
B Agricultural Land Service land-classification areas, 1964.
C A recent architectural view of landscape types, 1980.
D Structure plan and district council areas, 1981.

1900, for example, Dewar (Fig.11.1B) divided the county into eight well-tried and tested districts, although he re-inforced the unity of some of these by calling upon their literary associations. That part of the western edge of the Weald around Selborne he called "Gilbert White Country", while he identified the northern lowland fringe of the county with Charles Kingsley. Other writers, like Varley (1909) and still more recently Vesey-Fitzgerald (1949), took such associative ideas further by referring to the rather poorly-defined southeastern corner of the county as the home district of cricket. Collinson-Morley (1940) subdivided Hampshire into no less than sixteen districts in her guide, although one of the more popular of the numerous county books published in recent years has settled on no more than half-a-dozen areas, largely delimited on their physical attributes (Dutton, 1970)(Fig.11.1C). Whatever their number or boundaries, it is clear that, if the rural writer reflects popular perceptions, regions within regions are nowadays more recognised in Hampshire than two centuries ago.

Parallel, but less clearly seen, trends during this century in the presentation of information on Hampshire's countryside, which may also reflect the public's changing view of the county, have included some books playing down the differences between small districts. Some have viewed Hampshire as part of a broader, but only vaguely-defined region; others have seen it as composed of two types of country, namely those areas already well known to the tourist and inhabitant alike and other areas yet to be 'discovered'. Several titles, like 'We Wander in Wessex' (Herbert, 1947), and other 'Wessex' books (Grigson, 1951) have appeared in increasing numbers since the 1920s, linking Hampshire to its neighbouring counties to the west. As such, these are in keeping with the scale of the larger physical framework, the wider range of touring as offered by the car, and the growing popularity in the public mind of the concept of the Wessex region. During the same period other books appeared, such as 'Where Traditions Linger' (Fea, 1925) and 'Unknown Hampshire' (Holland, 1926), which purposely avoided consideration of the already well-known districts in favour of the little-visited areas off the main routeways and away from the main centres.

Perhaps the most important of these trends since the late nineteenth century has been the rise of a more scientific interest directed towards the county's rural areas and their various biological and topographical elements. This trend has emerged partly because of a clearer recognition of the threat overhanging these features as a result of economic and other changes in more recent decades. Many of these surveys also subdivide the county into various districts. However, few similarities are to be seen in the areas defined, mainly because the components and purposes of the surveys differ, but also because perceptions of where boundary lines should lie in a region of undramatic landscape have remained fluid. Whereas, for example among the earliest of these surveys, Townsend's report of 1883 on the botanical districts of Hampshire largely used drainage basin units, later county surveys, such as Green's land-use survey (1940) and the Ministry of Agriculture's land evaluation maps (1964), have largely reflected a physiographic basis to the definition of districts (Figs.11.1D, 11.2A and B). A recent architectural regionalisation of the county based on the distribution of its traditional building types and the main physiographic units has produced patterns different yet again and further demonstrates the range of elements that are seen to create the varied value of the countryside (Fig.11.2C).

THE PLANNING VIEW

With at least two centuries of changing and broadening views of the
Hampshire countryside behind us, it should come as no surprise that
over the last thirty-five years one might also detect shifts in the
approaches of those planners charged with planning for and conserving
that countryside. Since the Second World War, planning control for the
rural parts of the county has gone through a series of modifications,
reflecting the influence of evolving national policies and an
increasing, yet changing set of pressures on the countryside. Whereas
during the nineteenth century, when Hampshire's various rural areas
were poorly perceived, the rate of population growth in the county had
been well below that for the nation, since 1900, and particularly
following the Second World War, these relative positions have been
reversed. This reversal has been brought about by a combination of
raised birth rates, a buoyant economic base which has attracted people
into Hampshire, a policy of accepting overspill population from the
London area and a growing number of persons retiring into the county.
Most of this population expansion has been concentrated in either the
Tertiary basin around Southampton Water and within the semi-urban zone
stretching east to Portsmouth, or in the northern part of the county,
which has increasingly come under the influence of the spreading
metropolitan commuter belt. Separating two areas of rapid population
growth, there is the major block of the downs, distinctive in terms of
its physical landscapes, itsmuch higher value for agriculture, its more
nucleated rural settlement pattern and its lower overall population
density, whilst the sparsely-settled New Forest has acted as a buffer
within the Tertiary basin between the main urban zone of South
Hampshire and a secondary growth area based on Bournemouth and Poole to
the west. In this way, the post-war tendency for population to
concentrate in those parts of the county already more densely settled,
and away from the areas of more highly-prized and more rural
landscapes, seems only to confirm the established differences within the
county. Thus it became recognised that, unless some policy of
containment was to be applied, continuation of these growth processes
would soon spread pressures into the more rural areas, harming their
agricultural, landscape and other values.

This containment was brought about by the Hampshire Development Plan,
prepared under The Town and Country Planning Act (1947) and approved in
1955, whereby the county planning authority obtained a framework of
guidance for land-use development, using its powers to grant or refuse
planning permission. Under the Plan, a green belt (the only one
established in Hampshire) was drawn up to envelop the main area of
settlement expansion in the Tertiary basin and thereby to protect the
New Forest, the Chalk areas and various undeveloped parts of South
Hampshire, including stretches of the coast (Fig.11.3). Although its
role was eventually subsumed into the designated countryside areas laid
out in the South Hampshire Structure Plan, part of the green-belt
concept has survived within the country-areas policy of the draft S W
Hampshire Structure Plan area, where it is needed to link up with that
already approved for the adjacent area in Dorset. No green belt was
ever put forward for the northern growth area of the county, although

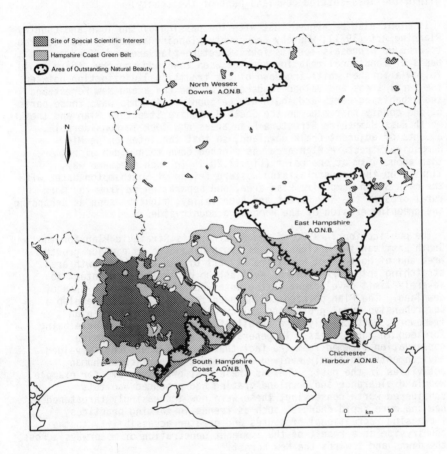

Figure 11.3 Special status land in rural Hampshire.

when Hampshire County Council objected to a London County Council plan to create a new town for overspill population at Hook, in an area already threatened with urban sprawl, the LCC accepted Hampshire's counter-proposal to guide the growth into the market towns of Basingstoke and Andover. So, for the first time, urban expansion, albeit on a restricted scale, was artificially stimulated at two points within the less-settled downland part of the county.

It might also be argued that with the passing of the Town and Country Planning Act (1971), whereby the county planning authority was required to draw up proposals for its four structure-plan areas defined on the basis of functional relationships between town and country, there would follow a further whittling down of the traditional distinction between the rural areas and valued landscapes of the Chalk and New Forest and the urbanising north and south of the county. In this way, those parts of the county that made up the South Hampshire Structure Plan and the North East Hampshire Structure Plan areas now took in considerable amounts of adjacent Chalk downland, so that the intervening Mid Hampshire Structure Plan area was pinched down to a width of no more than about 15km at one point (Fig.11.2D). In much the same way, linking up the industrialising western fringe of Southampton Water with the main South Hampshire Plan area, and separating it from the more rural area of the New Forest and Avon valley, might be seen as enhancing the creeping erosion of the Hampshire countryside.

The publication in 1970 of the Government's Strategic Plan for the South East saw the designation of South Hampshire as a major growth area and of North East Hampshire as part of yet another growth area stretching into Berkshire, as well as the declaration of intent to severely limit development in the intervening Mid Hampshire area of downland. The Plan pointed to the need for the county to develop a comprehensive rural protection policy within the structure-plan framework, particularly as a result of other changes that were being foreseen in rural areas. In general, the need for countryside conservation stemmed from the fact that many of the county's valued environments had slowly evolved as a result of particular human activities in the past. Whereas these past processes of, for example, woodland clearance and downland grazing had produced habitats considered worth conserving, these were now increasingly threatened by new and more rapid changes, such as trends in farming practices, increasing recreational pressures and greater accessibility to the countryside as a result of the imminent penetration of motorways across the downs and towards the New Forest.

For the South Hampshire Structure Plan area, Buchanan (1966) had earlier suggested a linear form of urban development between Southampton and Portsmouth, partly as a means of protecting the downs to the north, the coast to the south and various intervening countryside elements like the river valleys. This, to some extent, pointed the way for the Structure Plan approved in 1977. Although the linear-city concept was abandoned at a time of lower expectations of population growth, the Plan still places stress on protecting the rural and coastal environments by designating countryside areas. This same approach is also adopted and detailed in the Winchester Area Plan (1976), in which seven country areas were defined in recognition of the potential conflicts between settlement expansion, agricultural needs and recreational growth in an area close to urban South Hampshire. In North East Hampshire, where considerable areas are held by the Ministry of Defence The Blackwater River Valley Landscape Restoration and Recreation Study (1971) and The Blackwater Valley Landscape Report (1976) have helped in the development of plans for both the protection and, in some cases, the rehabilitation of countryside areas.

At a scale below that of the structure-plan area, it is not surprising to find that over the last twenty years much emphasis has been placed on planning for the protection of the highest-valued countryside areas of the county. Four Areas of Outstanding Natural Beauty (AONBs) have been set up partly or wholly within the county and another is proposed, so that these, together with the Sites of Special Scientific Interest (including the New Forest) and other reserves, now make up one-third the area of the county (Fig.11.3). To some it has seemed that too much stress has been placed on trying to protect these areas and too little time and effort given to meeting the planning and management needs of the other two-thirds of the rural areas, which come under the less strict policies of the structure plans and, in South West Hampshire, within the green belt. Certainly, the management problems of the protected landscapes have been studied in some detail. The East Hampshire AONB, established in 1962 under The National Parks and Access to the Countryside Act of 1949, was the subject of a detailed study (1968) to identify its major characteristics and the conflicts between different users. However, few actual management arrangements have followed from this report. A major survey of the New Forest (1970) by the County Council, the Forestry Commission and local interest groups produced more far-reaching results from the management viewpoint in terms of a greater control on camping and car access to the open forest, made necessary because of the impacts of the rapid growth of recreation on other uses of the Forest. Numerous studies of various aspects of the New Forest's flora, fauna and land use, following on its original designation as a major Site of Special Scientific Interest in 1959, have led to refinements of that management plan in recent years. On the southern edge of the New Forest, the South Hampshire and Christchurch Harbour AONB was set up in 1964, and enlarged in 1967, to protect an area of both scenic and wildlife value. Part of it has been the subject of a management study to deal with conflicts between land use, recreation and landscape consideration in an area largely under private-estate ownership (Chesterton, 1969). The Chichester Harbour AONB has also been investigated for conflicts between wildlife and recreational sailing. On the northern side of the county, the Wessex Downs AONB was designated in 1972 to include parts of Hampshire, Wiltshire and Berkshire. Although the Himsworth Report (Countryside Commission, 1980) has recommended that few more AONBs should be established, one of the few that was approved, that at Cranborne Chase and including a small part of the West Hampshire downs, is likely to be established shortly.

Two other longer-standing policies, which as with the AONBs are based on selecting areas of land for special status, should also be mentioned, because they have played a major role in rural recreation and wildlife protection in the county. Since the 1960s Hampshire County Council has established twenty-eight open spaces. Although they represent only 0.5 per cent of the county area, and half of that occurs in only four of the parks, by 1977 they were attracting an estimated 2.3 million visitors a year, about 40 per cent of the number annually attracted to the New Forest. Since 1951 the Nature Conservancy Council has, with the co-operation of various bodies like the Hampshire Naturalists Trust, established eighty Sites of Special Scientific Interest in the county (Fig.11.3). Much of the emphasis has so far been on the protection of mainly small sites in chalkland, heathland, marsh and intertidal habitats. Of the twenty-five sites set up by 1959, eighteen were of this type and the proportion has changed little in those established more recently, although in future more recognition of the need to protect some of the many small ancient woodland sites of the county can be expected.

While the establishment of further Sites of Special Scientific Interest can be confidently predicted, one is not likely to see more country parks set up in the county, particularly at a time when the growth in countryside recreation has levelled off and, in some cases, has even fallen. Access to coastal waters for recreational boating still presents problems. The demand for this type of recreation continues to expand rapidly but, as Reed (1981) points out, the construction of marinas provides no easy solution, because of the planning and environmental problems they present. The Solent Sailing Conferences, representing the county, harbour authorities, the boating interests and other bodies, have met irregularly since the late 1960s. They have surveyed pressure points and conflict areas and are currently examining the boating capacities of the coast and conflicts between various users of these waters.

As these programmes to protect and manage particular areas of countryside have developed in recent years and as increasing concern has been felt for the well-being of the rest of the rural area outside of these designations, the county planning authority has drawn up a Coast & Country Conservation Policy. First outlined in 1969, it was intended to better co-ordinate the diverse activities of both county and district planning and other bodies, and to institute a more detailed set of proposals for the whole of the county's countryside areas. Development in the 1960s also coincided with enhanced public interest in the environment. At the national level, this led to legislation concentrated on specific issues, like The Protection of Wild Creatures Act (1975), but it also spurred on The Countryside Act (1968), which made it possible to give grants for landscape protection to areas outside of National Parks and AONBs, so removing one of the few real distinctions between designated areas and the rest of the countryside. Since the countryside policy in Hampshire was first drawn up before the structure plans, outlining countryside proposals, were completed, it originally concentrated on limiting the harmful effects of settlement expansion in the countryside. Since then, it has undergone modifications reflecting the need to view the countryside as a set of dynamic components within a system under impact from various internal and external pressures. In particular the policy has been extended to include the coast, following concern expressed both nationally and locally about the development of the coastline, and also articulated in the work of the Countryside Commission's Coastal Heritage programme (1966). In 1979 the county's countryside policy was further refined, particularly to attempt to deal more effectively with the increasing impact on the landscape of changes in agricultural practices and, to a lesser extent, in forestry, as outlined nationally in the reports of the Nature Conservancy Council (1975) and of the Countryside Commission (Westmacott and Worthington, 1974), but its prime role remains as a guide to development control.

Indicative of this shift towards a more all-inclusive approach to the countryside of Hampshire by the county planning authority has been the launching of its Treasures Surveys and Heritage Policy. Following a pilot survey in the Petersfield area in 1967, each parish in the county has been surveyed to list all features of aesthetic, archaeological, historic, scenic or traditional interest. It is hoped that this information will not only establish the relative importance of individual features when affected by planning decisions, but that a greater public awareness of these treasures by both landowners and the general public will help to ensure their protection where statutory means of protection are often not available. This work led in 1979 to the Countryside Heritage Project to record the natural and semi-natural features of the countryside which are considered to have ecological, historic or landscape significance. A report on ancient trackways has already been produced for this project and surveys are underway for studies on the downlands, ancient woodlands, historic earthworks, formal landscapes, the heathlands and river valleys. A number of thematic studies dealing with such features as the coast and the New Forest will follow.

Over the last thirty years, then, the main emphasis in planning policies for the Hampshire countryside has been shifting from a concern simply for the protection of a few valued landscapes and habitats towards a broader approach for the management of all rural areas. Such a change of direction has, on the shorter time-scale of the planner, echoed the increasingly wider appreciations of the county's landscapes which emerged over the previous two centuries.

REFERENCES

ANON (1858), A Handbook for Travellers in Surrey, Hampshire and Isle of Wight (London, Murray).

BLACKMORE, R D (1866), Cradock Nowell: a Tale of the New Forest (London, Sampson Low).

BROWN, C R B (1979), The Hampshire Coast: Interim Report (Unpublished).

BUCHANAN, C and Partners (1966), South Hampshire Study (London, HMSO).

BULLAR, J (1801), A Companion in a Tour round Southampton (Southampton, Baker).

CAIRD, J (1852), English Agriculture in 1850-1851 (London, Longman).

CHESTERTON, E (1669), The North West Solent Shore Estates (London, Leonard Manasseh Consultants).

COBBETT, W (1830), Rural Rides in the Counties of Surrey, Kent, Sussex, Hampshire etc. (London, Cobbett).

COLEBOURN, P and HUGHES, M (1980), The Countryside Heritage: an Introduction (Winchester, Hampshire County Council).

COLLINSON-MORLEY, L (1940), Companion into Hampshire (London, Methuen).

CORNISH, C J (1895), The New Forest and Isle of Wight (London, Seeley).

COUNTRYSIDE COMMISSION (1980), Areas of Outstanding Natural Beauty: Response to the Countryside Commission Discussion Paper (the Himsworth Report)(London, HMSO).

CRESPIGNY, R de and HUTCHINSON, H (1895), The New Forest: its Traditions, Inhabitants and Customs (London, Murray).

CRAWFORD, O G S (1922), The Andover District (Oxford, Clarendon).

DENT, H G (1924), The Hampshire Gate (London, Benn).

DEWAR, G (1900), Hampshire with the Isle of Wight (London, Dent).

DOUBLEDAY, H A (1900), A History of Hampshire and the Isle of Wight (London, Constable).

DRIVER, A and W (1794), General View of the Agriculture of the County of Hampshire (London, Macrae).

DUTHY, J (1839), Sketches of Hampshire (Winchester, Jacob and Johnson).

DUTTON, R (1970), Hampshire (London, Batsford).

ENGLEFIELD, H C (1801), A Walk through Southampton (Southampton, Baker).

FEA, A (1923), Where Traditions Linger (London, Nash).

GILPIN, W (1791), Remarks on Forest Scenery and other Woodland Views (London, Blamire).

GILPIN, W (1804), Observations on the Coasts of Hampshire, Sussex and Kent, relative chiefly to Picturesque Beauty (London, Cadell).

GREEN, F H W (1940), The Land of Britain: part 89 - Hampshire (London, Geographical Publications).

GRIGSON, G (1951), About Britain Guides: Wessex (London, Collins).

HAMPSHIRE COUNTY COUNCIL (1976), Winchester Area Plan (Winchester, County Planning Department).

HAMPSHIRE COUNTY COUNCIL (1980-), Hampshire Treasures (various volumes) (Winchester, County Planning Department).

HAMPSHIRE COUNTY COUNCIL (1980), County Conservation Policy (Unpublished).

HARTE, S et al (1980), Landscape of Hampshire (Winchester, Hampshire Architects).

260

HERBERT, J (1947), We Wander in Wessex (London, Ward Lock).

HOLLAND, C (1926), Unknown Hampshire (London, Lane).

HUDSON, W H (1910), A Shepherd's Life (London, Dent).

HUDSON, W H (1923), Hampshire Days (London, Dent), 242-244.

JAGGER, M and HUGHES, M (1979), Hampshire's Heritage and a Policy for its Future (Winchester, Hampshire County Council).

KENDALL, J (1831), Picture of Hampshire (Hampshire Pamphlets 45, Cope Collection, Southampton University Library).

MANWOOD, J (1615), A Treatise on the Lawes of the Forest (London).

MARRYAT, F (1847), The Children of the New Forest (London).

MARSHALL, J (1798), The Rural Economy of the Southern Counties (London, Nicol).

MINISTRY OF AGRICULTURE   (1964), Agricultural Land Classification Maps (London, Agricultural Land Service).

MUDIE, R (1838), Hampshire (Winchester, Gilmour).

NEW FOREST WORKING PARTY (1970), Conservation of the New Forest (Winchester, Hampshire County Council).

REED, A (1981), A Geographical Investigation into the Provision of Coastal Moorings and Marinas in England and Wales and some of the Consequences of their Development (Unpublished M Phil thesis, University of Southampton).

SALMON, N (1731), New Survey of England (London).

SHOARD, M (1980), The Theft of the Countryside (London, Temple Smith).

SKELTON, E (1818), The Southampton Guide (Southampton).

SMART, A D G et al (1968), East Hampshire Area of Outstanding Natural Beauty: a Study in Countryside Conservation (London, Hampshire County Council).

SOLENT SAILING CONFERENCE (1972), Conference Report (Winchester, Hampshire County Council).

SOUTH HAMPSHIRE PLAN ADVISORY COMMITTEE (1969), Study Reports on Agriculture, Recreation, Rural Landscape and Forestry (Winchester, Hampshire County Council).

TOWNSEND, F (1883), Flora of Hampshire (London, Reeve).

VANCOUVER, C (1810), General View of the Agriculture of Hampshire (London, Phillips).

VARLEY, T (1909), <u>Hampshire</u> (London, Adam and Black).

VESEY-FITZGERALD, B (1949), <u>Hampshire and the Isle of Wight</u> (London, Hale).

WESTMACOTT, R and WORTHINGTON, T (1974), <u>New Agricultural Landscapes</u> (London, Countryside Commission).

12 Issues in the 1980s
C M MASON AND M E WITHERICK

The preceding essays have highlighted some of the dimensions of growth
and change in the Southampton area during the past two decades, as well
as revealed a number of the resultant implications. The evidence
presented leaves little argument that the city region does deserve its
'growth area' designation. Whether measured in terms of employment,
population or a range of other criteria, the Southampton SMLA has ranked
amongst the fastest growing urban areas in Great Britain. However, as a
number of the essays have pointed out, with the movement of the national
economy into recession during the 1970s, so Southampton's growth rate
has slackened as compared with that experienced during the heady, boom
years of the 1960s. With no sustained national economic recovery
currently in view and in the context of accelerating technological
change, the prospects for the area in the 1980s appear unpropitious,
although they are considerably less bleak than those for much of the
country.

Given the current forecasts for South Hampshire of a substantially
lower rate of population growth in the 1980s than was experienced during
the past twenty years (Hampshire County Council, 1980a), it seems likely
that attention will increasingly turn from the problems of population
growth in the Southampton area towards the many and varied issues
arising from age-specific demographic trends (Chapter 6; White, 1981).
The problems associated with a large and increasing elderly population
may well prove to be one source of anxiety during the 1980s,
particularly in those parts of the SMLA which have acted as receiving
areas for retirement migration. Although the growth in the number of
those aged 65 and over will decelerate during the 1980s, the proportion
of very elderly (75 years and over) is expected to continue to rise as
a result of the national trend of increasing life expectancy. As these

people grow even older, weaker, suffer reduction in real income and become unable to care for themselves and their homes, so greatly increased pressure will be placed upon the special housing, community care and personal welfare services of local authorities and the National Health Service (White, 1981; Hampshire County Council, 1980b). There is little reason to expect any fall-off in the level of retirement migration in Britain. Indeed, with early retirement (be it voluntary or forced), with increase in the real value of incomes put aside for pensions and with increase in owner-occupation, retirement migration may actually grow during the 1980s (Law and Warnes, 1981). Consequently, the elderly population in the Southampton SMLA will continue to be 'topped up' by in-migration, and thereby create additional demand for already over-burdened social services.

Fortunately, the younger cohorts are also significantly represented in Southampton's population structure (in part a result of the in-migration of young families during the 1960s), so the area is in a better position than many other parts of the South Coast to cope with the anticipated increase in its elderly residents. Nevertheless, as its youngest cohorts 'grow-up', it is expected that population-related problems of a different calibre will be created. For example, with the passing of the 1960s 'boom' babies into adulthood, so during the 1980s the under-16 age group will account for a progressively smaller proportion of the total population. The consequence will be falling school rolls and declining demand for childrens' social services. How to manage efficiently this particular contraction will undoubtedly present a major challenge for local and central government administrators. However, the opportunity to improve standards, for example by reducing teacher-pupil ratios, seems likely to be thwarted by the political and economic pressures to cut public expenditure. Because of the fall in the birth rate since 1971, secondary schools will be particularly hard hit by the shrinkage in the school-age population. On the other hand, primary schools may look forward to some reversal of the trend of falling rolls due to the very recent upturn in the birth rate and the increasing number of women entering the child-bearing age range (Hampshire County Council, 1980b).

The concomitant of this projected decline in the under-16 age group is an increase in the young adult population. Their numbers are expected to grow rapidly until the mid-1980s. As they begin to form new households (not just as a result of marriage), so there will be an increased demand for housing. But house-building in the public sector is currently at a low level and re-lets have fallen sharply, whilst in the private sector rising property prices, high interest rates, periodic mortgage famines and failure of the housing market's self-regulating adjustments to ensure the provision of an adequate supply of suitable accommodation may all combine to frustrate the housing aspirations of this young adult population (Eversley, 1981). Possibly of even greater significance is the projected increase in the size of the SMLA's working population caused largely, although not entirely, by the growth of the young adult cohort. Other contributory factors include the low numbers leaving the labour market through retirement (a reflection of the low birth rate after the First World War), the re-entry of many married women into the labour market and continued in-migration of economically-active people into the area. Without a corresponding increase in employment, these demographic trends imply a growing imbalance during the 1980s between the supply and the demand for labour.

The outlook for employment growth appears distinctly poor,
particularly when compared with the conditions prevailing up to 1974
when labour shortages were commonplace and unemployment was almost
invariably less than 3 per cent (Hampshire County Council, 1977).
During the 1980s the major components in the local economy seem unlikely
to generate many new jobs. Indeed, in some cases the tendency will be
to require fewer workers. For example, the size of the workforce
needed to run the port is already contracting, due to declining
throughput, increasing automation and improved labour productivity. The
loss of business is especially worrying and is attributed by many as
reflecting the recent deterioration in labour relations inside the port.
In part this may well be true, but it is imperative to recognise that
it is also a result of the keenness of competition from other ports for
a larger share of the container and cross-Channel traffic. This has
recently resulted in two container companies transferring their
operations to Tilbury and Felixstowe and the removal of a large part of
Townsend Thoresen's cross-Channel ferry operations to Portsmouth.
Indeed, Portsmouth is now a serious competitor to Southampton, and with
its planned £11 million investment to double the size of its RO/RO
ferry and container-handling facilities (Financial Times, 29.7.80), it
must be very well positioned to entice further business from Southampton
in the future (Chapter 2). Indeed, the proposed rundown of Portsmouth's
Royal Naval Dockyard might actually assist the commercial port in
overcoming its greatest operational constraint, the shortage of space.
Hence, rather than proceeding with the mid-1970s proposal to expand
Southampton's container port further up the Test estuary during the
1980s or early 1990s, the BTDB may well wish to relinquish some of its
land. Given the present shortage of land for industrial development
within the city boundaries, any release of land by the port and any
decisions about its possible use will undoubtedly assume a critical
significance. However, the effects of the worsening port prospects do
not end there, for the ranks of locally-based companies which service
the port in diverse ways all face a loss of business each time a
shipping company pulls out of the port. Furthermore, the transfer of a
shipping company's operations to another port removes the need to
maintain an administrative office in the city. In short, any further
loss of business by the port during the 1980s will have serious
consequences for all those ancillary activities on the port-city
interface, repercussions thus reaching well beyond the dock gates.

Future job prospects in manufacturing also appear unfavourable
(Chapter 3). For many locally-based firms, any improvement in demand
can be met, at least initially, by utilising spare capacity, while
companies undertaking new investment will, in many instances, achieve
increased output with a static or even declining labour force. A
number of companies with an important presence in the Southampton SMLA
are likely to face reduced demand and fiercely competitive market
conditions during the 1980s. Rather than taking on new employees, they
will require to shed jobs, through natural wastage and either
voluntary or enforced redundancy, in order to remain competitive.
Because Southampton has such a large proportion of its manufacturing
jobs in just a handful of multi-national companies, it also remains
vulnerable to the ever-present possibility that such enterprises might
decide to transfer their local operations to bases in other parts of
the world. The recent decision to cutback Ministry of Defence
expenditure will also have adverse consequences for industry in the

Southampton SMLA. A considerable number of the area's medium-sized and larger enterprises are major MoD suppliers and they, in turn, sub-contract various parts of the production process to numerous small local firms. Therefore, enterprises of all sizes in the Southampton area which rely directly or indirectly on MoD contracts, from warship-builders Vosper Thorneycroft downwards, seem likely to face an inevitable decline in the amount of government work and will accordingly have only a short period of time in which either to find alternative customers or to turn to new lines of production.

The outlook for jobs in the very significant local office sector is probably less depressing. Although there are few signs of an immediate increase in demand for office space (Southampton City Council, 1981), it is anticipated that any national economic recovery will at an early stage prompt renewed activity in this sector of the local economy. However, there must be some doubt concerning the scale of any future generation of jobs within the office sector (Chapter 4). The adoption of micro-processor technology in the office will displace many secretarial and clerical jobs. As such, these losses are unlikely to be fully offset by those jobs created by the new office technology which will not only be fewer in number, but will require substantially different skills.

This unfavourable employment context in conjunction with enlargement of the workforce will inevitably mean that rising unemployment becomes a major issue, no less in the Southampton area than nationally. Numbers out of work in Southampton have already risen dramatically over a short period of time. In June 1979 unemployment in the Southampton travel-to-work area was just 3.7 per cent, whereas by June 1981 18,753 were registered as out of work, equivalent to 8.5 per cent of the workforce. Certainly Southampton's current (June 1981) rate of unemployment remains well below the national figure of 10.9 per cent, nevertheless it is higher than the average for the South East (7.7 per cent). Moreover, the rise in unemployment in the two years since June 1979 has been particularly steep, increasing by 133 per cent compared with 61 per cent nationally; but possibly this is the penalty for being one of the last areas to feel the effects of recession. The majority of those registered as unemployed are either semi- or unskilled. Their chances of finding employment will become increasingly bleak, since those industries most likely to create new jobs in the future are in high-technology fields and consequently will wish to recruit many qualified and skilled workers; paradoxically, such workers remain in short supply. It is the young and the old who are also at considerable risk in this climate of reduced labour demand. Men made redundant in their fifties and sixties will certainly find it difficult to find another job, but there is much greater concern for the plight of the unemployed school-leaver. The scale of the present problem is illustrated by the fact that in the Southampton SMLA in June 1981 there were nearly 3000 youngsters registered with the careers service. Of these, only 56 were found jobs in that month compared with 254 in the same period a year earlier (Southern Evening Echo, 22.7.81). Thus for many school-leavers the Youth Opportunities Programme will offer the only hope of leaving the dole.

Despite this pessimism, there is nonetheless a brighter side to the economic outlook for the Southampton area. For a start, its diverse industrial structure may be regarded as a source of strength. More specifically, a considerable proportion of local industry is in high-technology fields, and the technological achievements of locally-based firms are consistently recognised in the annual Queen's Awards to Industry. In addition, there is a proposal for a joint University-City Council venture to develop a science park in order to attract to the area research organisations and the research and development units of high-technology manufacturing enterprises (Southern Evening Echo, 15.4.81 and 29.4.81). The prospects for the success of this venture seem sound. There is, for example, well documented evidence of a strong preference by research establishments for locations in the Outer South East and particularly for those which can offer proximity to a university, good communications (air, motorway, inter-city rail) and an attractive residential environment to assist in the recruitment of research staff (Buswell and Lewis, 1970). If the venture does proceed, then the technological spin-off to the local economy might be quite considerable, as for example through the setting up of new techno-logically-based firms close by, and because of the tendency for the commercial application of innovations to occur in factories located close to the innovating research and development unit (Oakey et al., 1980).

The commitment of private-sector investors to the Southampton SMLA remains strong and is confirmed in part by a high rate of new-firm creation (Chapter 3). At least two leisure groups (Crest and Holiday Inns) have plans to build new hotels in the Southampton area (Financial Times, 20.8.81). Property and investment companies remain active in developing industrial estates, generally in peripheral locations, and new units quickly attract tenants. Furthermore, a 20 ha site between the city centre and the docks is to be redeveloped as a shops, offices, industry and leisure complex. This ambitious scheme, the Western Esplanade Development, is to be undertaken by the Heron Group in conjunction with the National Coal Board Pension Fund and on behalf of the City Council, and should considerably enhance Southampton's status as a commercial centre as well as provide many hundreds of jobs. Future economic prospects also seem likely to be enhanced by Southampton City Council's decision to launch a large, and possibly overdue, initiative to attract firms and jobs to the city. In this campaign the council is considering aggressively advertising the city's advantages for commercial, tourist, residential and leisure activity, giving financial assistance to new and small companies and promoting training opportunities (Southern Evening Echo, 23.6.81).

Yet perhaps the brightest hope for Southampton in the 1980s relates to the possibility that it will become Britain's 'energy city'. Certainly the signs are promising. Southampton is to be the site of Britain's first commercial exploitation of geothermal energy. The City Council has recently approved a £3 million scheme (with £1 million of risk capital provided by the Department of Energy) to drill a borehole and tap an underground reservoir of water with a temperature of 70°C. This will provide heat for the planned Western Esplanade complex, the Civic Centre, the swimming baths and possibly the Pirelli cable factory. The first heat should be available by 1984 (Financial Times, 14.8.81). Eastleigh is hoping to embark upon a similar scheme (Southern Evening Echo, 11.8.81). Of even greater significance is the discovery of oil at Wytch Farm in Dorset (1973) and in Hampshire at Humbly Grove, near

Basingstoke (1980). This has prompted a number of companies to
undertake exploratory drilling at various sites in Hampshire, Dorset
and Wiltshire and at off-shore locations in the English Channel
(Chapter 9). The opinion of the oil industry is one of optimism that
further discoveries will be made. Indeed, one recently expressed view
is that the geology of much of Hampshire (especially the area surrounding Humbly Grove) makes it "the most attractive on-shore prospect in
Great Britain" (The Oilman, August 1981, 28). A positive outcome from
the present oil exploration activity would, of course, provide a
considerable boost to the Southampton economy, while an off-shore strike
would be expected to result in the use of the port as the main drilling
supply and service base. This, in its turn, would bring pressure to
develop or redevelop vacant land and buildings near, or with direct
access to, the waterfront; in this context the reclaimed land at Dibden
Bay would seem to be a prime site should a large-scale shore base be
required. But these prospects for the Southampton area must be kept in
proper perspective, for few, if any, are anticipating that the city will
become a second Aberdeen!

The extension of on-shore oil exploration in Hampshire is already
resulting in increasing conflict between the demands for environmental
protection and their possible retarding effects on economic growth.
Many of the proposed on-shore oil exploration drilling sites are in
environmentally-sensitive areas. For example, Shell UK is one of a
number of companies holding exploratory drilling licences and has
recently applied for planning permission to sink an exploratory well in
the New Forest. Its request, which is now to be decided by the
Secretary of State for the Environment, has stirred tremendous
opposition from environmentalist groups who have argued that such a
scheme would damage a priceless and irreplaceable asset and would not
be appropriate in an area of such ecological importance. Furthermore,
opponents of oil exploration fear that, although the Shell application
is only for one exploratory well, if oil were to be found, then it
would prove impossible to resist pressure to get planning permission to
extract it. The opposing argument is that it is in the national
interest to know, one way or other, the extent of on-shore oil reserves
and that it is also in the local interest to create as many new jobs as
possible. But, as Hall has pointed out, this is only one example of a
much wider national issue, and he suggests that the central question for
planning in the 1980s could be "how much do we care about the
conservation of what we have in our environment versus the generation
of new economic wealth" (Hall, 1980, 11).

The early indications are that oil exploration in the New Forest will
be allowed to proceed. According to Hall (1980), development will be
permitted in such situations on the grounds that conservation is a kind
of discriminatory public good, and that in an age of scarce resources
and public expenditure cuts conservation will be perceived as a luxury.
Although the decision concerning Shell's application is now to be made
by central government, the New Forest District Council has already given
its approval subject to certain conditions, and Hampshire County
Council is thought to be favourably inclined towards exploration. The
philosophy of the present government certainly seems well disposed
towards resource exploitation (O'Riordan, 1980). Thus it seems very
probable that in this particular instance the protection of the
environment debate will shift during the 1980s from being concerned with

whether or not drilling should take place to a concern that if
commercially recoverable deposits of oil are discovered, then
exploitation should occur in such a way that the least damage is done
to the Forest's aesthetic and ecological quality. It might be argued,
however, that the greatest threat to the New Forest during the 1980s
will in fact not come from the oil industry, but rather from even
greater recreational usage stemming from increased leisure time and
from major road improvements, notably the completion of the M3 and M27
motorways, which will increase considerably the day-tripper catchment
area. Outside the Forest, pressures on the environment will be no less
severe, as for example from such activities as aggregate working,
marina development, reservoir construction and modern agricultural
practices (Chapters 9 and 11).

A final issue which might be expected to emerge during the 1980s
concerns the future structure and form of the city region. The City of
Southampton, notably in its inner area, already displays most of the
symptoms of inner-city decline, such as lack of investment, selective
loss of population, high unemployment and poor housing; admittedly
those symptoms are not of the same degree and scale as are encountered
in the industrial cities of the North. This declining core co-exists
with a belt of affluent, prosperous and expanding post-war suburbs
outside the city boundary, and which extend from the edge of the New
Forest in the west to Fareham, just beyond the eastern limit of the
SMLA (Chapters 6 and 7). The continued growth of these suburbs during
the 1980s seems assured, given the desire amongst the middle classes for
semi-rural living, the much greater capacity of the SMLA periphery to
accommodate new development and given existing structure plan policy.
Commercial and industrial organisations have shown a similar preference
to develop at locations outside the urban core, and this preference is
again reinforced both by planning policy and by the availability of
industrial land (Hampshire County Council, 1980a). One possibility for
the 1980s is, therefore, that sub-centres such as Eastleigh, Fareham,
Totton and Winchester will become increasingly important as foci for
employment, retailing, leisure and other services, thereby resulting in
the gradual transformation of a core-dominated city region into one
which is multi-nuclear in structure and in which suburban centres
assume a much greater significance. Such a transformation will, of
course, involve a considerable reorientation of interaction within the
SMLA from an essentially north-south alignment (between core and
periphery) to more of an east-west pattern within the peiiphery itself.
Clearly, the completion of the 'missing link' of the M27 motorway
(scheduled for 1984) around the northern perimeter of Southampton will
help in this regard, providing as it will an unbroken motorway and
trunk road link from the Hampshire/Sussex border westwards into Dorset.

These changes in the basic structure of the city region will not be
without their social costs. For example, the difficulties of either
reverse or orbital commuting by public transport will create an
accessibility constraint for both inner-city and suburban non-car owners
attempting to reach the expanding sources of employment in the
periphery. Both the elderly and non-working wives, whose husbands
monopolise the family car during the day, will face similar
accessibility constraints in such contexts as shopping or visiting
friends and relatives. This evolving pattern of suburban development
and the resultant increase in car-borne journeys within the periphery

also have energy implications which should be given much fuller consideration in urban planning (Lee and Wood, 1980). If events since 1974 forebode more expensive and less reliable supplies of oil in the future, then this might serve to check the scale of suburban development. Energy shortages may even prompt a radical change in urban form, although numerous low-order changes in behaviour seem a much more likely outcome (Lee and Wood, 1980). For this reason alone perhaps now is the time to reconsider the desirability of permitting and perpetuating the decentralisation tendency within the SMLA.

Thus the specific issues which might be expected to face the Southampton area during the 1980s appear to be of a different order and complexity to those confronted during the previous two decades. For much of the recent past, it has been necessary to deal with the problems of accommodating the diverse manifestations and consequences of a rapidly expanding population and a high rate of commercial and industrial growth. In marked contrast, expansion in the 1980s will be at a greatly reduced scale (although still well above the national norm), investment will be much lower, whilst unemployment will remain high due to the seemingly unavoidable mismatch between an expanding population of working age and a poor level of employment creation. The issue which might be expected to gain popular attention is the threat to high-amenity environments posed particularly by oil exploration, but also by greater recreational pressures and continued residential development. However, the issue which is likely to prove more serious and intractable is intensification of the spatial imbalance within the SMLA. Employment creation, population growth and residential, industrial and commercial investment will increasingly be confined to the expanding districts outside the urban core. How to prevent the emergence of profound spatial and social inequalities will, therefore, provide a major challenge to the existing planning policies of the city region. As they now stand, these policies appear willing to passively accept market forces and to do little more than decide in which peripheral locations offices, owner-occupied housing and the necessary infrastructure may be built. There seems likely to be an increasing demand for planners to adopt what for them is an unfamiliar interventionist role, in order to ensure a more equitable allocation and redistribution of resources and opportunities within the city region. There is, however, no guarantee that the pursuit of this objective will not prejudice the traditional economic buoyancy and overall prosperity of the Southampton area. But in order to reduce the chances of future serious social unrest, it may be felt that this risk is worth taking.

REFERENCES

BUSWELL, R J and LEWIS, E W (1970), The geographical distribution of industrial research activity in the United Kingdom, Regional Studies, 4, 297-306.

EVERSLEY, D (1981), Household formation, the family life cycle and economic pressures - implications for future housing demand and residential location planning (Paper to Regional Studies Association South East Branch Conference).

HALL, P (1980), Dark prospect, Town and Country Planning, 49, 11-12.

HAMPSHIRE COUNTY COUNCIL (1977), South East Hampshire employment study: employment structure and trends, County Planning Department Research and Intelligence Group, Working Paper, 77/3.

HAMPSHIRE COUNTY COUNCIL (1980a), Hampshire Strategic Monitoring Report 1980 (Winchester, County Planning Department).

HAMPSHIRE COUNTY COUNCIL (1980b), Hampshire Facts and Figures (Winchester, County Planning Department).

LAW, C and WARNES, A (1981), Retirement migration, Town and Country Planning, 50, 44-46.

LEE, T R and WOOD, L J (1980), The city in an era of restricted car usage: some potential responses and adjustments to future oil shortages, Geoforum, 11, 17-30.

OAKEY, R P, THWAITES, A T and NASH, P A (1980), The regional distribution of innovative manufacturing establishments in Britain, Regional Studies, 14, 235-253.

O'RIORDAN, J (1980), Environmental issues, Progress in Human Geography, 4, 417-432.

WHITE, R (1981), A general appraisal of the planning implications of expected population changes in the South East (Paper to Regional Studies Association South East Branch Conference).